Random Arguments
A life of learning

Copyright © 2020 Jerry Diakiw

Jerry Diakiw has asserted his moral right to be identified as the Author of this work in accordance with the Copyright, Designs and Patents Act 1988.

All rights reserved. Apart from any use permitted under Canadian copyright law, this publication may only be reproduced, stored or transmitted, in any form, or by any means, with prior permission from the copyright holders. This book may not be lent, resold, hired out, or otherwise circulated without prior consent from the copyright holders in any form or binding or cover other than that in which it is published and without a similar condition being imposed on the subsequent publisher.

Paperback ISBN 978-1-7774634-0-3

First Printing, 2020

Dedication

For my granddaughter Hannah and her progeny.

Acknowledgments

Alan Wilkie, a student of mine at Richmond Hill High School in the mid-1960s and now a graphic designer and longtime resident of New Zealand, persisted for years in putting my random memories together in a book. He has put in hundreds of hours, correcting typos and laying out the book, page by page, using hundreds of my photographs. He has put up with my endless whining, complaining and changes of mind. He has never shown any frustration or impatience, though well warranted, often. It is inconceivable that either book would ever see the light of day without Alan's dedication and passion for this collection of stories. It just would never have happened. Thank you Alan Wilkie.

Thanks also to Casey Hrynkow (nee Diakiw), my talented niece, Senior Brand Strategist at Ion Brand Design for yet again designing a front and back cover.

My family is the centre of my life. My family is my heart and my pride. Ann, my wife of 58 years, supports and inspires me. I marvel at her return to teaching in 1976 and rapidly acquiring a B.A., B.Ed. and M.Ed. while working full time and raising two daughters. I learned so much from her about literacy, and learning. I am inspired by the life and career achievements of my daughters, Lindsey and Kate, and their respective spouses Jeff and Daniel. My lone granddaughter Hannah is the pride of my life. All of them have inspired me in everything I have achieved in my life.

Introduction

Jerome Bruner (1989) opened my eyes to the fact that argument and story are two ways of knowing:

"...two modes of cognitive functioning, two modes of thought each providing distinctive ways of ordering experience, of constructing reality . . . a good story and a well-formed argument are different, natural kinds. Arguments convince one of their truth, stories of their life-likeness."

In my book, *Random Memories: Reflections on a Life* (amazon.ca, kindle publishing, 2020), I included a hundred stories of my life in family, in schools and on the road in over a hundred countries alone. As Catherine Bateson expressed it, "Our species thinks in metaphors and learns through stories" (1994). In this volume, following Bruner's conception of two ways of knowing, I include many of my arguments about teaching and learning in schools, about equity and social justice issues, Canadian culture and identity, and antiracism. Most of these stories have been published in a variety of professional and general publications after I learned late in my career, that I could write well enough to be published, after a lifetime of believing I could not, that I lacked the ability to present my arguments clearly in my mind but I could not put them convincingly into writing. So from about 1980, some 20 years into my career in education, to the present has been a prolific period of writing both stories and arguments. In this volume I include many of my published arguments.

Contents

1. Literacy: Reading, Writing, Talking and Learning to Teach
- Let Them Play the Trombone 5
- The Power of Engaged Reading 8
- Storying 10
- Reading Recovery: A Social Justice Intervention 12
- Children's Literature and Canadian Identity 18
- You Can't Learn to Write by Rote 25
- Children's Literature and Global Education 26
- Reflections on Becoming a Teacher 31
- Evolution of an Anti-Racist Educator: A Life History Perspective 37

2. Preschools to High Schools
- Good for Kids, Good for Us 41
- It's Time for a New Kind of High School 48
- Why We Should Be Investing In Disadvantaged Children 50
- Thinking Outside the Box 52
- Put Bragging Rights on Hold, Canada 53

3 Racism and Multiculturalism
- A Dialogue With Black Students 54
- Say Goodbye Huck, Say Goodbye Shylock 56
- In One Generation... 57
- Our Culture's Native Roots 59
- Want infrastructure spending that pays off? Spend the money on kids. 60

4. Canadian Culture and Identity
- Strengthening the Ties That Bind 61
- Reconsidering Our Heritage 62
- The School's Role in Debating and Discussing Our Canadian Culture 64
- Building Bridges Around the World 78

5. About this and that
- Why We Travel: A Backpackers Ethos 80
- Dance In Toronto: East Meets West 82
- Slim Chance 84
- The Case for Extremes Taxes on Extreme Wealth 90
- Thinking About Paris 91
- A Superintendent and a Principal Write to Each Other 92
- Is Oman the Canada of the Middle East? 96
- Getting Old: The Dark Side & The Bright Side 97
- Old Age. It's All About Transcendence... Gerotranscendence 102
- Architecture as Symbols 105

1. Literacy: Reading, Writing, Talking and Learning to Teach

Let them play the trombone

If we are to teach a student to play the trombone, we must allow him/her to play the thing. Similarly, if we are to teach a student a language, or history, or mathematics, we must allow him/her to "play" that subject.

I had a dream in which I observed a teacher teach a music class, day after day all year, by demonstrating from the front of the room how to play each instrument while the students sat silently behind their black music stands with their hands folded empty in their laps, as I yelled "Give them the bloody trombone!" from the back of the room. Somehow this message often escapes us when it comes to "playing" language in our classrooms. Too often, the students sit passively while the teachers experiences the joys of playing language.

Let them do it

My daughter illustrated the point last year. She was studying for a test on the short story *The Painted Door*, by Sinclair Ross. I asked her what it was about and she recounted the plot of the story. Your class discussion must have been fantastic," I said. "The issues of fidelity, ambition, and love are so wonderfully yet chillingly focused." "What discussion?!" she said, and she went on to describe her teacher asking the class what short story had been assigned the day before. He then thumbed through his recipe box, pulled out the tattered "Painted Door" card and lectured to them on his interpretation of the story; the students sat silently without their instruments.

In contrast, the next evening she attended a night school class where the assigned reading was J.D. Salinger's *Nine Short Stories*. When the class was assembled the teacher asked one question: "Which one of the nine stories did you like best and why?" Exploding with interaction the students related their preferences, inevitably revealing the personal meanings they brought to the story. My daughter came home and wanted to talk all night about what was said. She said it was the most exciting class she had ever had – all from one question! This teacher gave them the trombone.

This incident also reminds me of an English teacher who was being evaluated by a Superintendent for a permanent contract. She was teaching *The Apprenticeship of Duddy Kravitz*, by Mordecai Richler. She opened her lesson with the question "Was Buddy Kravitz a moral person?" The class erupted in heated debate; so many of them had so much to say that the teacher quickly reorganized the class into small group discussions, then brought them back together at the end of the lesson to summarize the ethical positions presented. Later, with the supervisor, she apologized for not getting to her lesson plan – but she was given an excellent rating!

Understanding is at the point of expression

For years, I thought I understood the concept of Language Across the Curriculum. It certainly seemed like a simple enough notion until one day, in a discussion with Don Routledge, a colleague at the Toronto Board of Education, a penny dropped and I felt the "Eureka!" experience. I had suddenly attained another level of understanding of language and learning significantly different from my previous level. (I wonder how many more levels there are?) Don talked about the importance of "putting it in your own words", or as James Britton once said, "Understanding is at the point of utterance." Talking is clarifying; talking is thinking; talking is learning. Similarly with writing. James Thurber, when asked what he thought about something, said "How do I know what I think until I write it down?" The act of expression is critical to understanding, whether oral or written.

In the past, psychologists have viewed thought as something that originates within the individual and then is expressed socially. We now recognize that thought develops as a social process and is internalized only after it has been socially expressed. Jan and Gordon Wells (1984) succinctly capture this notion in the title of their article *Learning to talk and talking to learn*.

Don Routledge describes the excitement of watching the explanation of Einstein's Theory of Relativity on Jacob Bronowski's series *The Ascent of Man*. As the theory was explained, he leapt up shouting "I've got it. I finally understand Einstein's Theory of Relativity!" "Oh yeah?" his wife said. "Explain it to me then." Don started to speak and stalled... he didn't have it, he wasn't quite there. He had received all the data but he hadn't sufficiently sorted and sifted, talked and worked it over to be able to articulate it. Mucking about in the material and having the time to do it is critical to developing understanding. We need to wallow in it, to talk about it, to write about it, to play it, so to speak. The significance of these simple notions, for me, has profound implications for teaching. Put simply, we must give students the trombone.

Application in teaching

With young teachers I have often described one simple implication of this principle by describing a traditional classroom exercise such as asking students to write the causes of the French Revolution in their notebooks. Traditionally, students open their textbooks and with their index fingers search out the first cause. When they find it, the information travels up their arms, across their shoulders to their other arm, down to their pens, and on to the paper. The information virtually bypasses the brain. In contrast, a simple change in the teaching process can radically alter this learning experience. For example, if the students are asked to read the section of the text that describes the causes of the French Revolution, and then asked to close their textbooks and in their own words discuss the causes of the French Revolution, what a profoundly different exercise this becomes – understanding is at the point of utterance.

I recall complaining to my principal when I was in Grade 13 that my Biology teacher never taught any lessons. He simply had us make notes from our Biology textbook for a whole year. Biology turned out to be my highest Grade 13 mark. It was years later that I made the connection between my Grade 13 mark in Biology and the method of instruction. In Biology, I was at least interacting with the material on a daily basis and instead of the mechanical transcription of the text, I was making my own notes – putting it in my own words. In all my other classes, the method of instruction was pure teacher talk. I spent all my time listening to the teacher (my attention span was thirty-two seconds!). I daydreamed for hours every day. While discussing or explaining the Biology material would have been better, the daily activity of note making was far more productive for me than sitting passively daydreaming.

Implications for practice

Nancy Atwell (1986) recently said "American school children spend ninety percent of their time listening to teachers talk". In our jurisdiction, this is a preposterous figure; yet, the need for increased pupil to pupil interaction is still one of the most common recommendations on teacher evaluation reports. We need to search continually for strategies that place students in situations where they are required to put things in their own words, to explain things, to argue positions, and to take a stand, whether orally or in writing.

In the classroom setting, a teacher can employ a variety of strategies to increase that same effect.

Benjamin Bloom, in his article *The 2 Sigma Problem*, lists teaching strategies that have the most significant effects on increasing student achievement and positive attitudes towards schooling. Included are many strategies that clearly increase the amount of pupil-to-pupil interaction. For example, tutorial instruction – one-to-one teaching with corrective feedback – has an astounding effect on student achievement. In fact, in repeated studies, ninety percent of tutored students attained the final levels of achievement that was attained by only the top twenty percent of students taught in a regular class. Put another way, the average student taught through tutorial instruction with corrective feedback outperformed 98% of the students in the control group, a regular class taught in the traditional manner – even when taught by the same teacher.

Lucy McCormick Calkins reminded me that the books you remember best are those you talked about with someone else. Alan Purves said it perfectly: "It takes two to read a book". There is certainly sufficient evidence that when older students in remedial reading programs are required to work one-on-one with a grade 1 or 2 student with remedial reading problems, the reading levels of both students improve significantly. Tutorial instruction provides opportunities for much higher levels of pupil interaction even when the tutoring is between students. The students are talking, explaining, questioning, clarifying; therefore, it's not surprising that the level of achievement increases.

Bloom also identifies co-operative learning as one of the most significant strategies for increasing student achievement. A variety of cooperative learning strategies – such as jig-saws, and student team learning – place students in situations where they are required to depend on each other in order to put together all the information required to achieve success. The result is a highly interactive classroom.

Many of Edward DeBono's thinking strategies, for example, PMI (Plus, Minus, Interesting); the "Say Something Activity" (Harste et al, N.D.); the use of group consensus activities; peer conferencing; peer evaluation; classroom debates; simulations; and sometimes simply the provocative question provide students with ample opportunity to say things in their own words, to clarify their thinking, to develop new understanding through utterance, and through "talking to learn".

In short, there are many ways to "give the student the trombone." Such strategies should be at the centre of every teacher's instructional repertoire.

References

Atwell, N. (1986) Making time for reading and writing. Presentation at the Celebrating Literacy Conference, Toronto, Ontario.
Bloom, B. S. (1984) The 2 Sigma problem: the search for methods of group instruction as effective as one-to-one tutoring. Educational Researcher, 13(6).
Calkins, L.McC. (1986) The art of teaching writing. Portsmouth, NH: Heinemann Press.
Wells, J. & Wells, G. (1984) Learning to talk, talking to learn. Theory Into Practice, 23(3).

Originally published in Education Canada, March 2014. https://www.edcan.ca/articles/the-power-of-engaged-reading/

The Power of Engaged Reading

How to boost our children's life success? Instill a love of reading

The art of reading, particularly engaged reading as opposed to the mechanics of reading, is a powerful predictor of life success by any measure. It is not only the best predictor of who goes to university – regardless of socioeconomic background and parental education – it is the best predictor of life income, career options, even life partner choices. And neuroscience is proving that reading fiction is one of the most powerful means of developing sympathetic individuals, with better social skills and higher levels of self-esteem. The converse, especially for unengaged young male readers engaged in long hours of playing video games, is higher unemployent and dependence on social welfare, antisocial behaviours and increased crime rates. Never has there ever been such compelling evidence of the power of engaged reading for our youth and their future prospects.

Reading with pleasure, and especially reading fiction, is far important than we have ever imagined.

If I were a father living in poverty, I would dedicate myself to encouraging my children to be engaged readers of relevant, age-appropriate fiction. If I were a school teacher, I would dedicate my professional development time to learn strategies to promote and develop engaged readers of meaningful and relevant novels, short stories and drama, no matter if I was a Grade 1 teacher or Grade 12 Physics teacher. It is the most important thing I could do for a child, especially a boy.

A perplexing issue within this broad realization is the disturbing disconnect between boys and reading. It verges on a problem of epidemic proportions. Finding ways to develop engaged readers is important for every child, but particularly for boys.

The state of Arizona forecasts the number of future prison cells needed based on Grade 4 state reading scores. Perhaps we should examine what they know that we may not. Increasingly, new research across many countries is showing that the best predictor of future education achievement and life success is reading ability – or, more significantly, being an engaged reader. (The engaged reader, according to Guthrie, is "purposeful, intrinsically motivated, and socially interactive.") While most research has shown, for example, that family income is the best predictor of who goes to college, Ross Finnie and Richard Mueller at the University of Ottawa have shown that "the largest determinant of university participation, however, is the score on the reading portion of the PISA." Those reading scores proved to be by far the best predictor of post-secondary attendance, even pre-empting family income and parental education.

The connection between engaged reading and life success is, in a way, intuitive. But Timothy Bates and Stuart Ritchie, at Edinburgh University, have proven the connection between reading well and future job success empirically. They analyzed the relationship between early reading skills at seven and later socio-economic life, following more than 17,000 people in England, Scotland and Wales over 50 years from 1958. They showed that reading well at age seven was a key factor in determining whether people went on to get a high-income job. Reading level at age seven was linked to social class even 35 years on. "Children with higher reading and maths skills ended up having higher incomes, better housing and more professional roles in adulthood," the authors concluded.

By contrast, 79 of 100 people entering Canadian correctional facilities don't have their high school diploma; 85 percent of them are functionally illiterate, and the vast majority are male.

In his study of 4th Graders, John Guthrie at the University of Maryland found that engaged readers from homes with few material advantages routinely outperformed less engaged readers from the most advantageous home environments. "Based on a massive sample, this finding suggests the stunning conclusion that engaged reading can overcome traditional barriers to reading achievement, including gender, parental education, and income." This is a remarkable finding as we continuously search for ways to narrow the gap between the achievement of the advantaged and the disadvantaged children in society. Literacy is the key to economic and social power, regardless of socio-economic class. As we consider the growing gender gap between boys and girls, it is even more important.

What about the boys?

The aggregate data masks a major problem that exists for boys. The gender gap is a central element in understanding the power of engaged reading. A recent Ontario Ministry of Education report on boys' literacy cites declining achievement and concludes that boys score lower than girls on all measures of literacy. There is a literacy gap between boys and girls from Grade 3 right through to Grade 12. Boys dominate behavioural and other special education classes and are twice as likely as girls to be diagnosed with an attention deficit or learning disability. They are more likely to be held back and to drop out. If they do graduate, they are less likely to attend college or university. If they do go to college, they get lower grades than female students and are less likely to graduate. Concomitant social factors are equally troubling. For example, suicidal behaviours are increasing in boys; boys are twice as likely to abuse alcohol and have higher unemployment, crime, and incarceration rates.

I believe a major factor in this growing problem with boys is the exponential use of video games, especially violent ones. While playing video games may also have positive effects, Leonard Sax posits they are the major reason for boys' declining reading scores, school achievement and increasing social problems. He argues in *Boys Adrift*, for example, that the evidence is unequivocal. The more time a child spends playing video games, the less likely he is to do well in school, at every level from elementary to college. But it is not just declining achievement, it is declining social behaviour as well. According to Sax, playing violent video games such as Doom or Grand Theft Auto "clearly and unambiguously causes young men to have a more violent self-image and to behave more violently"; playing violent video games leads directly "to aggressive behaviour, aggressive cognition, aggressive affect, and cardiovascular arousal, and to decreases in helping behaviour." Boys who play these games, he argues, are more likely to engage in "serious, real-world types of aggression."

But engaged reading of fiction offers a powerful antidote to all these negative effects, particularly for boys.

The fiction factor

If all reading is helpful, reading fiction offers added benefits – in fact, astounding benefits! It has long been argued that reading great literature improves us as human beings. Neuroscience is proving this claim to be truer than we ever imagined. Functional magnetic resonance imaging (fMRI) studies show us that the same regions of the brain that are activated during a real event are activated while reading about it in a story. Reading a story produces a vivid replica of reality. Novels are not only a simulation of reality, but permit readers to enter viscerally into the thoughts, feelings, and problems of others.

Raymond Mar, at York University performed an analysis of 86 fMRI studies. He found narratives in novels offer a unique opportunity to engage what is called "theory of mind." He, along with Keith Oatley and others, reveal how we identify with the hopes, dreams and frustrations of the novel's characters, speculate about their motives, and follow their relations, conflicts and activities with friends, lovers and family, the same areas of the brain are activated as when experiencing real-life issues. Literature allows not just learning about emotions, but experiencing them, It is a form of practice for real life. It is, both psychologically and practically, immensely beneficial.

It appears from this growing body of research that individuals who read fiction are better able to understand other people, empathize with them and see the world from their point of view. These researchers found a similar result in preschool-aged children: the more stories they had read to them, the keener their "theory of mind." For example, five-year-olds exposed to egalitarian material showed more egalitarian responses on tests of stereotypes for women's occupations that persisted over time. These results indicate an improved capacity to empathize with a marginalized group. Exposure to narrative fiction was positively associated with empathic ability, whereas exposure to expository non-fiction was negatively associated with empathy. Reading fiction not only leads readers to be more empathetic, but also leads to personal growth and improves us as individuals. Reading fiction, these researchers conclude, leads to self-understanding, a relevant key to improving ourselves. They call this effect the Self-Improvement Hypothesis, wherein "changes in selfhood can occur as a function of reading certain kinds of fiction."

The act of reading, particularly engaged reading as opposed to the mechanics of reading, is a powerful predictor of life success by anymeasure. It is the best predictor of who goes to university regardless of socio-economic background and parental education. It is the best predictor of life income, career options, even life partner choices. And neuroscience is proving that reading fiction is one of the most powerful means of developing sympathetic individuals, with better social skills and higher levels of self esteem, resulting in increasing self improvement and prosocial behaviours.

The converse, especially for unengaged young male readers, especially many of those engaged in long hours playing video games, is higher unemployment and dependence on social welfare, antisocial behaviours and increased crime rates.

So, what's not to like? Let's get our kids reading!

the DIAKIW DIGEST

Storying

There are seminal moments in my life on the journey of learning to teach that explode with discovery about something so fundamental that up to the moment of illumination I did not know was there. But when it was exposed I often felt "Of course! Why did I not see that before. It makes so much sense". One such lightening bolt struck me some 20 years ago, listening to Gordon Wells talk about the power of 'storying' in the learning process. I began to truly understand, and incorporate into my teaching, the power of story and the importance of the role of 'storying' in the learning process. Now every course I teach on social justice and equity issues in classrooms, schools, and communities is built around this narrative model. I read a children's book on the theme each class, we read relevant novels, I tell and share many personal stories and students tell and share their personal stories. We read stories, reflect and write about those stories, share our stories in class and talk about the issues that emerge. Our class mantra is "reading and writing float on a sea of talk." (Britton,1972)

Storying is central to our understanding of social justice issues in schools. As Barbara Hardy stated, "Narrative is a primary act of mind" (1977), and as Joan Didion mused, "We tell ourselves stories in order to live." (2006) Jerome Bruner opened my eyes to the fact that argument and story are two ways of knowing, "two modes of cognitive functioning, two modes of thought, each providing distinctive ways of ordering experience, of constructing reality... a good story and a well-formed argument are different, natural kinds. Arguments convince one of their truth, stories of their life-likeness." (1986). Gordon Wells connected this concept to learning in schools when he stated, "storying... is one of the most fundamental means of making meaning; as such, it is an activity that pervades all aspects of learning." (1986) As Catherine Bateson expressed it, "Our species thinks in metaphors and learns through stories." (1994)

As I returned to my first love, teaching, it is Bruner's concept of story, as an alternative way of knowing, that I have now structured my courses.

Your Brain on Fiction

New light has been cast on this notion by neuroscience. In the Sunday *New York Times*, March 18, 2012, Annie Murphy Paul, in an article called *Your Brain on Fiction*, explores this new research. I herewith extract some of her ideas that appealed to me. Here's the link to the full article, http://www.nytimes.com/2012/03/18/opinion/sunday/the-neuroscience-of-your-brain-on-fiction.html.

While many have long intuitively understood the power of story in many aspects of life, new research in neuroscience provides amazing amplification of the power of reading narrative. Novels, it appears, are formidable learning and coping tools. Stories stimulate the brain and change how we live our lives! Different parts of the brain are activated while reading, other than the well known language zones (Broca) of the brain.

When one reads smell words like "lavender" or "coffee", for example, or texture words such "leathery" hands, or motion phrases, "He kicked the ball", different parts of the brain light up not just the language centres. Even within the motion center a phrase involving the leg area, "He kicked the ball" lights up differently then when one reads, "He tossed the ball". The more illuminated the brain the richer the experience.

More importantly the brain makes no distinction between reading about an experience and encountering it in real life; the same parts of the brain are stimulated! But unlike real life, it offers us the opportunity to enter the minds and feelings of others. Raymond Mar from York University points out that's there is an overlap in the brain's networks used to understand stories, and those used to figure out the thoughts and emotions of others. This has the remarkable effect of 'honing our real-life social skills'. We learn to see the world through the eyes of others; to empathizes with them; to understand them better. The more stories read to pre-school children the keener their "theory of mind", known as the capacity of the brain to construct a map of other people's intentions.

As Keith Oatley argues, novels, stories, and drama can help us understand the complexities of social life. We have long felt the great literature makes us better people, but now, "brain science shows this claim is truer than we imagined."

Reading Recovery: A Social Justice Intervention

Birth, Demise, and Rebirth of an Idea: A Personal Memoir

Jerry Y. Diakiw, York University, Toronto, Ontario, Canada

This is a story of a personal journey of my awakening to a startling discovery of the power of Reading Recovery and its societal impact. It is also a history of this innovation in one school system where it became a part of a reform agenda addressing literacy and poverty.

Schools have been lamenting their dropout rates for decades and administrators at all levels have been searching for better ways to keep our young people in schools until at least high school graduation. The societal costs of early dropouts are staggering: high unemployment and welfare rates; teenage pregnancy; social workers; higher crime rates; and more police, courts, and prisons. The data on life expectations of dropouts are disheartening; the relationship between poverty and dropouts is unequivocal.

In 1989, a Dropout Prevention Conference for school administrators, organized by the Ontario (Canada) Ministry of Education, offered many options of "best practices." I was a recently appointed area superintendent in a York Region District School Board with just over 100 schools at that time. I was attracted to an option called Reading Recovery, offered by two psychologists from the Hamilton Board of Education. Because of our board's priority on the role of language in the learning process, I attended their session. They argued that if students were not reading by the end of Grade 1, that the rate at which they began to lag behind others was exponential. When they hit Grade 7, the psychologists stated, those students were confronted with the wall of "the textbook" at reading levels well above Grades 7 and 8. These students were soon 3 to 5 years behind their peers. This gap widened in secondary school so that, by the time these students were 15 and 16, they experienced frustration, loss of self-esteem, and shortage of credits. They soon become dropouts.

It was a compelling argument, especially since our board had been hearing presentations by Gordon Wells on his seminal work called the Bristol Study (1990). Wells followed the language acquisition of children from the age of 3 through to higher levels of schooling. His study concluded that children of the poor acquired oral language skills at the same rate as children of the wealthy, but as soon as they attended school, children from higher socioeconomic groups leapt ahead of those from lower socioeconomic levels.

The children from higher socioeconomic families lived in literate environments where most were read to daily and where parents were readers. As well, they traveled more, visited galleries and museums, and attended concerts and plays at a much higher rate. When they attended school, children knew how books worked; they knew how stories worked and they instantly understood the codes and conventions. They could imagine a different time when they heard, "Long ago when the King

---

This is a story of a personal journey of my awakening to a startling discovery of the power of Reading Recovery and its societal impact. It is also a history of this innovation in one school system where it became a part of a reform agenda addressing literacy and poverty.

---

of Spain..." These more "literate/booky" children understood story language, school language, a sense of history, and an understanding of world geography. They had acquired an important schemata or understanding upon which schoolwork could be attached, and they took off academically.

I was predisposed at this workshop to understand how one group of children could rocket ahead and another group struggle. It was a "eureka" experience. It all tumbled together – to understand how that early advantage for some students results in school success while another group slips behind incrementally followed by a declining self-esteem, even shame, before a devastating difference emerges as the student enters the intermediate grades. By the end of Grade 8, these students are "passed on," sadly, to the high school by elementary school teachers at promotion meetings. They just feel that these students, who are years below their peers, would be better off in a new setting in a high school rather than repeating Grade 8 (often having already repeated 1 or more years). I knew how this happened in school after school. I was involved in other initiatives examining the Grade 7/8 problem, especially boys. It is one of the most-painful experiences Grade 8 teachers undergo in their careers – struggling over what is the best thing to do with a student performing way below his or her grade level.

This is the great narrative of school system failure from the early days of the establishment of the public school system. It has been a chronic failure of the system at every level to address the issues of poverty in our schools, as well as students with special needs. It is a great sweep of failure that clearly begins in Kindergarten and Grade 1. The correlation between income and school achievement is overwhelming. The recent report on the reading results in Ontario, for Grades 3 and 6, showed a direct correlation in achievement between income and school achievement (O'Reilly, J. & Yau, M., 2009).

As Levin (1995) states:

> Thirty years of careful social science has provided overwhelming evidence that socioeconomic status has been and continues to be the best predictor of how much schooling students will obtain, how well they will do at their studies and what their life prospects beyond school are. (p. 31)

The Hamilton psychologists offered one proven intervention called Reading Recovery, developed in New Zealand in the mid-1970s by Dr. Marie Clay, a developmental psychologist. It was a viable solution to the problem. I was sold. Reading Recovery fit with everything I knew about early learning and early reading and what I knew about adolescent failure in Grades 7, 8, and 9. Teachers provide daily one-to-one lessons which are always based on whole texts in both reading and writing and incorporate all aspects of reading instruction.

I invited the Hamilton Reading Recovery advocates to meet with principals and introduced the feasibility of attaining literacy for all Grade 1 students. Some argued that students should not be pushed; that they would all become readers in their own time. Others saw how the difference between readers and nonreaders at that early age correlated with the eventual achievers and nonachievers at graduation time.

I was eager to push this Reading Recovery narrative forward and accelerate the prospect of widely implementing the Reading Recovery model. I asked if any principal was willing to pilot the Clay methodology. Frank Brathwaite, a new principal, jumped at the idea. At this point, all we had was Marie Clay's recent book, Becoming Literate: The Construction of Inner Control, outlining the process. He happened to have a teacher working on her doctorate in early reading who was keen to try. I remember thumping on Clay's book with my hand as I gave it to Frank and had him assure me that he would stick to the program. Unfortunately, his new teacher did not run a successful pilot. I was very unhappy at the phonics only presentation to principals on her progress and argued that it was not the Clay model, as Clay was far more holistic with whole texts as central to early reading, not solely a program on phonics, but incorporating all cueing devices.

It is indicative of the difficulty experienced trying to implement a new initiative with limited resources and only a strong feeling of the need to forge ahead. I remember my frustration at not being able to move forward with this initiative as fast as I would like. I experienced how a new innovation is often filled with pitfalls and setbacks.

Robert Dunn, my special education co-coordinator, also became deeply committed to the program after researching the long-term effect of Reading Recovery student success in follow-up years.

> I felt that, if confronted with my decision, I could justify working on the Reading Recovery program in my little domain of 25 elementary schools in the board, and work toward the goal of all my Grade 1 children reading at grade level. I believed this was a really good idea for students and that Reading Recovery would have its day. Reading Recovery was a social justice issue addressing low achievement and poverty better than anything I knew.

He was also able to research a longitudinal study of Reading Recovery costs based on the proven reduction of special education classes if students are reading at the end of Grade 1 (Lyons, 1990). Along with Frank, he also became an ardent supporter of Reading Recovery. We began to float the idea that it should be our goal to have all students reading at grade level by the end of Grade 1. It was a central part of our 5 year reform agenda, of what we called at the time, "The Fifteen Language Development Concerns". But, it was not just a literacy issue; it was a social justice issue.

In the meantime, the University of Toronto, in partnership with the Scarborough Board of Education, had opened a Reading Recovery Centre. Hazel Dick, a talented and committed special education teacher, took the training to be a Reading Recovery teacher which qualified her to be work with struggling Grade 1 students.

But, to reach our goals of full implementation and all Grade 1 students reading at grade level by the end of Grade 1, in all schools in the region, we needed to have a Reading Recovery teacher leader/trainer. This would allow us to train our own teachers. Hazel was keen to take the next step, but to become a teacher leader she had to take a year off from teaching to take the intensive yearlong coursework. First, I had to obtain the funding to release her to take the training. Robert and Frank pushed me take the next step, but I was fearful of the response.

Armed with all the research provided by Robert and accompanied by Frank, who was now also a superintendent, I arranged to put our Reading Recovery proposal on the agenda at the weekly Superintendent's Council. At this regular meeting of 18 superintendents, I simply proposed that one staff equivalent be taken off the total region staff allocation so that the board could send Hazel to be trained as a Reading Recovery teacher leader. I argued that it was consistent with our literacy initiative. We described the Reading Recovery intervention. But as we explained the process, the director bristled at being asked to finance any teacher to work individually with students. His vociferous reaction thwarted further discussion or explanation and conveyed the futility of pursuing the topic further. Immediately, he exclaimed "Let's not waste any more time, let's vote." His abrupt dismissal was shocking. There was a cold shudder around the room, as it was obvious this plan was dead.

Crestfallen, I went back to my area and met with Hazel to give her the news. She was disappointed, of course, but still felt committed to taking the training. I looked at my staffing allocation and felt I could get away with taking half a staff member off the top of my own area staff allotment. She thought about it, and felt that she could afford to be on half salary for a year. The deal was struck.

It was a dramatic decision for me to make that move 'against the grain', given the director's outburst and the vote of colleagues. I felt that it was possible I could have a career ending reprimand and possibly terminated for this, but I just had to be true to myself. I felt that, if confronted with my decision, I could justify working on the Reading Recovery program in my little domain of 25 elementary schools in the board, and work toward the goal of all my Grade 1 children reading at grade level. I believed this was a really good idea for students and that Reading Recovery would have its day. Reading Recovery was a social justice issue addressing low achievement and poverty better than anything I knew. I was comforted by the maxim, yet again – it is better to beg forgiveness than it is to seek permission.

Hazel's study-leave letter in response to her decision to train stated that "there was no commitment to implement Reading Recovery in York Region." I wondered how this story would end. It was now out of my hands.

> The York Region District School Board, a diverse and growing school district in the Greater Toronto area, currently has 161 elementary schools. In 2009-2010, 86% of all Grade 1 students were reading at grade level upon entering Grade 2. Over 13,000 students have now received Reading Recovery assistance.

The former director never knew that I took my own area staffing to initiate Reading Recovery. Bill Hogarth became the new director and had visited the Scarborough Board's Reading Recovery program. Upon arrival in York Region Board, this visionary leader was already committed to Reading Recovery and found a large number of principals already knowledgeable and committed to the program and a trained teacher leader! Frank Brathwaite, Robert Dunn, and Hazel Dick were a formidable team with exceptional implementation skills. All they needed was a supportive director who understood the potential of this intervention. As well, they had a committed and supportive Superintendent of Curriculum, Lyn Sharratt.

The York Region District School Board, a diverse and growing school district in the Greater Toronto area, currently has 161 elementary schools. In 2009-2010, 86% of all Grade 1 students were reading at grade level upon entering Grade 2. Over 13,000 students have now received Reading Recovery assistance. Controlling for first language spoken in the home other than English (39%), the discontinuing rates (former lowest students who met grade-level expectations after a full series of Reading Recovery lessons) have averaged 88% with a range of 85–91% (RRCNA Website, Jan.30, 2012). York Region achieved the highest Grades 3 and 6 test results in the province. The Grade 10 literacy test results also rank among the highest in the province, and York's dropout rates are among the lowest.

The Reading Recovery Council of North America recognized the outstanding work done by the York Region Board as part of their 25th anniversary celebrations in 2009-10. York Region has consistently outperformed the median for all districts in Ontario on the grade 3 and 6 literacy tests. Bill Hogarth was awarded an honorary doctorate by York University for his contribution to early literacy. Lyn Sharratt, Superintendent of Curriculum, masterfully implemented Reading Recovery systemwide. She hired Hazel Dick, in a new leadership position for implementing RR, outside of the federations, so that she could have frank conversations with superintendents and principals about the effectiveness of their teachers. She incorporated Reading Recovery as the essential part of an early intervention component of a comprehensive literacy plan.

The remarkable level of achievement of the York Region District School Board in province-wide testing at Grades 3, 6, and 10, is attributable, in my opinion, to the implementation of reading recovery in every school and taking the lowest achievers in Grade 1 (about 20% of the cohort annually) in the population and providing then with intensive help to attain grade level by year's end. This, despite a remarkably diverse multicultural population.

Commenting on the independent evaluation of Every Child a Reader (ECaR) in the UK, (Department of Education 2010), Douetil, writes:

> "It presents hard evidence of the significant impact of the programme on children who would otherwise be at serious risk of failing in such a central aspect of learning, especially boys and children living in poverty or with a disruptive home life" (2011a).

What is not often discussed are the attributes of those students most in need of assistance in Grade 1. Reading Recovery is centered on the belief that all children can learn to read. Douetil notes that not only do schools over-diagnose special education needs as a solution for children struggling with learning in school, but there is a clear over-representation of children in poverty among those listed as having special education needs (2011b, p. 7). These pupils are disproportionately from disadvantaged backgrounds, are much more likely to be absent or excluded from school and achieve less well than their peers both at any given age and in terms of their progress over time (Office for Standards in Education, Ofsted, 2010).

With over one in five, or 1.7 million children of school age in England identified as having special educational needs, authorities considered it vitally important that both the identification process, the kind of support students receive, work in the best interests of all children in the UK. Reading recovery is clearly the best alternative to this over identification of children with special education needs (Ofsted, 2010).

Douetil also points out:

> Children entitled to free school meals were two and a half times more likely to be identified for the intensive early literacy intervention than their more advantaged peers... Children in poverty were also more likely to be at the very bottom of the attainment curve. (2011b, p.7)

Another major report by Harrison, Johnson, & Purdon (2011) recently published in England shows that Reading Recovery, targeting the literacy levels of the lowest-achieving children in primary schools, had a significant impact. It was amongst this low-attaining group, who were disproportionately from low income families, that the most-significant results were reported. Clearly, poverty need not be a barrier to progress as, once in Reading Recovery, children entitled to free school meals made just as much progress as others.

Most encouraging is that Reading Recovery clearly has long term positive impact. As Jean Gross, former director of the Every Child a Reader Trust and England's first Communication Champion for Children, stated:

> It is fantastic to see the long term positive effect of Reading Recovery. These are very vulnerable children, with all sorts of ongoing difficulties in and out of school, so the immediate impact of the programme might easily have disappeared over three years. It hasn't, and the children now have a real chance in life (Leading education and social research, 2010).

It was also found that children provided with Reading Recovery were significantly less likely to be identified at the end of year three as having special educational needs.

Reading Recovery is not just a reading intervention; it is a social justice and equity intervention. While many argue it is too expensive, one needs to have a longer view...

The Reading Recovery program in the UK was delivered to over 23,000 students in approximately 1,600 schools in England in 2009–10. Any study would show a disproportionate number of the lowest achievers in any school come from low-income homes, often with a hard-working single mom, where these children struggle to get a healthy meal and rarely have any books in the home. In Toronto, children with parents earning over $100,000 per year outperformed students from families earning less than $30,000, by over 30 percentage points in both grade 3 and 6 (O'Reilly, J. & Yau, M. 2009). These children had at least one of the following demographic characteristics: racial minority, single parent, male, low parental education, English as second language in the home, or recent immigrant status. Reading Recovery has now been proven to erase any or all of these disadvantages to learning to read.

Reading Recovery is not just a reading intervention; it is a social justice and equity intervention. While many argue it is too expensive, one needs to have a longer view and not only compare the cost to school boards for costly special education programs but the long-term costs to society from unemployment, dropout rates, and other societal-related costs like courts, police, and prisons. In the scheme of things, Reading Recovery is cheap. The correlation between poverty and school achievement is inescapable. As Levin stated, "Poverty is such an enormous negative influence that it must be part of the educational reform agenda whether justified on grounds of economic interest or of social justice" (1995, p. 21).

As David Moriarty of the Reading Recovery Council of North America put it:

> Reading Recovery steps into a child's life at a critical time – before the cycle of failure begins. It remains worldwide as an example of the most powerful, effective staff development program available, yielding the best-trained teachers of reading in their districts, and compared to other programs that go on for years and never get children reading on grade level, Reading Recovery is a bargain (RRCNA website, November 2010).

In the great narrative of the historic school systems' failure to address the needs of children in poverty and with special needs, I really do believe that Reading Recovery is one of the best high school dropout prevention programs there is. Reading Recovery is a powerful intervention in the issue of the persistence of child poverty.

This is a personal story of my observations and participation in the journey of the implementation of Reading Recovery in one district. It demonstrates the ways in which ideas can be extinguished and the ways in which ideas can be ignited. It is also about the magic of learning to read, what Alberto Manguel calls "the most human of creative acts" (2010). At a time when one in six Canadians still cannot read a headline, understanding the process of learning to read is still an issue of great concern.

For me, it all started with a workshop option at a high school dropout prevention conference focusing on a Grade 1 reading program! It seemed odd, but it works!

References

Clay, M. M. (1991). Becoming Literate: The Construction of Inner Control, Toronto, Pearson Education Canada.

Department of Education (2011). Evaluation of Every Child a Reader (ECaR) in the UK, London, UK.

Douetil, J. (2011a, May). Hard Evidence That Reading Recovery Works, Institute of Education, University of London Website, http://www.ioe.ac.uk/newsEvents/53063.html.

Douetil, J. (2011b, May). At last, some good news about children in poverty, Literacy Today, Summer No. 66, p7.

Harrison, C., Johnson, G., & Purdon S. (2011). Evaluation of every child a reader (ECaR), (Research Report DFE-RR114). Department for Education by the National Centre for Social Research (NatCen), the Institute for Fiscal Studies (IFS), the University of Nottingham, and Bryson Purdon Social Research (BPSR), London, NatCen.

Leading education and social research (2010). New Report Reveals Success of Every Child a Reader Programme, Institute of Education, University of London, London, UK. http://www.ioe.ac.uk/newsEvents/35492.html.

Levin, B. (1995). Educational responses to poverty, Canadian Journal of Education, 20(2), 211–224.

Literacy Trust (2012). New research reveals ongoing success of every child a reader programme, Literacy Trust Website, Jan 18, 2012. http://www.literacytrust.org.uk/news/1475.

Lyons, C. A. (1991). Reading Recovery: A Viable Prevention of Learning Disability, Reading Horizons, 31(5), pp. 384-408.

Manguel, A. (2010, December 3). Host of Empire of the Word, [Television series]. Four-part documentary based on his 1996 book, A History of Reading. Television Ontario, TVO. Available on YouTube at http://www.youtube.com/?v=iZWj9u88uEo&feature=youtube_gdata_player.

Office for Standards in Education, Ofsted, (2010). Ofsted Report on Special Educational Needs. Children's Services and Skills, UK.

O'Reilly, J. & Yau, M. (2009). Parent Census, Kindergarten-Grade 6: System Overview and Detailed Findings, Toronto District School Board.

Reading Recovery Council of North America (2012). Website, Jan. 30., www.readingrecovery.org.

Wells, G. (1985). The Meaning Makers: Children Learning Language and Using Language to Learn. Portsmouth, N.H, Heinemann.

Originally published in Canadian Children's Literature Quarterly, Fall 1997.

Children's Literature and Canadian Identity
A Revisionist Perspective

Canadian children's literature can play an important role in affirming a Canadian culture and identity. The school has always played and, whether we like it or not, always will play, an important role in promoting a national perspective. This article argues that there are commonplaces of our Canadian culture and identity that are inclusive of Canadians of all racial and ethnocultural origins and from all parts of Canada. The promotion of any national viewpoint is usually directed at the secondary level where Can-Lit and Canadian history become a focus for study. This viewpoint has traditionally been a Eurocentric perspective that has ignored the reality of Canada's current diversity. A focus on the secondary level ignores the fact that most societies have traditionally focussed on inducting their youth into the "tribe" before the age of thirteen. Therefore elementary schools have an important role to play in telling the Canadian story through children's literature, a literature that can not only reveal the splendour of our regional diversity, but one that can promote equity, justice and fairness through the richness of our multicultural literature.

Many Canadians believe that there is such regional, cultural, linguistic and religious diversity in this country that we do not in fact have an overriding culture or identity. But even those who express this belief are quick to distance us Canadians from our American neighbours and from our British and French roots. I would like to argue that there are in fact powerful commonplaces in our culture and identity – shared values that most Canadians can identify with – and that the school is an important place to explore, discuss and debate these commonplaces. I especially want to suggest that, because story and literature are important ways to reveal these commonplaces, there can be a powerful connection between Canadian literature and Canadian cultural identity, a connection educators should take advantage of. Nor is it just a matter of including Canadian literature at the secondary school level. Since it is in the early years before puberty that who we are really comes into focus, I believe it is imperative that we give young children access to the rich body of Canadian children's literature.

Schools in Canada and elsewhere have always conveyed cultural and political views, and they will continue to do so whether we like it or not. In the past, of course, these views were dominated largely by the white male European perspective of the most dominant powers in society; but as the conviction of so many that there is no over-riding Canadian culture suggests, this is no longer true. The culture and identity we all share is multi-faceted, and not dominated by any one group. The difficult task schools now face, therefore, is determining how to convey our culture and identity in a way that is inclusive of all Canadians, so that justice and equity are underlying principles of the curriculum.

How Cultures Have Traditionally Transmitted Their Values

In most culturally homogeneous countries, children grow up hearing and learning the stories that define their culture: myths, legends, folklore, historic tidbits, tales of heroes and villains, miraculous tales and tales of courage and achievement. These shared stories lie at the heart of a culture's identity. Literature, arts and crafts, music, dance, film, and poetry blend together over time to crystallize an image that says, "This is who we are." The shared stories provide a culture with its values and beliefs, its goals and traditions. The myths, legends, folk tales, histories, and experiences of any cultural group bind the individuals together to form a cohesive society which allows people to communicate with each other and to work together with a shared purpose. These common stories become the foundation of public discourse, and they are a source of pride in their community.

The education of children is central to this process. According to E.D. Hirsch Jr., "The weight of human tradition across many cultures supports the view that basic acculturation should largely be completed by age thirteen. At that age Catholics are confirmed, Jews bar or bat mitzvahed, and tribal boys and girls undergo the rites of passage into the tribe" (30). Hirsch traces how Korean children traditionally memorize the five Kyung and the four Su. In Tibet, boys from eight to ten read aloud and learn the scriptures, in Chile the Araucanian Indians use songs to learn the customs and traditions of their tribe. The Bushmen children of South Africa listen to hours of discussion until they know the history of every aspect of their culture.

Hirsch also traces how the education system has been used to convey a national culture in modem nations. Traditionally on any particular day in France, for example, each child in each grade would be reading the same page in the same textbook. In the history of American education, the text book has been a constant source of debate over attempts to control the culture transmitted through the schools.

Hirsch cites an example of the influence of one particular document in defining a culture. In 1783, Hugh Blair, a Scot from the University of Edinburgh published *Lectures on Rhetoric and Belle Lettres*, intended as a compendium of what every Scot needed to know if he or she were to read and write well in English. This book had enormous impact on curriculum in school systems throughout the English-speaking world. Widely used in Great Britain, US and Canada between 1783 and 1911, the book went through 130 editions! Blair defined English literary culture for use initially by the Scots, later by colonials like Canadians and Americans; and eventually it became the standard for educating Englishmen and women.

In *Nations & Nationalism* (1983), Ernest Gellner argues that, viewed from a historical perspective, it has been the school and not the home that has been the decisive factor in creating national cultures in modern nations. Literate national cultures, he maintains, are school-transmitted cultures. He asserts that the chief creators of the modern nation have been school teachers; they helped create the modern nation state. They perpetuate it and make it thrive. The history of Europe has shown that the schools play a major role in the creation of a national culture. Even in the United States with its many disparate groups, the schools have done much to create a national culture through such common shared stories, both real and imagined, as George Washington, Daniel Boone, Tom Sawyer, and Casey at the Bat, as well as through the promotion of strong central shared values and symbols of patriotism.

The history of the evolution of nationalism in country after country indicates clearly that a national culture is an artificial, created construct. Discussing how nation builders use a patchwork of folk materials, old songs, legends, dances, and historical tidbits, selected and re-interpreted by intellectuals to create a national culture, Gellner says, "The cultural shreds and patches used by nationalism are often arbitrary inventions, any old shred or patch would have served as well… Nationalism is not what it seems and above all, not what it seems to itself. The culture it claims to defend is often its own invention".

While these readings and discussions have illuminated for me how culture has been transmitted during our recent world history of colonialism and nationalism, they have unsettling implications. Hirsch, for instance, laments what he sees as the disintegration of central core values and a shared common knowledge in recent years. He argues for the need to identify what every American needs to know, and works to promote a return to a narrowly Eurocentric curriculum based on the glories of Greek civilization, the British Empire, and the Bible. While the European civilizations, and in particular, British and French traditions, are an integral part of our identity, they are but one significant facet among many facets.

Yes the school is, and always has been a major purveyor of a national viewpoint. But what kind of a viewpoint do we want to promote for the future? Any examination of the curricula of the past reveals a program of indoctrination into the culture and mores of those in power. The old African proverb is still true: "Until lions have their own historians, tales of bravery and courage will be told about the hunter." Or, as Napoleon put it more bluntly, "History is a set of lies agreed upon." History is written by winners (Wright). The winners write the school curriculum and decide what stories will be told and what literature will be read.

As the child of immigrant Ukrainian parents in grade seven and eight in Toronto in the late 1940s, I vividly remember spending hours memorizing the Kings and Queens of England in chronological order. Later in high school I read the required stories and novels of Rudyard Kipling, Charles Dickens and Jane Austen, and the poetry of Tennyson and Wordsworth. I do not recall ever reading any Canadian authors. The children's books in the local library reflected this Anglocentric curriculum. I grew up feeling that I was somehow an outsider in Canada despite the fact that I was born in the country. Nor was I alone: My current research into the life histories of racial minority teachers in Canada reveals time and again that as students these young Canadians did not see themselves reflected in the curriculum of their schools. These experiences illustrate how recently in our history educators perceived the transmission of traditional culture as a major function of schools. It was clear who the winners were.

Revisioning the Traditional Culture

Since Prime Minister Trudeau proclaimed the policy of Multiculturalism in 1971, there has been a remarkable change in our official notions about our culture. It is no longer officially English or French-based or Eurocentric. Indeed, Trudeau said, "While we have two official languages we have *no official culture*, no one culture is more official than another" (italics mine). I have long celebrated Trudeau's statement; but the longer I ponder it the more I have difficulty with the words, "we have no official culture…" It seems to imply what many have said for decades, that Canada has no cultural identity at all. The insistence on no official culture has resulted in a backlash against multiculturalism, while multiculturalists struggle to stem the tide of racism and disempowerment.

Education, then, is caught between conflicting demands. As Grossberg suggests,

> "On the one hand, there is the discourse of multiculturalism and liberation which calls for a democratic culture based on social difference and which is usually predicated on a theory of identity and representation. On the other side there is a discourse of conservatism based on canonical notions of general education and a desire to impose what it cannot justify – the existence of an illusory common culture."

Simply, there is a lament over the loss of a culture rooted in Western civilization and values, and there is also the cry for equity and a multicultural curriculum. Must there be a dualism? Is there an alternative to these two positions? Amidst the remarkable diversity of this country are there inclusive commonplaces? Can a patchwork quilt of our stories welcome all Canadians?

It is helpful to review some history surrounding some of these issues. We have been inundated the last few years with critical examinations of the meaning and purpose of multiculturalism and its affects on the curriculum in the school. Popular best selling books like Hirsch's *Cultural Literacy*, Bibby's *Mosaic Madness* and Bissoondath's *Selling Illusions* have promoted a return to a traditionalist view. In Henry Giroux's view, they have "argued that multiculturalism posits a serious threat to the school's traditional task of defending and transmitting an authentic national history, a uniform standard of cultural literacy, and a singular national identity for all citizens to embrace". The heated position of the traditionalists is best demonstrated by Roger Kimbal's provocative statement:

> "Implicit in the politicizing mandate of multiculturalism is an attack on the idea of common culture, the idea that despite our many differences, we hold in common an intellectual, artistic, and moral legacy, descending largely from the Greeks and the Bible/supplemented and modified over the centuries by innumerable contributions from diverse hands and peoples. It is this legacy that has given us our science,

our political institutions, and the monuments of artistic and cultural achievement that define us as a civilization. Indeed it is this legacy, insofar as we live up to it, that *preserves us from chaos and barbarism*. And it is precisely this legacy that the multiculturalists wish to dispense with." (italics mine)

This position is widely held in Canada as well. The notion that our cultural mosaic and regional and ethnic differences can promote "chaos and barbarism" is a form of extremism that is not useful in promoting a constructive dialogue.

An alternative is to think of culture as, in Gates's words, "a conversation among different voices." Is it possible, by identifying a set of commonplaces, to balance the traditionalist objective and yet incorporate a multicultural, inclusive and liberating perspective? Is it possible for diversity to be a source of cultural identity? Is the idea of multiple loyalties and identities possible within the framework of a national culture and identity?

I personally identify with my Ukrainian heritage, my Toronto and Ontario regional roots, with immigrant cultures, as well as feeling an overriding identity with Canada and even a pervading global outlook. Survey data indicate strong regional loyalties and identities in many parts of Canada, far stronger than any regional loyalties in the United States; yet the evidence shows that the stronger the regional loyalty, the stronger the identity with Canada (Lipset).

As individuals we hold a complex set of loyalties and cultural identities, particularly in Canada. We have a strong bond to place – neighbourhood or community; often a strong affinity to our bio-region – the Maritimes or the Prairies, for example; often also a bond to our ethnic and/or our linguistic heritage, and to our religious group; and finally, to our country. For many Canadians there is even a strong feeling of loyalty to, and identity with, the planet. We move in and out of our various "tribes" with ease and comfort. The complexity of our "tribal" relations is in fact quite extraordinary. We are a mass of hierarchical, overlapping, shifting, often contradictory and conflicting loyalties and identities.

Given this complexity, one might ask why national identity and culture are so controversial. Among many academics, nationalism is a concept in disrepute. At one extreme, David Trend declares, "Nationality is a fiction. It is a story people tell themselves about who they are, where they live and how they got there." And in *Imagined Communities: Reflections on the Origin and Spread of Nationalism*, Benedict Anderson demonstrates how nationalism is only a recent phenomenon in human history. He finds its origins in the late eighteenth century, and points out three paradoxes about it. The first is "the objective modernity of nations to the historian's eye vs. their subjective antiquity in the eye of nationalists." The second is "the formal universality of nationality as a socio-cultural concept – [the idea] in the modem world that everyone can, should, will 'have' a nationality, as he or she has a gender..." The third paradox is "the 'political' power of nationalisms vs. their philosophical poverty and even incoherence." Anderson comments that, as Gertrude Stein referred to Oakland, one can quickly conclude with respect to nationalism that "there is no there there".

But despite his unwavering scorn for the concept of nationalism, Anderson reflects on the continuing process:

> "And many 'old nations,' once thought fully consolidated, find themselves challenged by 'sub'-nationalism within their borders – nationalisms which, naturally, dream of shedding this sub-ness one happy day. The reality is quite plain: the 'end of the era of nationalism,' so long prophesied, is not remotely in sight. Indeed, nation-ness is the most universally legitimate value in the political life of our time."

Why culture and identity need to be addressed in the schools

Regardless of how we feel about this debate, nation-ness is with us. Nationalism is clearly not going to go away. It is unlikely we can do much about it. We can, however, make every effort to ensure that the manner in which our nation-ness is promoted in the school is based on democratic principles of justice and equity, concepts which also lie at the core of our Canadian commonplaces. As a pragmatist educator I am confronted with the problem of observing a gathering of fundamentalist, traditionalist and conservative forces which are erupting across this country and whose views are consistent with those of Roger Kimbal – that the legacy of western civilization and the Bible saves us from "chaos and barbarism." They are fanning a backlash and are profoundly influencing the policy-makers and practitioners to bring back their "common culture," a move which they see as a return to essentially an exclusive Eurocentric Christian society. They view the schools as having a central role in transmitting their view of our common culture through a common curriculum.

"Some argue that in an increasingly multicultural society there is a need for a common literacy; others propose that we are moving toward a culture of many literacies." (Trend) I propose bridging these two positions – that we work towards a common literacy as long as the common literacy is inclusive of all Canadians.

This sort of bridging of these positions requires a revisioning of our traditional notions of our culture. For example, we have to recognize the temporal character of culture. As Tomlinson points out, "There is no such thing as a single national culture that remains the same year after year. Nations are constantly assimilating, combining and revising their national characters" (Trend). In a speech given by Sheldon Hackney, Chairman of the National Endowment for the Arts in 1993, he claims, "All ethnic groups have permeable boundaries, and the meaning of any particular identity will change over time... History has a way of changing who we think we are." Hackney postulates a view of America that I believe is equally true of Canada: "There is an American identity that is different from the identities of any one of the ethnic groups that comprise the American population, that is inclusive of all of them and that is available to everyone who is an American."

Commonplaces of Canadian Culture and Identity

One way in which culture and identity can be addressed from a revisionist stance is by approaching the issue from the perspective of commonplaces of our culture accessible to all. It is important to identify these commonplaces, not because they are finite, correct, or complete enough to end the debate, but simply because they can provide a starting point for further debate and discussion. As Richard Rorty has argued, it is not so important to arrive at the absolute truth as it is to "keep the conversation going".

While Canadian culture is constantly evolving, I am convinced that it is tied together by a number of commonplaces which most Canadians consciously or unconsciously accept, promote and take pride in, commonplaces which permeate many aspects of our society and reveal some central truths about our country. Elsewhere, I have discussed ten such commonplaces in some detail. Let me list them here:

1. Canada: A wilderness nation, a land of awesome size and grandeur, with savage beauty and incredible obstacles. Despite our largely urban existence our wilderness preoccupies our psyche, our literature, our arts, our mythology.

2. Canada: A country of diverse and distinctive regions with powerful regional identities – Quebec, the Maritimes, the Prairies, for example.

3. Canada: A democratic, multi-faith nation with remarkable freedoms. Equity is enshrined in our Charter of Rights and Freedoms, but we are nevertheless a nation marked by equity struggles yet unfolding, for First Nations, women, people of colour, and French Canadians.

4. Canada: A nation with a strong sense of social welfare. A social safety net is part of our tradition, a tradition that is the envy of many of our neighbours to the south.

5. Canada: Home of our First Nations. Our Native roots are deeply entwined in our Canadian way.

6. Canada: A nation of immigrants. We cherish our multicultural mosaic, our immigrant culture – this immigrant culture has forever attracted adventurers, inventors and entrepreneurs.

7. Canada: A nation state founded initially on the cultures of France and England. They have profoundly contributed to many of our institutions, laws and principles. Most of us respect and support our bilingual society and our distinct Francophone culture centered in Quebec.

8. Canada: A nation of enormous resources with a vibrant, inventive economy. Our identity is in part a product of this economy, one that permits one of the highest standards of living of any nation in the world.

9. Canada: A nation of rich cultural traditions in the arts, sports and popular culture. We have a legacy of distinctive creative and artistic achievement in all the arts, provided by institutions such as the CBC, the NFB, the National Ballet, the Montreal Symphony, the Canadian Opera Company as well as by individuals like Bryan Adams, Alanis Morriset, Celine Dion, and our many comedians.

10. Canada: Peace-keepers for the world and a partner with all nations. Our long history as peace-keepers and mediators, our participation in international organizations, our long involvement with developing nations, and our comparatively open immigration and refugee polices, confirm our global commitment as global citizens and our family ties to virtually every country in the world.

Note: Since publishing this article I have added two more commonplaces. Canada: A Northern Nation, and Canada: Not the USA. See The School's Role in Debating and Discussing Our Canadian Culture, *p64.*

In struggling to identify these commonplaces, I asked myself a series of questions. Do they provide ample latitude to address critical issues in our society? Do they provide for a new multicultural curriculum that provides opportunities for students to become, in Henry Giroux's words, "border crossers"? As Giroux states, "Teachers must be educated to become border crossers, to explore zones of cultural difference by moving in and out of the resources, histories and narratives that provide different students with a sense of identity, place and possibility". And finally, do the commonplaces reveal that there is a Canadian identity that is different from any one of the ethnic or regional identities that comprise the Canadian population, and are also different, for example, from an American identity?

I believe that the answer to all these questions is, yes. Canada is a complex nation with multiple characteristics and identities. Its identity is comprised of layer upon layer of physical, regional, linguistic, ethnic, religious and cultural variations. While any one of the commonplaces I listed may also be characteristic of other nations, the layering of them, one over another, creates a unique Canadian culture. But despite this complexity, there is a Canadian culture and identity that emerges from this layering that is different from any one of the regional, cultural or ethnic cultures and identities that exist within Canada. Nevertheless, this national culture and identity is inclusive of all groups and individuals and is accessible to all Canadians. All regions and ethnocultural groups can relate to these commonplaces.

Most significantly in terms of literature, these commonplaces are rich with stories that are part of our "community of memory." There are gripping and fascinating stories that emerge from them, whether through narratives of events or through biographies of remarkable women and men who exemplify them. While there is room for considerable debate and discussion here, these commonplaces are the "stuff" that myths are made of. The big stories of Canada are embedded in them.

The Role of Story and Literature

Story is a powerful and traditional way to provide a common bond for members of a society and to familiarize children with a culture. According to Postman, "Human beings require stories to give meaning to the facts of their existence… nations, as well as people, require stories and may die for a lack of a believable one". And Bellah states:

"Communities in the sense that we are using the term, have a history – in an important sense they are constituted by their past – and for this reason we can speak of a real community as a 'community of memory,' one that does not forget its past. In order not to forget the past a community is involved in retelling its story… These stories of collective history and exemplary individuals are an important part of the tradition that is so central to a community of memory."

It is through stories that our central values and commonplaces are shared. It is through stories that we can preserve and enhance our Native roots, our rich multicultural heritage, while still revealing an understanding of the historic traditions and structures that created the Canadian nation state. Our stories explore and reveal our commonplaces. In *Survival*, Margaret Atwood argues for the important understanding of how our culture is revealed in our literature:

> "I'm talking about Canada as a state of mind, as a space you inhabit not just with your body but with your head. It's that kind of space in which we find ourselves lost.
>
> What a lost person needs is a map of the territory, with his own position marked on it so he can see where he is in relation to everything else. Literature is not only a mirror; it is also a map, a geography of the mind. Our literature is one such map, if we can learn to read it as our literature, as the product of who and where we have been. We need such a map desperately, we need to know about here. Because here is where we live. For the members of a country or a culture, shared knowledge of their place, their here, is not a luxury but a necessity. Without that knowledge we will not survive."

Toward Understanding Our Culture and Identity

Because our identities, our attitude to people of different races, our sense of self and therefore probably our sense of a national identity or lack of it, is largely fixed by the end of elementary school, children's literature can be a powerful way of sharing a nation's stories. Fortunately, furthermore, there is now a rich body of Canadian children's literature which can provide our children with knowledge of our culture and identity – "a map, a geography of the mind." Many titles provide rich insight into many of the commonplaces I have identified, and reveal a revisioned Canadian culture consistent with the heritage of our young Canadians from across Canada of all races, religions, and cultures. A loose collection of such titles, if profiled and shared across Canada, could bind all Canadian school children together in the knowledge that in every school from White Horse to St. John's, whether Black, First Nation, Chinese, French Canadian or fourth generation English Canadian, they would all be reading and discussing many of the same Canadian stories, stories in which they can see a reflection of themselves. Through this process they would be inducted into the Canadian "tribe." These central conceptions and the shared stories, tales, histories, and poems would be the starting point for the beginning of our student's understanding of a Canadian culture.

In a country in which educational curricula are controlled by individual provinces, however, no authority exists to set any such canon. But at the secondary school level, at least, an unwritten canon has evolved amongst teachers across Canada. A central core of titles has emerged through word of mouth, through articles and journals, through courses, and through discussions at conferences and meetings. On the Can-Lit discussion group on the internet, for example, scholars and teachers from across Canada share their views about titles and authors they suggest for serious study. No such process has developed at the elementary level, where perhaps the need is greatest. Our students are more familiar with the wonderful children's authors from England, the United States and Australia than they are with our own Canadian authors and illustrators. In the faith that a loose list of shared Canadian materials would be of great value, I would like to offer some suggestions about what it might contain.

- Pre-primer alphabet books such as R.K. Gordon's A Canadian Child's ABC, Ann Blades's By the Sea (a BC alphabet book). Erica Rutherford's An Island Alphabet, about PEI, Elizabeth Cleaver's ABC, Ted Harrison's A Northern Alphabet, Stephanie Poulin's Ah! Belle Cite, A Beautiful City, ABC and A Halifax ABC. Through these alphabet books, young children become familiar with many of our Canadian icons.

- Children's stories by some of our finest writers: Margaret Lawrence's Olden Days Coat, Gabrielle Roy's Clip Tail, Mordecai Richler's Jacob Two Two and the Hooded Fang, W.O. Mitchell's Jake and the Kid, Farley Mowat's Owls in the Family, Ralph Connor's Glen Garry School Days, Lucy Maud Montgomery's Anne of Green Gables, Marshall Saunders' Beautiful Joe.

- Richly-illustrated picture story books that have entered into our canon, such as Robert Service's Cremation of Sam McGee and The Shooting of Dan McGrew illustrated by Ted Harrison, William Kurelek's Prairie Boy's Winter, Roch Carrier's The Hockey Sweater, and perhaps even Robert Munsch's Paper Bag Princess.

- Stories of our multicultural heritage such as Ian Wallace's Chin Chiang and the Dragon Dance and The Sandwich, Ann Blades's Mary of Mile 18, Paul Yee's Curses of the Third Uncle, Mary Hamilton's The Tin-lined Trunk, Sing Lim's West Coast Chinese Boy, Kit Pearson's Guests of War Trilogy about war-time guests from England, Laura Langston's No Such Thing as Far Away, a story set in Chinatown, Ann Alma's Skateway to Freedom, and Marlene Nourbese Philip's Harriet's Daughter.

- Historical novels such as Susanne Martel's The King's Daughter, set in New France; Barbara Smucker's Days of Terror, Barbara Greenwood's A Question of Loyalty, Geoffrey Bilson's Fire over Montreal, Marsha Hewitt's One Proud Summer, James Reaney's The Boy With An R in His Hand, Bernice Thurman Hunter's Booky series, and Janet Lunn's The Root Cellar, to name just a few.

- We need to provide opportunities to have children appreciate and celebrate our spiritual and religious diversity through such books as Kathleen Cook-Waldren's A Wilderness Passover, the Divali story in Rachna Gilmore's Lights for Gita, Kim So Goodtrack's ABC's of Our Spiritual Connection, as well as Christmas stories such as Bud Davidge's Mummer's Song, about Christmas in Newfoundland.

- The readings should also include stories that capture the majesty and savage grandeur of the country in wilderness survival tales such as Jan Truss's Jasmin. First Nation stories such as Markoosie's Harpoon of the Hunter, Jan Andrews's The Very Last First Time, Grey Owl's The Adventures of Sajo and the Beaver People, James Houston's Tikta Liktak: An Eskimo Legend, and Kevin Major's Blood Red Ochre.

- Fairy tales and legends from Eva Martin's Canadian Fairy Tales, Maurice Barbeau's The Golden Phoenix and other Tales from Quebec and Claude Aubry's The Magic Fiddler and Other Legends of French Canada, and First Nation myths and legends, such as William Toye and Elizabeth Cleaver's How Summer Came to Canada or The Loon's Necklace as well as children's literature written and illustrated by Native Canadians, for example, Michael Arvaaluk's Arctic 1,2,3.

- Poetry selections from anthologies such as Mary Alice Downie and Barbara Robertson's The New Wind Has Wings; Poems from Canada and David Booth's Till All the Stars Have Fallen.

- There are many titles that capture the essence of our many distinctive regions. The Prairies, as one region for example, are portrayed evocatively through such visually splendid titles as Jo Bannatyne-Cugnet's A Prairie Alphabet, A Prairie Year and Grampa's Alkali, David Booth's Dustbowl, William Kurelek's A Prairie Boy's Summer, Jim McGugan's Josepha: A Prairie Boy's Story, Marilynn Reynolds's Belle's Journey, a story of the Prairies in the twenties, and of course, the works of W.O. Mitchell. These and many other titles can convey a sense of the Prairies to young people from across Canada. Similar collections could be pulled together for each of the regions of Canada with the exception of Quebec. It is lamentable that the rich body of children's literature that exists in Quebec is not widely available in English nor is much of the literature in English available to children in Quebec.

- Biographies too, have an important role to play in creating a Canadian identity, not just the traditional figures included in the curriculum such as our adventurous explorers, founding fathers and sports figures, but including women, aboriginal and Black heroes in such sources as: Susan Merritt's Her Story: Women of Canada's Past, Jo-Ann Archibald et al's Courageous Spirits: Aboriginal Heroes of our Children, and Rosemary Sadlier's Leading the Way: Black Women in Canada.

- A rich body of recent historical works are available with the lively retellings of historic events by Pierre Berton, the Adventures of Canadian History series, Marsha Boulton's Just a Minute: Glimpses of Our Great Canadian Heritage, and Barbara Greenwood's A Pioneer Story, as well as compelling new historical biographies such as Jean Little's His Banner Over Me, the story of one of Canada's early female doctors, and new biographies for children including those of Nellie McClung and Roberta Bondar.

- But the Canadian story is not only about successes and heroic deeds. As Bellah says, "A genuine community of memory will also tell painful stories of shared suffering that sometimes creates deeper identities than success... And if the community is completely honest it will remember stories not only of suffering received but of suffering inflicted – dangerous memories, for they call the community to alter ancient evils. The communities of memory that tie us to the past also turn us toward the future as communities of hope. They carry a context of meaning that can allow us to connect our aspirations of a larger whole and see our own efforts being contributions to a common good." (153)

- Thus, the list should include stories of the Japanese internment, such as Joy Kogawa's Naomi's Road and Shizuye Takashima's A Childhood in Prison Camp; stories about early slavery and emancipation in Canada, such as Barbara Smucker's Underground to Canada; stories about discrimination like Jean Little's From Anna, Brian Doyle's Angel Square, Paul Yee's Tales of Gold Mountain and Ghost Train, Ann Walsh's Shabash in which a Sikh boy confronts racism, and Michelle Marineau's Road to Chlifa, in which Karim emigrates from war-torn Beirut and faces discrimination in Quebec.

While discussion and debate would be necessary to identify a core body of exemplary materials, as it has over time at the secondary level, it is important hat they reflect the central commonplaces of Canada's culture. The selection of these stories would be like creating a patchwork quilt. Each patch or story would be an individual creation of merit in its own right, but collectively, they would blend together to create a total image. Together these patches would tell the new emerging Canadian story.

While we do have some outstanding resources to begin, it is not enough. We still need to find new ways to tell tales about our heroes, not textbook biographies but fireside tales – tales about our First Nations, our explorers, our fur traders, our pioneer women, our artists and musicians, our great athletes and scientists; about the settlement of the west, the discovery of our minerals, and the building of our railways, the contributions of our new immigrants; about our international accomplishments, our Nobel Peace Prize winner; and in particular, we need sources about French Canada to bridge the two solitudes. We need to tell more stories that capture our multicultural heritage –stories about the Jewish fur traders and settlers who were here even before the English; about the Black Canadian men and women who lived in Nova Scotia two hundred years ago in greater numbers than Scots; about the Chinese workers who built the railways; about the English, Scottish, Irish, Ukrainian, Finnish, German, Sikh, and Japanese immigrants, to name just a few who broke ground across this country to make Canada what it is today.

Parekh defines multiculturalism in a way that fits appropriately within the intent of my conception of the commonplaces of our identity: Multiculturalism doesn't simply mean numerical plurality of different cultures, but rather a community which is creating, guaranteeing, encouraging spaces within which different communities are able to grow at their own pace. At the same time it means creating a public space in which these communities are able to interact and enrich the existing culture and create a new consensual culture in which they recognize reflections of their own identity. (Cited in Giroux 7)

We know that the school is a major purveyor of a political viewpoint. It always has been, and always will be. If we recognize this influence, we can promote a viewpoint that is reflective of all Canadians and that commits us to a continuing search for equity and a society for the new millennium that is free of racism and inequities. The "big" themes or commonplaces of Canadian culture can assist us in suggesting a core of readings for reading aloud, for study or discussion, for every grade from Kindergarten to grade nine in every school in Canada, that contributes to a truly just, equitable and inclusive society. Through this collective patchwork quilt of shared stories we create "a community of memory," and we reveal our Canadian culture and identity in a way that allows Canadians from all regions, French and English speaking, of diverse racial and ethnocultural backgrounds to "recognize reflections of their own identity" – a way that says, "this is who we are."

References

Anderson, B. *Imagined Communities: Reflections on the Spread of Nationalism*, rev. ed. New York, Verso, 1991.
Atwood, M. *Survival*, Toronto, Anansi Press, 1972.
Bellah, R., R. Madsen, W. Sullivan, A. Swidler, and S Tipton. *Habits of the Heart*. Berkeley, University of California Press, 1985.
Bibby, R.W. *Mosaic Madness*, Toronto, Stoddart, 1990.
Bissoondath, N. *Selling Illusions: The Cult of Multiculturalism in Canada*, Toronto, Penguin, 1994.
Diakiw, J. *The school's role in revealing the commonplaces of our national culture and identity a multicultural perspective*, Multicultural Education The State of the Art National Study, Report #4, Ed. Keith A McLeod, Winnipeg, Canadian Association of Second Language Teachers, 1996.
Gates, H.L. Jr. *Multiculturalism a conversation among different voices*, Rethinking Schools, Oct/Nov 1991.
Gellner, Ernest, *Nations and Nationalism*, Ithaca NY, Cornell UP, 1983.
Giroux, H *Living dangerously identity politics and the new cultural racism*. Grossberg.
Giroux, H *Curriculum, multiculturalism and the politics of identity*, National Association of Secondary Principals' Bulletin 76(548[1992]) 1-11.
Ghosh, R. *Redefining Multicultural Education*, Toronto, Harcourt Brace, 1996.
Grossberg, L., Ed. *Between Borders*, New York, Vintage, 1993.
Hackney, S. *Beyond the culture wars*, Speech to the National Press Club, 1993.
Hirsch, E.D. Jr. *Cultural Literacy: What Every American Needs to Know*, New York, Vintage Books, 1987.
Kimball, R. *Tenured radicals: a postscript*, The New Criterion, Jan 4-13, 1991.
Lipset, S.M. *Continental Divide*, New York, Routledge, 1990.
Postman, N. *Learning by story*, New Yorker, Dec 1984, 119-124.
Rorty, R. *Philosophy and the Mirror of Nature*, Princeton UP, 1979.
Trend, D. *Nationalities, pedagogies and media*, Grossberg.
Wright, R. *Stolen Continents*, Toronto, Penguin, 1992.

Learning to Write by Rote

My article pasted below was in the *Globe and Mail* many years ago. It was very controversial then and probably still is. Readers fall into two camps. Those who agree with its basic premise and those who know, deep in their hearts, that I am dead wrong. I am baffled. For me, those who disagree are like climate-change deniers, or even those who hold a biblical view of life on earth and deny evolution. They know from experience I am wrong. The evidence supporting my view is conclusive and irrefutable.

Yet famous writers, journalists, even teachers of writing persist in believing that the teaching of formal grammar is what gave them their superior skills with the written language and continues to be the best way to teach young writers.

No topic in education has been researched more, and no topic has had such convincing, replicated data for over 100 years. After reading much of the research I would be prepared to bet my total net worth on the results of comparing two groups of students.

With one group, I would provide them with 100 hours of the best available instruction on grammar and spelling, and with a second group I would provide them NO instruction (just to prove the point, but it is not what I would do if it was my class) and provide them with 100 hours of quiet reading and writing time, providing them with excellent age-appropriate books in a reading-writing workshop model.

I am NOT denying the importance of spelling and grammar. I am arguing here that it is best dealt with as it emerges in context from the student's own writing. Underlying all of this, is the simple fact that the more you read, the better you write and the more you write, the better is your writing. Working with a draft document with a coach/editor can address complex grammar issues within the context of the story or argument written.

Starting from the this premise of immersion in reading and writing there are some fascinating models of teaching writing in practice today without a systematic grammar program. I have seen the results of student writing that emerges from a reading writing workshop model where grammar and spelling are systematically dealt with in context through student, parent and teacher editing sessions.

You Can't Learn to Write by Rote

Originally published in The Globe and Mail, Wednesday, February, 1991

As a superintendent of schools, the most common complaint I receive comes from parents who feel that the schools aren't teaching spelling and grammar – that work comes home riddled with errors.

The problem is that the parents' conception of how we should teach spelling and grammar is radically different from what we now know about learning to spell and write. Our reactions as professionals are not unlike the way we would expect a doctor to behave if a patient requested bloodletting.

However, parents want us to teach these skills the way they think they learned them. How do you begin to explain that bloodletting doesn't work any more and never did? How do you tell articulate, well-educated parents that teaching spelling and grammar in isolation through daily lessons, drills and exercises and the use of a graded speller and a grammar text probably impaired their development as writers? Research has shown conclusively for 80 years that this approach does not work.

Spelling and grammar need to be taught in a different way and with an emphasis on correctness at a different time. How do we get parents to understand that the development of spelling is not unlike the child's development in painting and drawing? As parents, we proudly display our children's art work on the refrigerator door. We would never dream of putting red marks across it – "no neck, one arm too long." Neither would we charge back to the school saying, "You sent this home with all these errors unmarked." Spelling too, is a developmental process, well researched, with well understood stages, with appropriate teaching strategies for each stage.

Spelling and grammar are important, but they need to be taught in context. Students learn best when what they are learning is related to what they are doing, reading or writing. The learning then has personal meaning, it's natural. In a writers' workshop format, students create and manage, in consultation with the teacher, their own spelling lists that emerge out of their reading and writing, rather than using unrelated words listed in a speller that are out of context. Teachers help students correct grammatical errors in their own writing rather than through meaningless, isolated exercises.

Parents generally place an undeserved emphasis on spelling, and at the wrong time. An ability to spell well is also not a reflection of intelligence nor an indication of an ability to write persuasively or clearly.

As preschoolers we learn an average of 20 new words a day and absorb sophisticated grammatical structures in speech at a rate that staggers credibility. We accomplish this without a single formal lesson or grammar text. We learn language naturally because we need to communicate. We are coached by family and friends, not drilled on new words of the day. Our pronunciation and grammar are refined and corrected naturally as we converse.

We want children to learn to express themselves and to communicate with others in writing. The least important aspect of the process, initially, is spelling and grammar – not unimportant, just the least important. In classrooms where spelling and grammar are taught formally and emphasized strongly, students produce short, stilted works with limited vocabulary. Why risk getting punished for using a word you use in speech but don't know how to spell? In classrooms where writing topics are self-selected, where students "own" the process, and time for writing is provided, what a difference in the writing! Samples from process writing classrooms are lengthy and creative and often deeply personal. They reveal the writer's voice. Students' arguments are persuasive. Their work, however, may be filled with spelling and grammatical errors in early drafts. Students in traditional classrooms tend to hate writing, and students in process writing classes hate to go out for recess.

A key to understanding how spelling and grammar should be taught lies in the way writers write and what they write about. Writers write about what they know or what they are interested in. They normally write a rough first draft and try to get as much out onto paper as they can.

They focus initially on their thoughts, ideas and feelings. As they move through the stages of second and third drafts and as they polish and shape their ideas, they move closer to a final correct draft that goes "public."

When most of us write a letter, a memo, a report or a book, we get a friend or colleague, secretary or editor to check it over before it goes out. Why would we expect less of our students?

When a student's work goes public, the teacher demands that it be perfect. Going public for students takes a variety of forms: handing in final drafts for marking, posting a piece on the bulletin board, sending it home, or publishing it for the school library. Parents should expect to see many school drafts coming home with many spelling and grammar errors. But they should also expect final pieces to be perfect.

One teacher I observed decided to try teaching spelling by eliminating the formal spelling program she had conducted for years. Out went the graded spellers, the weekly spelling tests, the daily phonics instruction, and in came a daily reading and writing workshop with spelling, grammar and phonics taught in context. She administered traditional standardized spelling instruments used throughout North America as pre-tests at the beginning of the year and different versions of the same tests at the end of the year to confirm her personal observations. Not one student in the class went up less than two grade levels in spelling as measured by these tests.

The most powerful way for any of us to learn to spell, to increase our vocabulary, to improve our grammar and punctuation is through reading and writing. A skilled teacher, like an effective coach, can enhance this growth.

My years as a student convinced me that I could not write. In the productive, purposeful environment of the writers' workshop, students view themselves as writers and authors. What an amazing revelation. After all these years, these happy youngsters taught me that I too could be an author.

Children's literature and global education: Understanding the developing world

Diakiw is Superintendent of Schools, Area E, for the York Region Board of Education, Ontario, Canada. He also serves as a member of the Development Education Committee of UNICEF Ontario.

The Development Education Committee of UNICEF Ontario has been researching children's literature suitable for teaching development education issues since 1986. Thanks to funding from the Canadian International Development Agency in the summer of 1988, members of a curriculum writing project produced Children's Literature: Springboard to Understanding the Developing World. This flexible, integrated curriculum support document, intended for Grades 3 to 8, is a contribution to the growing movement towards a literature-based curriculum and is intended as a contribution to the International Year of Literacy in 1990. Within the broad framework of global education, development education concerns itself with gaining an understanding of the less developed regions of the world. These regions, normally the least studied across the curriculum, are the source of the majority of immigrants and refugees to North America and Europe. While development education issues include poverty, famine, and the problems of economic development, these problems are balanced by the search for the universal values common to all cultures throughout the world and by an understanding of the interdependence of all nations.

The UNICEF project was based on two premises: first, that children can and should deal with development education issues far earlier than is common in schools; and second, that children's literature can be a powerful device for gaining an understanding of a world far from students' own reality. The UNICEF document is one example of an approach based on these premises. However, using the recommended titles and approach suggested herein, teachers will find that the positive student response will lead naturally to a variety of reading and writing activities based on global issues.

Current research indicates not only that elementary children are developmentally ready for a global perspective, but that this may be a more appropriate age at which to introduce it. Charles Evans's (1987) summary of the research in this area shows that children ages 10 to 13 are receptive to learning about people from other countries; after age 14, however, attitudes formed about people from other countries are somewhat negative. He reports on a number of studies of primary school students in social studies programs with a strong global education focus. These students developed more positive attitudes not only toward themselves but also toward people from other countries. These students saw more similarities than differences between themselves and others. Evans affirms that children can deal with a global perspective earlier than we normally present it.

Importance of children's literature

Children's literature is a powerful medium for understanding the world. Young children find it easier to assimilate new information when this information is presented within the structure of a story, as Gordon Wells (1986) sites in his book The Meaning Makers:

> What I want to suggest is that stories have a role in education that goes far beyond their contribution to the acquisition of literacy. Constructing stories in the mind—or storying, as it has been called—is one of the most fundamental means of making meaning; as such, it is an activity that pervades all aspects of learning. Through the exchange of stories teachers and students can share their understandings of a topic and bring their mental models of the world into closer alignment. In this sense, stories and storying are relevant in all areas of the curriculum. (p. 194)

Stories can be a powerful way to transport students to distant countries with cultures and traditions far removed from their own. Children need the bridge that stories provide in order to link their growing understanding of other cultures to their personal experience and background knowledge.

Bruno Bettelheim (1976) believes in introducing children to unexpurgated traditional fairy tales because he feels they directly address the deep inner conflicts originating in our primitive drives. Like Bettelheim, we can argue that the ugly realities of the outside world — slums, famine, war—can best be addressed in the caring, sensitive environment of the classroom, rather than alone in front of the television set. Jonathan Kozol (1975) eloquently articulates this position:

> Teachers often respond to me with words like these: "Isn't it too much of an interruption to bring these agonizing, and enormously disturbing, matters to the lives of children?" I hear their words. I look into their eyes. It is as if they were to speak about another planet, or a world they dream of, or a world that they recall within a passage of Vivaldi or a painting of Renoir. They tell us that we must not "bring in" rage and pain. I ask them then: What shall we do when rage walks in the door? (p. 59)

Perhaps children's literature can address these issues in the same way that fairy tales address children's deeper fears. Lisa Paul (1988) states it another way:

> What we, as teachers, have to remember is that stories create a space where moral and social issues can be explored safely—without threat. And therein lies their value.... Injustices of society can be tempered through the sustenance of imaginative art. (p. 4)

The selection of titles recommended in this article includes traditional folktales and fantasy as well as contemporary realistic fiction. They affirm the powerful need of all people to tell stories. They demonstrate the universal questions and fears that cultures all over the world explore in their folklore and literature, and they raise moral and social issues about the significant differences that exist between one part of the world and another.

- *Instructional approaches*

Regardless of whether a teacher wishes to develop a single lesson or a whole unit, children's literature is the recommended starting point. The story becomes the common

Children's literature can be a powerful device for gaining an understanding of a world far from our own reality.

knowledge for the class—it is the scaffold, the schema, upon which students' understandings and interests are explored and new knowledge is added. Teachers are encouraged to avoid traditional comprehension questions; rather they are encouraged to provide wait-time for spontaneous responses, and to ask open-ended questions that allow the reader or listener to respond from her/his own background experience or interests. Questions such as these could be asked: What do you think this book is about? What did it remind you of? What were you thinking about as I read the story? As Sylvia Ashton-Warner (cited in Partnow,

1977) expressed it, "I follow them into their minds and fraternize there" (p. 8). The student response then becomes the basis for follow-up activities.

The UNICEF curriculum guide is based on this approach. Consisting of four units—African Folktales, Global Interdependence, Latin American City Life, and India—it is intended for teachers of students in Grades 3 through 8. The units are very flexible in that a third-grade teacher can pick and choose titles, activities, and approaches suited to the class just as easily as an eighth-grade teacher. A teacher who has access to only one title in a unit and little time may wish to read the story aloud, use some of the questions suggested, and perhaps invite the students to select one or more of the many activities provided that explore development education issues. Another teacher with more time and resources available can establish an integrated theme approach where language arts, history, geography, and values education are all dealt with under a common theme and a more open activity-centre approach is taken.

The picture storybooks suggested are as useful with eighth graders as they are with third graders. They are like poems, reducing an issue, scene, or emotion to its essence, thus permitting one to see the whole more clearly. For the teacher, the picture storybook can be read in a short amount of time allowing follow-up activities to be developed over a longer time period. While picture storybooks are the core of each unit, junior/intermediate novels are also included and can be used as readalouds during the course of the unit or, with more senior grades, as novel studies on their own. The curriculum guide provides hundreds of follow-up ideas that teachers or students can pick and choose from including reading and writing activities, research questions, games, simulations, and case studies as well as suggested audiovisual resources.

Suggested units

• African Folktales

The titles in this recommended unit tap the rich treasury of illustrated African folk-tales in order to explore what African cultures have in common with our own. They reaffirm that we are more alike than we are different. The tales may also be used as a stimulus to study topics such as modern Zimbabwe, water, famine, or the customs of an African tribe.

Suggested titles include Mufaro's Beautiful Daughters by John Steptoe, Anansi the Spider by Gerald McDermott, The Village of Round and Square Houses by Ann Grifalconi, and three by Verna Aardema: Bringing the Rain to Kapiti Plain, Who's in Rabbit's House?, and Why Mosquitoes Buzz in People's Ears. There is also a junior/intermediate novel, The Calf of the November Cloud, by Hilary Ruben, suitable for a read-aloud or for an indepth study of the novel.

Although the focus of this unit should be on the unity of humankind, the subject matter of the stories permits an easy and natural springboard to development education issues. Two Masai tales, for example, lead to a study of a proud, independent tribe at odds with a modern economy. Mufaro's Beautiful Daughters portrays a sophisticated ancient civilization. The book can be a starting point for raising questions about what happened to this civilization or for drawing comparisons with the achievements and problems of modern Zimbabwe. Bringing the Rain to Kapiti Plain is a natural springboard for identifying the importance of water in the developing world, and particularly the relation of drought to the recurring famine in Africa. The contribution of the sons in Anansi the Spider is a useful analogy for discussions about the importance of international cooperation.

Many of these books depict an exotic tropical paradise, a garden of Eden of tribal simplicity, or idyllic village life. In reality, however, the developing world is urbanizing at an astonishing rate. Over 35% of the population of Africa is urbanized, and this figure is increasing rapidly.

It is important that the teacher maintain a proper balance through the use of other media and activities and avoid the risk of reinforcing the stereotype of the backward uncivilized native. Otherwise, these books of folktales may obscure the reality of an Africa with modern, bustling, progressive cities; established universities; many enlightened and articulate leaders; and a rich, growing literary and artistic tradition.

After reading these stories, students are able to draw connections between these African tales and familiar traditional tales such as Cinderella and Henny Penny. Through such stories, whether they are African, North American, Asian, or European, we learn that people around the world are more alike than we are different.

- *Global Interdependence*

The focus of this unit is realizing the importance of global interdependence. The three picture storybooks suggested in the unit, The Expedition, War and Peas, and The Sea People, are powerful contemporary satires on international relations. They confront the issues of development education head on. Like classic satires such as Gulliver's Travels and Animal Farm, they employ fictitious settings or animal characters to mirror contemporary society and allow us to see ourselves more clearly. The three titles make provocative reading and raise critical questions about the way in which we relate to economically less fortunate countries.

War and Peas, by Michael Foreman, satirizes a country of plenty with its fat and greedy king and his gluttonous army, grown flabby and weak from excess. The brilliant wordless storybook, The Expedition, by Willi Baum, recounts how a ship's crew plunders the treasures of a remote tropical island. It raises questions about who is really being exploited; it is a perfect metaphor for the relation between developed and developing nations.

The Sea People, by J. Muller and J. Steiner, portrays the way of life of two adjoining fictitious islands, through powerful, detailed illustrations. The inhabitants of Greater Island are ambitious and aggressive in their feverish expansion while the inhabitants of Lesser Island live quiet, gentle lives in balance with their environment. The confrontation between the two islands and the resolution provide opportunities for thought-provoking discussion and debate. After reading these books aloud to a class of 10 year olds and inviting the children to respond in writing about their feelings, one student wrote:

> Dear Planetmate,
> I wrote this letter because I want you to know how I feel about countries sharing with each other, not giving to each other, and taking from each other. I think that we should be proud of being on one planet and we should feel lucky as we are the only one with life on it yet discovered. Because we are so lucky, we should protect our country by helping each other to enjoy what we have. We aren't one country or one city, we are one planet, one world. I suggest that we use what we have properly.
> Christina

- *Latin American City Life*

The unit on Latin American city life attempts to balance the traditional view of simple village life in the developing nations with the reality of urbanization. The unit recommends children's literature that explores the urban experience in the third world and the pull to a life in the cities. Over 70% of the population of Latin America lives in cities, and this figure is growing rapidly. In most South American cities, up to 70% of the inhabitants live in shantytowns with no water, electricity, or sewer systems. Brazil alone has over 20 million street children.

The Ballad of the Burglar of Babylon, by Elizabeth Bishop, is a poem of the search for Micicti, a young burglar from the shantytown of Babylon in the hills above Rio de Janiero. The Streets Are Free, by Kurusa, explores the actions of a group of youngsters from the shantytowns of Caracas. Lito the Shoeshine Boy, by David Mangurian, tells the life of Lito Chirinos through a photographic essay. The Crossing, by Gary Paulsen, is a junior/intermediate novel that recounts the story of a 14 year-old street child from Juarez, Mexico, whose aim in life is to cross the Rio Grande into the United States. The Most Beautiful Place in the World by Ann Cameron is another short novel that explores optimistically the life of a street child.

- *India*

The literature in this unit helps students begin to understand the problems of one of the world's largest and most complex developing countries, an immense nation of 750 million people. The richness and diversity of Indian culture opens up before the students, engages their interest and motivates them to learn more.

The core of the unit is Village by the Sea, by Anita Desai, a powerful junior/intermediate novel suitable for a read-aloud or more advanced novel study. It is an inspiring and fast-paced story of two children from a small fishing village who are faced with adult responsibilities when their parents fall ill. The book is a sensitive portrayal of India's struggle in the modern world.

Two picture storybooks, Jyoti's Journey by Helen Ganly and Gita Will Be a Dancer by Barbara and Eberhard Fischer, provide strong stories of the daily lives of young girls growing up in India today.

Children's books cited

African Folktales

McDermott, G. (1972). Anansi the spider. New York: Holt, Rinehart. & Winston. Unpaged. 0-03-088368-7.

Aardema, V. (1981). Bringing the rain to Kapiti Plain. Ill. by Beatriz Vidal. New York: Dial. Unpaged. 0-8037-0809-2.

Ruben, H. (1977). The calf of the November cloud. London: Pan Books Ltd. 128 pp. 0-330-29932-3.

Steptoe, J. (1987). Mufaro's beautiful daughters. New York: Lothrop, Lee & Shepard. Unpaged. 0-688-04045-4.

Grifalconi, A. (1986). The village of round and square houses. Boston: Little, Brown. Unpaged. 0-8037-0809-2.

Aardema, V. (1975). Why mosquitoes buzz in people's ears. Ill. by Leo and Diane Dillon. New York: Dial. Unpaged. 0-8037-6088-4.

Aardema, V. (1977). Who's in rabbit's house? ill. by Leo and Diane Dillon. New York: Dial. Unpaged. 0-8037-9550-5.

Global Interdependence

Baum, W., & Edizionne, E. (1985). The expedition. Reproduced in D. Booth & C. Lundy (Eds.). Improvisations: Learning through drama. Toronto: Academic Press. 0-7747-1211-2.

Muller, J., & Steiner, J. (1982). The sea people. London: Victor Gollancz. Unpaged. 0-575-03088-7.

Foreman, M. (1978). War and peas. New York: Puffin. Unpaged. 0-14-050243-2.

Latin American City Life

Bishop, E. (1968). The ballad of the burglar of Babylon. New York: Farrar, Strauss & Giroux. Reprinted by permission in Children's literature: Springboard to understanding the developing world. Ontario: UNICEF.

Paulsen, G. (1987). The crossing. New York: Orchard Books. 114 pp. 0-531-05709-8.

Chirinos, L. (1975). Lilo the shoeshine boy. Trans. by David Mangurian. Photos by David Mangurian. New York: Four Winds Press. Unpaged. 0-531-05709-8.

Cameron, A. (1988). The most beautiful place in the world. Ill. by Thomas B. Allen. New York: Alfred A. Knopf. 57 pp. 0-394-89463-4.

Kurusa, (1985). The streets are free. Ill. by Monika Doppert. Trans. by Karen Englander. Scarborough, Ontario: Firefly Books. Unpaged. 0-920-30307-02.

India

Fischer; B., & Fischer, E. (1986). Gita will be a dancer. Ill. by Dinanath Pathy. New York: UNICEF 32 pp. 3-907999-142.

Ganly, H. (1986). Jyoti's journey. London: Andre Deutsch. Unpaged. 0-233-97899-2.

Desai, A. (1986). The village by the sea. London: Heinemann Educational Books (New Windmill Series). 157 pp. 0-435-12290-8.

Conclusion

A growing volume of children's literature about the developing world allows us to approach this world in a way that is meaningful for young people. It allows us to deal honestly and sensitively with the many complex issues that confront developing nations. It provides us with the opportunity to develop values-driven curricula through which we can cherish and celebrate our similarities and our differences.

The curriculum guide Children's Literature: Springboard to Understanding the Developing World is available for CAN$10.00 from UNICEF ONTARIO, 333 Eglinton Avenue East, Toronto, Ontario, Canada M4P 1L7 Tel.: (416) 487-4253.

References

Bettelheim, B. (1976). The uses of enchantment: The meaning and importance of fairy tales. New York: Alfred Knopf.

Diakiw, J., Baker, C., Ledger, G., Leppington, S., & Pearce, G. (1989). Children's literature: Springboard to understanding the developing world. Ontario: UNICEF.

Evans, C. (1987). Teaching a global perspective in elementary schools. Elementary School Journal, 87, 545-555.

Kozol, J. (1975). The night is dark and I am far from home. Boston: Houghton Mifflin.

Paul, L. (1988). What stories have to do with life. Growing with books. Ontario: Ministry of Education.

Partnow, E. (Ed.). (1977). The quotable woman. San Francisco: Corwin.

Wells, G. (1986). The meaning-makers. Portsmouth, NH: Heinemann.

Reflections on Becoming a Teacher

An Auto-Ethnographic Life History

At long last I have learned to teach. I taught for 57 years in elementary, and high schools, to university from 1958 to 2015. Over all that time, three dominant themes emerge from my story of becoming a teacher.

First, my passion for social justice and equity that permeated every seminar or class I taught.

Second was my discovery of the profound connection between language and thought. It became central to all aspects of the teaching learning process, regardless of the subject matter or the age of the students. (Lev Vygotsky, *Thought and Language*, 1962). Every seminar in my final university teaching years was structured with this fundamental understanding of the need for students to put things in their own words, in a multiplicity of ways.

Thirdly is my understanding of the importance of the role of "storying" in the learning process. As Barbara Hardy stated, "narrative is a primary act of mind." (1977) And as Joan Didion mused, "We tell ourselves stories in order to live." (2006) Jerome Bruner (1989) opened my eyes to the fact that argument and story are two ways of knowing:

> "...two modes of cognitive functioning, two modes of thought each providing distinctive ways of ordering experience, of constructing reality... a good story and a well-formed argument are different, natural kinds. Arguments convince one of their truth, stories of their life-likeness."

Gordon Wells connected this concept to learning in schools when he stated, "storying... is one of the most fundamental means of making meaning; as such, it is an activity that pervades all aspects of learning." (1986). As Catherine Bateson expressed it, "Our species thinks in metaphors and learns through stories." (1994). Traditional schooling is all about 'argument'. It is within Bruner's concept of story, as an alternative way of knowing, that I have structured all of the courses I taught. Story is also how I will reveal my philosophy of teaching, in this reflection.

Life history methodology

This auto-ethnographical reflection is explored through a life history methodology. Life history is one form of narrative research. The importance of narrative in educational inquiry is, as Connelly and Clandinin (1990) believe, "that humans are storytelling organisms who, individually and socially, lead storied lives. The study of narrative, therefore, is the study of the ways humans experience the world." (p. 2). Within this broad field, research into teacher's work is well documented through a life history methodology. (Goodson, 1992; Cole and Knowles, 1993; Bullough, 1991; Ball and Goodson, 1985; Measor and Sykes, 1992; Polkinghorne 1995; Tripp, 1994).

Dhunpath argued:

> "I want to suggest boldly, therefore, that the life history approach is probably the only authentic means of understanding how motives and practices reflect the intimate intersection of institutional and individual experience in the postmodern world." (2000, p. 544)

As Clemons, R.F. and Tierney, W. G. in *The Uses and Usefulness of Life History* argued:

> "Life history has experienced a renaissance as researchers acknowledge the method's flexibility and usefulness... in illuminating and, ultimately, contesting inequitable social, economic, institutional and political forces."

It is the examination of one's life, particularly with reference to epiphany and the critical incidents that forge new insights that lead to professional growth and understanding. (Denzin, 1989; Tripp 1994) Life history research advocates a concern with the phenomenal role of lived experience, with the ways in which individuals examine and interpret their own lives and their world around them. The crucial focus for life history work for Goodson (1992) is a highly contextualized narrative; to locate the teacher's own life story alongside a broader contextual analysis, to tell a narrative of action within a contextualized theory.

All life history is narrative, but not all narrative is life history. As Bertaux stated, "Life history is sociologically read biography." (As cited by Measor and Sikes 1992, p. 210). Life history and narrative always focus on the meaning-making systems of individuals.

In as much as it is humanely possible, life history inquiry is about gaining insights into the broader human condition by coming to know and understand the experiences of other humans... that every indepth exploration of an individual life-in-context brings us that much closer to understanding the complexities of lives in communities. (Ward and Delamont, Chapter 24, p270, 2020).

A life history researcher tries to understand how the larger issues in society are examined over time, internalized by an individual. It, in fact, becomes autoethnographical.

> "Autoethnography places the self within a sociocultural context... It uses the self as a starting point from which to explore broader sociocultural elements, issues or contacts." (Gannon, 2020)

In my case, I explore how my immigrant family experiences, my early school life at an Anglo-Saxon bastion of 'British' education, and experiences in Apartheid South Africa shaped my educational career. As Wordsworth, noted, "The child is father to the man." (1888)

Ben Levin, wrote about my story:

> "It's an interesting life story; we could benefit from more such life histories in education because they provide specificity and historical reality as a balance to the theoretical material that people like me write." (Personal communication, August 28, 2011).

Similarly, Ken Leithwood wrote:

> "The idea of publicizing the work of people who toil close to the action, but frequently are not widely acknowledged for their work, is an excellent one. We can learn from successful educators and they should be encouraged to tell their stories. (Personal communication, August 22, 2011)

Within the context of my own story of becoming a teacher I explore how each of the themes of social justice, language and thought and the importance of 'story' emerged in my life and how they became central to my views of teaching and learning.

My story: How I came to be a teacher and how I learned to teach (in press)

In 1958, following completion of my Bachelors degree, I experienced a transformative five months, working on the West Driefontein Gold Mine in South Africa. I also hitch-hiked over much of the country, including Basutoland and Swaziland. It was at the height of oppressive Apartheid period. I had been accepted to Osgoode Hall Law School, then in Toronto, but I began to feel drawn to the idea of being a high school geography teacher, not a lawyer as my father had urged and planned for me! Upon returning to Canada, I was still troubled by my decision to study law, I wandered up to the Geography Department at University of Toronto, where I had completed my undergraduate degree in Geography. After a chat with the Department Head, who was excited to hear of my experiences with Apartheid in South Africa, out of the blue, he offered me a teaching fellowship, since a recipient from the UK had cancelled due to a serious illness. I dropped out of Law school and joyfully began my career in teaching as a teaching fellow with a dream of becoming a high school teacher. I have never regretted that decision.

It was my experience of working in an oppressive apartheid regime on the gold mines of South Africa working along with my own team of 12 Zulus, where the evils and atrocities of racism were lived out daily at every level of society contributed strongly to my lifelong passion for antiracism and for my career passion for equity in the school system. As well, my early life as a child of illiterate immigrant parents and through a strange quirk of fate, whereby I attended my five years of high school at Upper Canada College, ingrained me with a profound feeling of being, 'othered'. It was there they attempted to squeeze every gene of my immigrant identity out of me, to induce me to be a proper English gentleman in a school environment, taught mainly by an all male, retired British military staff, under an imported British Headmaster, and daily church of England prayers, within an anti-immigrant, anti-Semitic, racist culture. That experience still has an indelible affect on my teaching.

After my M.A. years in Geography at university, I accepted a job at Richmond Hill High School and began my career as a high school educator. A trait of my personality have been characterized as an innovator. As Gordon Cavanaugh stated in his profile, *A Champion of Innovation in Education,* "He was an educator for whom innovation and change were coded into his marrow. He was a change agent from his early days as a teacher." (2011) This trait continued through my career right up to my final years of teaching social justice and equity issues in schools and communities in the Faculty of Education at York University .

At Richmond High School, from the very beginning, a deep seated global perspective was at the heart of my teaching. I had absorbed this perspective from my multiple travels, through Asia, Africa, Europe, and the South Sea Islands and Australia; my human and economic geography studies at U of T; a passion for social justice and equity from my observations of the inequities observed in the developing world; and my antipathy, as an "other" to my privileged private school experience. I told stories of all that I had seen and learned around the world.

As a high school geography teacher I quickly developed innovative strategies, intuitively understanding the role of 'storying' in learning by eschewing geography textbooks in exchange for novels. I substituted *Nectar in the Sieve* (Kamala Markandaya) for my textbook unit on India, and James Michener's *Caravans* for the study of the Middle East. I also began to understand the value of interdisciplinary studies and proposed and developed a school wide independent interdisciplinary study project where 30 students spent the entire spring term on individually designed interdisciplinary research.

I was selected by the provincial geography inspector to present a paper at the National Council for Geographic Education in New York City and later was invited to sit on that board as the representative from Canada, and on several Ministry of Education curriculum writing teams. My efforts were recognized at home by receiving the first Distinguished Teacher Award offered by my School Board. A few years later I was appointed Director of Instructional Services at an innovative new high school, called Thornlea Secondary School. It was based on a trimester system with a cadre of highly motivated teachers and a remarkable offering of creative 13 week courses that quickly attracted provincial attention from visitors and researchers, including Michael Fullan who wrote about the school in a book called *Thornlea Secondary School: Case Study of an Innovative School* (1971). He wrote about me as Director of Instructional Services,

> "Partly because of his role and partly because of his personality the director of instructional service is the most influential idea man in the school. He is one of the main sources of information on pertinent literature, current theory, and new ideas in education." (p16)

As one former pupil wrote:

> "The teachers treated their students as adults, the curriculum was innovative as was his inquisitive mind, and especially for new ideas being implemented. He was there for many years as a secondary VP who led many innovative curriculum thrusts." (Cavanaugh, 2011)

Another teacher wrote:

> "It was a unique school with a unique philosophy. I would say it was ahead of its time and people like Diakiw allowed for this school and its students to thrive."

And finally, a third teacher at the school commented:

> "I also remember his enthusiasm for educational innovation, his unflagging interest in both students and teachers; quite frankly Thornlea Secondary School would not have been such a pioneer in education without Diakiw's participation." (Cavanaugh, 2011)

As principal at the Baden Sr. School, (1974-76) in West Germany, an Ontario Grade 7-13 school for children of military families with Department of National Defence, I launched a flurry of innovations including the establishment of an International League of Schools; an extensive school wide co-op program; a program in the arts for opera, ballet and symphonies, where the artists came to the school the day before the performance to talk about their work; an active physical education program including a school-wide ski week for all students, 'run for your life' community runs, and cycling trips through the Alps; and a highly successful house system based on participation, not just winning. My Director, Don Vinge, wrote:

> "As a high school principal he inspired the staff with his innovative approaches to organization and curriculum delivery. Few S.S. principals that I know have been able to consistently maintain a focus on students, their interests and needs." (personal note, 2011)

But when one examines all the innovations there are some emerging common threads. There is a prevailing concern for social justice and equity; a social justice need for narrowing the gap in achievement between the "haves and the have nots"; reducing the dropout rate; a heightened development of literacy or language across the curriculum; a global perspective, and meeting the diverse needs of diverse students, through the arts, co op education and alternative education.

As a teacher, from my earliest novice beginnings, I believe I followed the intent of Fullan's dictum (Fullan, 1993), and affirmed by Cavanaugh (2011):

> "Moral purpose keeps teachers close to the needs of children and youth; change agentry causes them to develop better strategies for accomplishing their moral goals."

This was the meaning that I found later in my work as a school superintendent. I used varied techniques of change agentry to achieve my goals, such as in my development of the first high school International Co-op Program in Thailand, and, defying advice of superiors when I was convinced I was right, in developing the Reading Recovery Program in grade one, as a social justice issue to lower dropout rates in high school.

I consumed vast amounts of new knowledge about teaching and learning through books and journals about education during this period. My wife would bring me my morning coffee in bed, while I continued to read aloud the latest educational journals and we would argue and discuss the readings till it was time for me to get ready to go to work.

> "Teachers as change agents are career-long learners, without which they would be able to stimulate students to be continuous learners." (Fullan, 1993)

Even as a superintendent I still thought of myself as a teacher and I enthusiastically shared my readings on new ideas about language and thought, and about social justice issues in schools through excerpts, notes on research and in my monthly, *The Diakiw Digest*, including a special issue on *Storying*. My history verifies that I was successful at combining the mantle of my passion and moral purpose with a commitment to change as Fullan stated:

> "Moral purpose without change agentry is martyrdom; change agentry without moral purpose is change for the sake of change... In combination, not only are they effective in getting things done, but they are good at getting the right things done." (1993)

As a teacher and administrator, colleagues were asked by Cavanaugh about my interest in and impact on multiculturalism and antiracism:

> "Diakiw was the poster boy for promoting multiculturalism/anti-racism before its time. His empathy for new Canadians and his intolerance of racism was a model to everyone." (personal note)

That theme is present in every one of my seminars at York University, in a wide variety of interesting, diverse and challenging ways, including readings, movies, video clips, CBC and NPR radio documentaries and clips, engaging students through a process of varied interactive strategies.

As another principal wrote: "His work in racism was system-changing". For example, I assigned a Black educator from the classroom who had the same passion for equity as I did and who was also concerned about the lagging achievement of Black students in our area. He became the first community liaison worker, mentoring and coaching reluctant Black students who were at risk in grade 7 and 8. He wrote:

> "At a time when most school and system administrators in York Region, and indeed in the Greater Toronto Area (GTA), were preoccupied with the daily, banal, minutiae of managing a school or school system, Diakiw, in his capacity as Superintendent of Schools for the old Area E in the York Region Board of Education, showed superior foresight and vision in beginning conversations and setting up structures to efficiently and effectively address the issues related to the management of race, community and cultural relations... A very powerful relationship was developed with stake holders in the Black Community of York Region that resulted in a Saturday School Program that has since become the model for all such programs not only in York Region, but in the GTA as a whole. All other racial, cultural and linguistic groups have sought and demanded and gotten similar programs from their School Boards."(Paul DeLyon, personal note, 2011).

My passion for equity in my courses at York University can be traced back to my very early years as a classroom teacher until it flowered and flourished into a plethora of innovations as a superintendent. In 1989, at a Dropout Prevention Conference for school administrators, for example, organized by the Ministry of Education, which offered many options of

"Best Practices, for Dropout Prevention", I was attracted to the counter-intuitive option, called Reading Recovery for Grade One Students! (RR). It was not just a literacy issue; it was a social justice issue. The majority of students identified in need of help in grade one, come from families with several of the following demographic characteristics: living below the poverty line; mostly with English as their second language; single moms; minority families; immigrants; mostly boys; and low levels of parental education. These are the children who would end up as dropouts with enormous long term costs to society. As one colleague observed:

> "There is now a Reading Recovery teacher in 147 English-language K-8 elementary schools in York Region School Board in 2009. 90% of all grade one students were reading at grade level upon entering grade 2. Over 12,000 students have now received Reading Recovery assistance. York Region dropout rates are among the lowest. That was the day that reading recovery was born and as I said before, implemented into the total system and stands to this day. This is probably the most significant of all the initiatives he did. I think that is why this board tests so high in the province." (Gord Maunder, Principal, personal note to Gord Cavanaugh, 2011)

Another principal wrote, "I was so motivated by him... I witnessed the creation of some programs that then spread to another area, then to the all schools in the area... then to the system, and still are in operation to this day".

I felt the need to meet the needs of students in ways beyond the traditional curriculum allowing underachieving students to find ways of expressing themselves and gaining the confidence to do better.

Another example was my effort to create a grade 6-8 elementary school of the arts. Despite the repeated blockage of the proposal by the Superintendent of Curriculum, who was finally out-voted by the executive council, Baythorn Public School still thrives over 25 years later.

My transformative months working on the gold mines in South Africa as a young man were the stimulus for the pursuit of a dream of an international co-op program for senior students to experience living and working in an emerging economy. The experience of living and working in a foreign country allows student to see the world through another keyhole. I wanted students to have that kind of experience. As an area superintendent there was nothing in my portfolio that would indicate any responsibility for such an initiative. After months of searching, and many meetings with a variety of NGOs I finally found AFS International. They were able to provide placements and host families in Northern Thailand. It was the ideal structure I was looking for. I applied for Canadian International Development Agency funding to permit students from all socio-economic families to participate, not just the well to-do students for this very expensive program for me that was key. Stephen Lewis, Canada's UN Ambassador wrote in a personal note, "Diakiw, your international coop is inspired. You are consistently creative". (1990).

It is this broad global perspective that I incorporate into my courses. For example, when we are examining issues of boys and girls in the classroom, we also examine world statistics about child attendance and literacy rates, particularly regarding the shocking low rates for educating girls.

Language development was a multi-year school board priority. Derived from extensive discussion among all superintendents, consultants and principals, the priority was elaborated in a guiding document called the Fifteen Language Development Concerns. It advocated an understanding of the powerful role of language in the thinking process – it applied to all subjects K-OAC. This was an explosive period of my own professional learning. It was this period that made me decide to return to university. I did complete my doctorate shortly after retiring and the focus of my work at OISE and in my thesis was consistent with the themes of this reflection – my life history methodology listening to the stories of my research participants in *Becoming an Antiracist Educator: Black, South Asian and East Asian Perspectives*. (1999)

In the Board, we developed an all pervading common vision of the power of language across that curriculum. I was, and am, committed to a holistic progressive view of the role of language in the thinking process based on many thinkers like Lev Vygotsky, (1962) "New knowledge is only internalized when it has been socially expressed." This notion is central to the way I organized and presented my seminars at York.

I also became aware of the power of story through children's literature and became a promoter of children's literature as a powerful tool for initiating an issues-approach to curriculum. I developed a fascination with, and passion for children's books. I grew up in a home with no books and had never had a children's book read to him. I advanced the concept with this work with UNICEF. "He read aloud children's books at principal meetings", one principal noted, and I modeled interactive group challenges that demonstrated vividly the power of structured group problem-solving. As another teacher noted,

> "As a high school history teacher, I was very aware of his stimulating presence as an educator and superintendent... Language across the Curriculum deepened my teaching... arranging my classroom in clusters of four, fostered reflection and dialogue about the material. These clusters encouraged teamwork and learning different roles." (Cavanaugh, 2011)

I was also committed to my monthly Diakiw Digest because it kept everyone on the same page of the common vision of social justice and equity and promoted the latest understandings of language and thought and storying.

One teacher wrote:

> "I do remember his Diakiw Digest that he wrote for our Area teachers. The monthly digest was one of my favorite reads – it was abundant with research articles on expanding your methodology and classroom practices with students." (Personal note to Cavanaugh, 2011)

I was also reaching out with extensive writing about multiculturalism, Canadian culture and identity, literacy and children's literature in a variety of professional journals, the Huffington Post, the Globe and Mail, and the Toronto Star. Even today, years after leaving the Board, I continue to write about better ways to meet the needs of diverse students, about the achievement gap, with articles like, *Thinking Outside the Box: The postmodern high school*,(2008); *Reading Recovery*, (1999); *Alternatives to Black focussed schools* (2009), *Reading: the importance of early reading*, to name a few. All these articles are on the themes central to this reflection and to my teaching.

As Don Vinge, my former Director in West Germany during the 70s emailed:

> "The impact of your writing, your teaching, your leadership… and by just being! You find ways to turn the results of inquiry into action. Your creative spirit is an inspiration to me and to many more than you will ever know. I keep sharing your writing with many former colleagues here and overseas." (Personal email, 2017)

As one principal expressed it, "It was a wonderful culture within which to work and learn".

And it is this culture for learning I was committed to, in developing each of my courses at York. Through a lifetime of teaching, travel, reading and researching five guiding principles evolved for me to consider in planning each class or unit of study.

Rather cheekily, I named them the "Diakiw Laws". While none of them are original, they pull together current research around a central issues that emerged out of my life in and out of schools.

Herewith are the Diakiw laws:

1. Give them the trombone! (Diakiw, 1989)

I kept having this recurring nightmare of visiting a grade 8 music teacher to confirm his permanent contract and during all 40 minutes observing the class he demonstrated how to play the flute, playing brilliantly, while students sat in their seats listening with their instruments on their laps. In each subsequent dream he was demonstrating and playing a different instrument, and it went on and on, day after day, never allowing the students to begin to learn to play their assigned instrument. In my final nightmare, I screamed "Give them the bloody trombone!"

It became a metaphor for how much, many teachers like to hear themselves play their own verbal trombone by elucidating from the front of the class, hour after hour and day after day, after day. John Goodlad commented: "Typical classroom possessed a flat neutral emotional ambiance where boredom is a disease of epidemic proportion." (1984) Walking through the halls of schools today one can still hear the steady drone of teacher talk in many of the classrooms or lecture halls. Students need to play their own instrument of language, the most powerful instrument they have for thinking and learning.

It was my goal to create 'the one question lesson plan' or seminar in my classes at York University, to phrase the opening question, or issue in a way that immediately engages and challenges the students, so that at the end of the three hour seminar, including a variety of formats, they wonder where the time went. That is a typical reaction to my seminars when mentioned in course evaluation.

This 'trombone' approach lies at the heart of a constructivist classroom. I try to talk for no more the 5-10 minutes in a seminar, then an engaging provocative group activity, followed by class summary and perhaps another 5-10 minute wrap-up, Q and A, by me. The pattern however varies from class to class, with a wide variety of media breaking up the routine. We know that when students can play their 'language instruments', learning can happen. Poor grade 8 readers, for example, working one on one with poor grade one readers, both have rising reading scores.

So, 'giving the students the trombone' leads to active and interactive learning. My favourite mantra is "Reading and writing, float on a sea of talk", or "Understanding is at the point of utterance" (J. Britton 1970). In preparation for a seminar I ask them to read one several articles from our course kit and prepare a written maximum one page response based on the reading. They then share their writing about their reading with colleague, talk about their reading and writing at each and every session. I argue the work is internalized at a deeper and deeper lever with each version of reading, writing, talking, telling and re-telling as new knowledge is really only internalized when it has been socially expressed. (Vygotstsky 1982). This understanding directs me to find a way in each seminar for students to become actively engaged in a group setting within this notion of 'giving them the trombone'. Metaphorically, I search for a challenging, engaging one question lesson plan for each seminar.

I know how important oral expression is, in knowing and learning. As one student once said, "How do I know what I think until I hear what I say." (Paraphrase of E.M. Forster) or as the Chinese proverb states, "Tell me and I forget, show me and I remember, but involve me and I understand." Students need to wallow in the subject at hand: To talk to learn and learn to talk.

Giving them the trombone is a metaphor for constructivist pedagogy. It is generative; it is holistic; it is interactive; it is transactional; it is student-centered; it is meaning making; and it is ultimately transformative. The ideal class is students engaged in heated discussion and debate in small groups.

2) Immerse them in the "it"

Students will engage with curriculum when they perceive it to be relevant to their lives. I believe teachers need to mediate relevance for students and this is best done in the introduction of new content, e.g. introduction to a new concept, to a lesson, or to a unit of study. I try to present students with the most real 'thing', the 'it': under study, perhaps by activating prior knowledge. It may be as simple as having students share their experiences with 'it'.

But it is best to take them to the 'it', bring in an 'it', let them see an 'it', feel it, play with 'it', e.g. a field trip first, not as a culmination. If you can't take them to 'it', bring in a video, or pictures, e.g. if studying whales, start with a video about whales.

In my course on Foundations of Education, in which the underlying issues of social justice and equity permeate the course, I introduce the course by showing the film *Freedom Writers*. The movie is my 'it' for this course. The movie brings the viewer into an anti-racist classroom based on constructivist and critical pedagogical principles. Alternative ways of introducing the 'it', are by telling personal, or other stories about 'it' or having students share their own stories and experiences with 'it'. At the very least I read a picture story book about 'it', regardless of the age of students.(Carr, K.S et al. 2001). Constructivist teachers, "Follow them into their minds and fraternize there." (Sylvia Ashton Warner). And as Dewey stated, "Accept the child where the child is".

Providing students with some form of 'it' enables them to have a narrative or framework upon which to build new knowledge and insight. The experience of 'it' is like a scaffold for elaborating and building on the essence or content of the topic under study.

3) It's about the human condition!

Regardless of the subject matter or the age of the students, a primary question I ask myself is, "What is there about this topic or unit of study that can illuminate some central value or understanding about our humanity?" I choose literature, essays, articles, topics that are relevant to their lives. It's about love, truth, trust discrimination, friendship, beauty, loyalty and tragedy, to name a few themes. The study of language and literature, for example, is not about the mechanics of language. We read because of the power of literature to give meaning to our lives. I apply this line of thinking to almost every other subject on the curriculum. If the curriculum dictates that I teach 'the paragraph', I carefully select sample paragraphs from great writers about some aspect of humanity. So from relevant value, I move to the mechanics of 'the paragraph. The law can be applied to other subjects in the sense that we are always looking for the big issues, the big questions that illuminate the human condition, which activate relevance for the student. I aim to not get bogged down in the trivia. Think big!

4) Invite, don't dis-invite

I have learned you never know how what you say to a student, either positively or negatively, will profoundly alter their lives. I am reminded of the times a teacher said something that lit up a student like a candle or squashed him like a bug. I wish I recorded the hundreds of times that I heard students tell of teachers or counsellors telling students they do not have 'it' for university or they should take courses at the practical level, or to tell them they should not count on graduating. What do we know what they can become with the right guidance and maturity? Those hurtful comments have often been proven wrong. I avoid putdowns and negative comments at all costs I strive to invite students by making encouraging meaningful compliments at every opportunity The most innocent, timely affirmation about some achievement or skill can ignite self-esteem and will never be forgotten, and a putdown can squash one's spirit.

> "He put his hands on my shoulder that first day of class and it burned clear through to my heart." David Hanson, Teacher of the year.

5) Race matters!

'Race matters' stands for all forms of discrimination that exist in our society. For the first time in the history of Canada the children of minority immigrants feel less Canadian than their immigrant parents. Race, class, ethnicity, faith, gender and gender preference are some of the underlying elements of social justice and equity issues and should be central to our thinking about curriculum. These issues lie at the heart of a critical pedagogy. The most divisive issue facing our schools and our society is racism... along with all the other forms of discrimination and inequitable treatment. Equity issues should be the driving force behind school policies, the curriculum, human interaction, as well as the hidden curriculum.

Good constructive pedagogy often stays within the classroom. Critical pedagogy, however, is initiated in the classroom but moves out into the community to make life a little better. For me critical pedagogy lies at the heart of 'race matters'. Critical pedagogy is constructivist pedagogy plus, the Hebrew phrase, 'TIKKUN', 'to heal the earth'. To name it, to reflect on it and to act, is a mantra of critical pedagogy.

It is transformative for the student, the teacher and society; it critiques the status quo; it believes we, society, can do better; and it believes schools can change society. This law is at the heart of my teaching. We share our stories; we read our societal his-stories and the students stories. Through story we peel back the multiple layers of the onion to expose the inequities that so many of our students face. Regardless of the topic or grade level there is almost always an equity race or multicultural twist that can be incorporated. It may be as simple as a primary school teacher using a picture book about a Black family, such as *Amazing Grace* (1991), or a high school math teacher introducing a new math topic by demonstrating its roots in Arabic history, or relevance to architecture or building construction.

Conclusion

The themes of social justice, the role of language and thought, and the role of story in learning, emerged from my early life history, and my days as a student and as an educator. I have never stopped learning. This is my story of learning to teach.

Each and every new insight of my understanding about teaching and learning emerged from the 'boiler rooms' of differing communities and contexts. 'Boiler rooms' such as my immigrant family, my 5 year British Etonian style high school community, my Apartheid mining community, my multiple but differing university communities, from my undergrad Geography B.A. and M.A. degrees, my M.Ed. community in curriculum, to my OISE doctoral community focussing on Social Justice and Equity issues in schools. Each new school or career assignment incorporated and layered these new learnings acquired in each and every previous context.

All of these experiences gave birth to my identity as an anti-racist educator and my five 'Diakiw Laws'. More specifcally, three themes preoccupied me and guided me: the role of language in thinking and learning; story as an alternate way of knowing; and social justice and equity issues as a preeminent goal for all teachers regardless of age or grade. This life history study demonstrates how, "The child is father to the man", and how we are shaped in our careers by the social experiences of our history.

Evolution of an Anti-Racist Educator: A Life History Perspective

I have had cause in my passing years and COVID-19 isolation, to reflect on the evolution of my life passions, how events in my life shaped my views and commitments, personally and professionally. The longer I taught, the more passionate I became about several educational interests. As a teacher, school administrator and school superintendent, one of my driving interests was my evolving understanding and promotion of the role of language in learning: In Vygotsky's ideas that new knowledge can only be internalized when socially expressed; that talk, was thinking, as in, 'How do I know what I think until I hear what I say'; that talking to learn and learning to talk are synonymous. I wrote about my learnings in my first published article, *Give them the Trombone*.(1)

My travels abroad and the maxim, 'think globally, act locally' propelled me to become more active in international cooperation and learning. I applied and served overseas with the Department of National Defence Schools Overseas in West Germany as a consultant and secondary school principal where I created an international league of schools comprised of local international British, French, American, and German schools who cooperated together to plan events from everything from common dances to shared themed conferences in the Black Forest, athletic competitions, to fine arts events.

Upon return after 5 years, I became active with UNICEF's education committee. I promoted, and along with a team, developed 2 curriculum documents for school use; *The Girl Child* and *Children's Literature and Global Understanding*. I published an article in the Reading Teacher on the topic of using children's literature to develop international understanding.(2)

As a superintendent I sought a way to send students abroad to obtain their last 4 credits for graduation by working with the Hill Tribes in northern Thailand for the final 4 months of their graduating year. This international coop program still exists 30 years later.(3) As Steven Lewis commented (in a personal note): "Your international coop program is inspired".

I also became interested in the nature of being a Canadian and developed and wrote about 12 commonplaces of Canadian Culture and identity that could be basis of a program debating and discussing the veracity of these commonplaces.(4)

But it was in the field of anti-racism that I feel most confident and the greatest satisfaction for the huge growth curve I experienced in my career.

Growing up in a working class neighbourhood in Toronto with immigrant neighbours beside us and Jewish neighbours across the street, I was oblivious that my Ukrainian immigrant-family identity was relevant. But upon entering grade 9 at Upper Canada College I entered an Anglo-Saxon bastion and my 'otherness' became glaringly apparent. I hid my Ukrainian background and no one ever met my parents till I graduated.

I had never met a Black person till after university. There were no Black students at my elementary public school, at UCC, nor at Victoria College at University of Toronto. My only connection to Black people was learning to read, using the now banned, *Little Black Sambo* in grade 1. Only on reflection am I aware how Anglo-centric my curriculum was. In grade 8, for example, at Williamson Road Public School, I had to memorize the kings and queens of England in chronological order and I was never required to read a book by a Canadian author in any year from K-13, ever!

Two experiences shaped my identity and passion for social justice and equity: Attending Upper Canada College from grade 9-13, where I was institutionally 'othered' and secondly, working on the gold mines in South Africa for 4 months at the height of the apartheid era.

As soon as I entered UCC, as a son of Ukrainian immigrants, I felt 'othered' in the school culture. I systemically felt to be inferior to the white British exemplars of our school – English headmaster, and teaching masters, daily English rituals and routines, our English founders and patrons, and English traditions. We were modelled after the British public school, Eton. We had Church of England prayers in the prayer hall every school day for 5 years. While I do not know a word of my Ukrainian Orthodox Church upbringing, I can sing dozens of English hymns and traditional psalms, prayers and popular biblical passages. I was taught to be a proper English gentleman and instantly upon my arrival was ashamed of my family and background. My fellow students came from the highest socio-economic classes in Toronto. I felt I didn't belong. My classmates would find my feelings hard to understand. My life long friendships are from my grade 9 pool of UCC students. I met my wife through Lionel and Judi Conacher. Lionel and I were classmates and teammates for years at the school.

My second seminal experience was working as an 'official learner' (apprentice) on the West Driefontein Gold Mines, outside of Johannesburg, South Africa, in the summer of 1958, with UCC classmate 'Butch' Powell. We worked our way over and back on Norwegian freighters. It was in the prime of the Apartheid era, where 3 million white citizens ruled 11 million South African Blacks. They had no voice, no vote, no freedom of movement, primitive, inadequate, or non-existent schooling and essentially they were kept on the 'reservation' and let out to be a nanny or to work the fields and mines. It was a brutal era of oppression unlike anywhere in the world at that time. It was a visceral introduction of one extreme of racial hatred. Black Africans were treated like a sub-species of humans, yet on the job, underground, the 12 Zulus I worked with were exceptionally competent at their job, planning and laying down a dynamite pattern of drilling into the rock face and working together as an effective team, while I looked on. They displayed a camaraderie and bond that revealed a strong sense of community.

In May, 1957, I entered my new room at the Royal Canadian Navy training base, HMCS Hochelaga for my 2nd summer session as a midshipman. I introduced myself to my new bunkmate, Milton Zysman. He responded to my Ukrainian name, saying. "Ah, another Black man". The lights went on for me and for the first time memories tumbled back of my years at UCC and I understood being 'othered' there. Of course it had no equivalency to the experience of being Black, but it was another form of exclusion from the dominant white non-immigrant Canadian culture: a Jew, a Black man, and a Ukrainian all knew they didn't belong. We were outsiders.

Though it may surprise many, I have never had high self-esteem, still don't. It particularly affected me at UCC. It is the root I think of my neediness for recognition and compliments. It is a paradox that while I avoided leadership roles and the 'limelight', I've always suffered from a neediness for compliments and assurances. Whether I was socialized to feel 'subservient' or was genetically coded to do so, it was a recurring pattern throughout my life. I was often selected by my superiors for leadership roles or recognition and often rejected the opportunity for leadership and couldn't understand the recognition. For example, after only a handful of years teaching, at a crisis point in my high school's administration, Sam Chapman, the Superintendent of Schools, asked me to be the new vice-principal. When I reported to him, I thought I was going to be fired, I felt so lacking in the ability to take such a position. "Who me? Why me? I can't do something like that." Yet this pattern of being asked to do things by a superior persisted throughout my career. Another manifestation of this same reticence was my unwillingness to talk about or promote any innovation I had developed. I do know I have a fierce drive to try something new, often some radical innovation. I was so predisposed to 'giving it a try', or the axiom 'ready fire, aim', that I was often moving on to another innovation before I had successfully completed the last one. As one principal noted (in a personal email to Gordon Cavanaugh):

> "And really important, an understanding of how creative thinking people operate. I in particular am very right brained, and often a random thinker. So is Jerry, and people like us often take on too much in our enthusiasm, and occasionally let some balls drop. The knowledge that he understood this gave us the courage to admit when things had gone wrong, but to keep on going."

In Michael Kirton's theory of adaptor-innovators, he noted, 'Adaptors are the agents of stability and progress. Innovators are agents of change and reactiveness, often found in visionary leadership positions."(5)

Over the intervening years from working on the gold mines in 1958, I followed events in South Africa with dismay, as I did with the Civil Rights Movement in the USA. Yet there were few Black students in my life as a teacher or in my immediate community. I had no Black students in any of my schools where I taught, until the 1970s. Those I knew were excellent students. I recall supervising a school dance. I kept my eye on three troublemakers, all white, while I noted the off duty police hired for the dance were following 3 black students who had never created a problem in school or in the community. I challenged the police on it.

But with the growing population in York Region, with more public housing, and more lower income families moving in, the complexion of the schools changed dramatically. During the early 1990s, I became increasingly concerned about the level of disengagement I observed in some Black male youth in the schools I administered as a superintendent. For example, the dropout rate was disproportionately higher among Black youth.

Without any specific plan I just intuitively began to fire off 'shots' with a variety of spontaneous initiatives hoping that somehow something would bear fruit. I was very active in establishing a Reading Recovery program in my Area after being turned down for help from my superior colleagues.(6) I believed strongly Reading Recovery was a social justice intervention in grade 1, that would lead to a far higher graduation rate for disadvantaged youth. Reading Recovery helped all the students living in poverty to catch up to their peers by the end of grade 1. Too large a group of those living in poverty were Black kids with single moms.

I invited any Black teacher who was interested to come and exchange views on any issues facing Black teachers and particularly on their views of disengaged black youth. It was a remarkable first meeting. This group became the Black Educator's Network. I also sent out a request for principals and staffs to identity any disengaged or under-performing Black youth in grade seven and eight, with the intention of providing them with support, encouragement and mentorship. This created an uproar with some board members who interpreted this identification initiative as a racist move. The Black wife of a Board member was outraged that I would target and label Black students in this way, but I persisted. A couple of Years later she contacted me to express her regret at her reaction. She apologized and said I had done an admirable service to Black youth.

I collaborated with a Black teacher, Paul DeLyon, from one of my schools who had expressed a similar concern for the progress of some Black students. I pulled him out of the classroom and assigned him to counsel and mentor the identified struggling Black students in grade seven and eight. I advertised in the York University student newspaper, seeking volunteer Black students who were willing to mentor young, struggling Black students. Dozens applied. The mentoring program evolved into a Saturday Morning School for Black students with extensive parental involvement and carried on for over twenty years.

I also met with a group of Chinese parents to discuss their concerns about Chinese Canadian students in the schools. The major problem they identified was that there were a disproportionate number of students with absent fathers who were back in Hong Kong and Beijing. A new itinerant Chinese Community Liaison was appointed to replicate the highly successful work that Paul DeLyon, the Black itinerant counsellor had achieved. Neither staff members assigned to do this had any support from my seniors in head office. I was doing it alone, again.

As one principal wrote about my efforts:

> "His work in racism was system-changing". When colleagues were asked whether I had any impact on antiracism, one colleague responded, "Do bears shit in the woods? Jerry was the poster boy for promoting multiculturalism/anti-racism before its time. His empathy for new Canadians and his intolerance of racism was a model to everyone."

In one issue of my monthly Diakiw's Digest, *A Dialogue with Black Students*,(7) I interviewed over twenty Black students in my three high schools. It shattered perceptions in each school staff's pride in a belief they were teaching in a racist free school environment. I also published articles in the board's Pathways to Equity Newsletter, such as one on religious tolerance around issues of Christmas celebrations and another on the need to reconsider the use of *Huckleberry Finn* and the *Merchant of Venice* based on current theories of the 'Role of the Reader'.(8)

While it may not appear to others reading this reflection, I always felt I was working quietly, without fanfare, flying below the radar. Ironic, considering I was writing articles about these initiatives. I didn't mind writing about my initiatives, I was uncomfortable about talking or promoting them personally. It was always a surprise the way others viewed my work in anti-racism compared to how I viewed my work. It never came close to how others viewed me. Paul DeLyon, the first Black counsellor I appointed, for example, commented on my impact:

> "Jerry understood, and sought to get colleagues as well as the teachers, caretakers, school administrators and other Board personnel under his supervision to begin meaningful dialogue with respect to race, culture, multiculturalism, community involvement and language acquisition."

Gordon Cavanaugh(9) in his monograph on my leadership style reported that:

> "He was subsequently nominated for the Senator Yuzyk National Multiculturalism Award for lifetime achievement in 2012."

In his letter of support Stephen Lewis wrote:

> "I'm delighted to support this nomination. I first observed Jerry Diakiw's devotion to Canadian multiculturalism almost exactly twenty years ago. In the interim, he has never wavered in promoting the best of multicultural Canada. Rare is it that such commitment is shown to the principles of tolerance, inclusion and social justice. Mr. Diakiw would make a sterling recipient of this award."

After I retired as a school superintendent in 1993, I decided to continue the work of my several interests by completing a doctorate at the Ontario Institute for Studies in Education. These interests included Canadian culture and identity; role of language in learning (Vygotsky); multiculturalism; international studies; and anti-racism.

It wasn't long before I focused my studies on the latter. Dr Patrick Solomon of York University, one of the leading intellectuals on anti-racist theory in Canada invited me to share in the teaching of his new foundation course, 'Urban Diversity' a course on social justice and equity issues in urban schools and communities. That experience and my research led to my thesis title, *Becoming an Anti-Racist Educator: Black, South Asian, and East Asian Perspectives*. (10) After Dr. Solomon retired, he requested that the university appoint me to teach his beloved and landmark Urban Diversity course at York University. So, for the last 20 years of my active career I ended up back in teaching after decades of being a principal and superintendent. Teaching was the reason I originally left law school.

Raised in a Caucasian society, in a dominant Anglo-Saxon culture, I never met or talked with a Black person until after graduating from university. My life's career arc was irrevocably altered by my personal experiences of being institutionally 'othered' at UCC, and my real life experience living and working in an Apartheid state. These experiences profoundly affected my enduring commitment to social justice issues in our schools. How do others come to a deep understanding of racism in our society?

In the absence of any visceral experience of racism, one alternative is through the education of teachers who could carry their deeper understandings into their classrooms. I found teaching the Urban Diversity course at York University provided a platform for teachers to better understand the corrosive way that white privilege and racism leads to a failing, unequal democratic society.

The course was designed to bring multiracial students (50% white, 50% racialized students) together to read, write, discuss, argue, and debate the inequity issues we face, in a trusting environment with a minimum of lecturing and a maximum of small group mixed race discussion groups. My motto was 'Reading and writing, float on a sea of talk'. Each seminar had a foundational reading, and students were required to write a half page personal response for each seminar. (How do I know what I think until I see what I write?)

Stephanie Renaud, one of those students emailed me recently:

> "It was thanks to the work we did in the Urban Diversity Program that I had my eyes opened to white privilege, anti-racism, and the history I was never taught. It was thanks to all of this that I have been in this work now for 15 years. Prior to that time, I was utterly blind to privilege, would have said All Lives Matter and had no idea why and how it was deeply wrongheaded and tone deaf. Thank you. And thank you to my fellow classmates. I honestly give you credit for not throwing things at me for some of the ignorant questions I asked as we did this work together. I truly didn't know any better, and it's thanks to all of you that I now do."

And Laura Jones a student from another class wrote:

> "I still remember the class in 1996 when you shared Peggy McIntosh's *White Privilege: Unpacking the Invisible Knapsack*... immediately feeling gratitude for having a Prof who I felt was an ally in my own journey towards becoming an Anti-Racist Educator. I have done so much in the field since and it absolutely started with you!!"

In over 20 years of teaching this course, my hope was that all my students would respond this way, years after taking the course. As Laura responded in another email, "... and I have taught over 1000 students, worked with over 500 teachers... impressing upon them lessons learned from you! Imagine if even half of your former students are doing the same?!"

The mushrooming effect of teachers who have taken the Urban Diversity program or others like it in other faculties of education demonstrate the promise of education as a powerful way to positively influence social justice and equity issues in Canadian society.

References

1 Diakiw, J. (1989) Give them the Trombone, The Canadian School Executive

2 Diakiw, J. (1990) Children's Literature and Global Education: Understanding the Developing World https://www.jstor.org/stable/20200368?seq=1 The Reading Teacher. Vol. 43, No.4d

3 Diakiw, J. (2016) Building Bridges Around the World: International Coop https://diakiwsdigest.wordpress.com/2020/01/03/building-bridges-around-the-world- international-coop/

4 Diakiw, J. (2016) The School's Role in Debating and Discussing our Canadian Cultureand National Identity https://diakiwsdigest.wordpress.com/2020/01/03/the-schools-role-in-debating-and-discussing-our-canadian-culture-and-national-identity/

5 Kirton. M. (2020) Adaptor-Innovator Theory. https://kaicentre.com

6 Diakiw, J. (2012) Reading Recovery: A social justice intervention https://diakiwsdigest.wordpress.com/2020/01/03/reading-recovery-a-social-justice-intervention/

7 Diakiw, J. A Dialogue with Black Students

8 Diakiw, J. (2016) Say Goodbye Huck, Say Goodbye Shylock. https://diakiwsdigest.wordpress.com/2016/01/15/say-goodbye-huck-say-goodbye-shylock/

9 Cavanaugh G. (2013) A Champion of Innovation in Education: A Life History Study of Jerry Diakiw. A Culture Change Leader. (Kindle E-book)

10 Diakiw, J. (1999) Becoming an Anti-Racist Educator: Black, South Asian, and East Asian Perspectives. Doctoral thesis, Ontario Institute for Studies in Education. Collections Canada. https://www.collectionscanada.gc.ca/obj/s4/f2/dsk1/tape7/PQDD_0032/NQ63823.pdf

JERRY DIAKIW

Good for Kids, Good for Us
Socio-emotional skill development in the early years

Everything I need to know I learned in kindergarten

Most of what I really need
To know about how to live
And what to do and how to be
I learned in kindergarten...

ROBERT FULGRAM

Developing social emotional soft skills with young children early is good for kids because a socially competent 4-6 year old kid's life chances are significantly higher than one with poorly developed socio-emotional skills. And it's good for us, because investing in early childhood education, focusing on soft skills – especially for children living in disadvantaged circumstances – has a far greater positive impact on the economy than any other economic national investment!

Unfortunately, we are missing this huge economic and social opportunity. We have national policies aimed at stimulating our economy with investments in infrastructure, such as roads, solar, bridges and pipelines, but we ignore the power of investing - even before kindergarten – in our children. Economist James Heckman, the 2000 Nobel laureate, points out that investing in infrastructure has a 1-2% rate of return, whereas investing in early childhood education has an 8-10% rate of return. He maintains that paying focused attention to the young children of low-income families is not some warm, fuzzy notion – it's a hard-nosed investment that pays off in lower social welfare costs, decreased crime ratios and increased tax revenue".

It is refreshing to hear a celebrated economist speak passionately about early childhood education and who centres mothering, family and mentoring in his economic work. We are not investing enough in our families – this is particularly devastating for families headed by single moms who bear the brunt of the pay gap, inadequate system supports and an increasingly precarious labour market that impacts women – and there is a growing inequality gap as a result. An increasing percentage of children are growing up in poverty across Canada. This has an understandable and often profound impact on their learning.

The inequality gap

Even though Canada has the narrowest gap in academic achievement between low and high socio-economic status children according to international testing (PISA TIMSS), the current gap is still shameful.

In the last census report by the Toronto District School Board that correlated family income level to achievement on the EQAO, math and literacy results in Grade 3 revealed a 20-30% difference in achievement between students coming from the 26% of families earning over $100,000 per year and the 28% of families earning less than $30,000. The gap widened to over 30% by Grade 6. This 30% point differential is indefensible, especially when we know we can do something about it.

Toronto has a wide range of families of diverse economic status living together in nearby neighbourhoods. In affluent neighbourhoods, only 16% of students drop out of school, while in nearby neighbourhoods (dominated by families earning under $30,000). 43% of kids drop out of school. Research on the social and economic indicators of health also point to lower life expectancy and poorer health and well-being for marginalized families, including those living in low income communities. The skills gap, which is so apparent at age 18, is actually already in place by age three.

Socio-emotional skills

While academic achievement metrics are easy to obtain and widely available, they mask the far more important socio-emotional skills that are harder to measure yet critically predictive of life success. These soft skills include self-regulation, self-awareness, establishing good healthy interaction with adults and peers, and task completion.

"Early childhood experiences can be very consequential for children's long term social, emotional and cognitive development," says Sean F. Reardon, professor of poverty and inequality in education at Stanford University. "And because those influence educational success and later learning, early childhood experiences cast a long shadow." This is underscored by a growing body of studies in North America, the UK and New Zealand that affirms the long term predictive power of socio-emotional skills in young children, and reinforces the need to rethink our emphasis on testing for cognitive skills to the detriment of a more balanced program incorporating the soft skills.

In July 2015, the *American Journal of Public Health* published a study that looked at what had happened to a group of over 700 kindergarten students, 13 to 19 years after they left kindergarten. In the 1990s their teachers rated each student's social competence on a five point scale. It proved to be a powerful indicator of future outcomes. The greater the difference between social competence scores in kindergarten, the more significant the differences in all areas of life by the age of 25. Children who scored higher on social competence were not only more likely to have graduated from high school; they were also were four times as likely to graduate from college than those who scored low, and held far more well-paying jobs.

Academic achievement tests do not adequately capture character skills such as conscientiousness, perseverance, self-regulation, sociability, and curiosity – all of which are valued in the labour market, in school, and elsewhere. Sadly, we continue to ignore the importance of non-cognitive soft skills. As James Heckmnan points out, academic test score grades have only a 7% impact on life time earnings, whereas socio-emotional skills have a 27% impact!

Further, Claire Miller noted recently, class differences in childrearing are on the rise; privately obtained socialization, dietary and learning

OUR SCHOOLS/OUR SELVES

experiences provided by well-to-do parents ate exacerbating the achievement gap for both cognitive skills and socio-emotional skill.

Early interventions pay off

Heckman and colleagues completed a definitive economic cost-benefit analysis of investing in disadvantaged children early by examining the Perry program (Head Start Program) in Ypsilanti, Michigan. The cost per pupil of free instruction was $17,759 per year (2006 dollars). The Head Start program was initially considered a huge disappointment because early academic gains at age four were apparently lost by age 10 (later program adjustments maintained the early gains). But as participants reached age 40, the program was considered to have had a 6-10% annual rate of return, a virtual tie with the average annual rate of return in investing in the U.S. stock market from 1946-2008. The researchers pointed out that each dollar invested at age four returned between $60 and $300 by age 65, and within the targeted population there were significant health improvements. Heckman found similar results from the Abecedarian Childhood Program in North Carolina. A recent reanalysis based on 40 years of data tracking long-term outcomes for participants from the Perry Project from the 1960s, showed that the $15,166 spent for every child in the Perry project saved $195,621 in social costs. As McKinzie and company pointed out, achievement gaps, in evidence from birth, are the equivalent of a permanent national recession".

Quality, persistence and thoughtful and relevant measurements are essential to actualizing the promise of quality early childhood education. The Abecedarian preschool program in North Carolina started at birth and provided parental education, health, nutrition, and early learning up to age five. After over 35 years of follow-up study on the treatment and control groups it was the only early childhood program that provided educational and life skills which, in combination, delivered greater returns in educational achievement. employment, and, most importantly, health.

There are a few existing early intervention programs in Canada that dramatically alter cognitive skills and improve socio-emotional skills in our Canadian youth. These programs need to be expanded, but far more needs to be done for disadvantaged families with preschool children.

Early reading ability is a bellwether of future academic and economic success. The Reading Recovery program targets non-readers in Grade 1, in intensive one-on-one sessions with a qualified Reading Recovery teacher to bring them up to grade level by the end of Grade 1. The York Region Board of Education began implementing the Reading Recovery Program over 20 years ago with a Reading Recovery teacher in nearly every York Region school. It is expensive, but highly successful.

In Toronto, the Regent Park Community Health Centre, along with Toronto District School Board, and York University initiated a program called Pathways to Education, targeting youth in low-income neighbourhoods, focusing on both cognitive and socio-emotional skills. The long-term benefits are conclusive. The Boston Consulting Group concluded that every $1 invested in Pathways has yielded a social rate of return of $24, a cumulative lifetime benefit to society of $600,000 for every Pathways graduate. Not only did high school graduation rates double, but also there has been a 300% increase in post-secondary attendance.

In 1992, in Quebec the report, *Quebec Fou Ses Enfants,* based on the success of the Perry and Abcedarian programs caused a revolution in provincial thinking about early childhood education, leading to the highly successful Carrefour de la petite enfant, (CPE) with high quality day care available to all for $7 a day (while the upfront cost remains roughly the same, the program has since been modified to reflect the income of parents on their tax returns). The success was immediate, yielding $1.04 in payback instantly just from taxes from women now able to enter the workforce.

In Ontario, the ground-breaking Pascal report summarized all the known benefits from research across the globe advocating full day programs for all four and five year olds and galvanized the government to mandate full day kindergarten.

Generally, the earlier the intervention, the higher the rate of return. Policies that provide thoughtful, systemic and properly-funded support for disadvantaged families not only reduce inequality, but also raise productivity. As Heckman has pointed out, such investments have higher rates of return than any other national economic investment.

When it comes to thinking about marginalized children and poverty, it's worth remembering that investing in early education is a morally and an economically good thing to do. Far more needs to be done for developing socio-emotional skills in 3-6 year olds especially in disadvantaged families. It's part of a necessary anti-poverty, pro-equality strategy that's good for kids, and for all of us.

ENDNOTES

1. The family plays a dominant role in shaping adult outcomes, but in the U.S., 40% of children are now being raised by single moms. Celinda Lake, founder of a top Democratic research firm in U.S., predicts that by 2018 50% of all kindergarten students in the U.S. will be from households headed by single mothers. In Toronto, in families earning under $30,000 per year, single moms are the defining characteristic of that population. In 2011, single parent families in Toronto had an average household income of one-half that of two-parent households.

REFERENCES

Boston consulting Group. 2011. "BCG assessment of Pathways to Education: Executive summary". Online presentation retrieved from http://www.pathwaystoeducation.ca/sites/default/files/pdf/BCG%20 Assessment%20of%20Pathways%20%28February%202011%29.pdf.

Dalziel, Kim M., Dale Halliday and Leonie Segal. Feb. 2015. "Assessment of the cost benefit literature on early childhood education for vulnerable children: What the findings mean for policy." Feb. Sage Open Access. Retrieved from http://dx.doi. org/10.1177/2158244015571637.

Diakiw, Jerry. 2012. "Reading Recovery: A social justice intervention". The Journal of Reading Recovery. Spring. Volume 11. Number 2. Pages: 35-42.

Government of Quebec. 1999. "Un Quebec fou de ses enfants - Rapport du groupe de travail pour les jeunes". 1999. Publication number 94-849, Government of Quebec.

Greeley, Brendan. Jan 16 2014. "The Heckman Equation: Early childhood education benefits all". Article retrieved from http://www.bloomberg.com/bw/articles/2014-01-16/ the-heckman-equation-early-childhood-education-benefits-all.

Heckman, James. July 17, 2009. "What's the 'rate of return' on social skills". Video retrieved from https://m.youtube.com/watch?v= 5BrCv_N.

Heckman, James, Seong Hyeok Moone, Rodrigo Pinto, Peter Savelyev and Adam Yavitz. 2009. "A reanalysis of the HighScope Perry Program". Chicago Illinois, University of Chicago.

Heckman, James and Flavio Cunha. 2009. "The economics and psychology of inequality and human development". Journal of the European Economic Association, Vol. 7(2) 320-364.

Heckman James. April 2, 2010. "The economics of investing in children". Video retrieved from https://m.youtube.com/watch?v= Rt a0 5PmJmS8.

Heckman, James. 2015. "The economics of human development". Retrieved from https://heckman.Chicago.edu/page/current-projects-0/.

Heckman, James. Oct 15, 2015. "Quality early childhood education: Enduring benefits". Article retrieved from http://heckmanequation.org/content/quality-early childhood-education-enduring-benefits.

Jones, Damon, E., Greenberg, Mark and Crowley, Max. 2015. "Early Social-Emotional Functioning and Public Health: The Relationship Between Kindergarten Social Competence and Future Wellness". American Journal of Public Health: Vol. 105, No. 11, pp. 2283-2290.

McKinzie and Company. 2009. "The economic impact of the achievement gap in America's schools". Social Sector Office, McKenzie and Company.

Miller, M. Cain. 2015. "Class differences in child-rearing are on the rise'. New York Times. Dec 17.

O'Reilly, Janet, and Maria Yau. 2009. "Parent census, and kindergarten-grade 6: System overview and detailed findings". (Report No 08/09-16). Toronto Ontario, Canada (Toronto District School).

Organization for Economic Cooperation and Social Development. 2004. "Messages from PISA 2000". Paris.

Robert Woods Johnson Foundation. 2015. "How children's social skills impact success in adulthood: Findings from a 20 year on the outcome of children screened in kindergarden". Robert Woods Johnson Foundation.

Sowell, Elizabeth. 2015. "Family income, parental education and brain structure". Nature Neuroscience. Vol. 18. 773-778.

Yau, Maria, and Janet O'Reilly. 2007. "2006 Student census, grades 7-12: System overview". (Report No. 07/08-01) Toronto, Ontario, Canada. Toronto District School Board.

Yau, Maria, Lisa Rosolen, Bryce Archer. 2015. "Census portraits: understanding our students' backgrounds, socio-economic status reports. (Report No 14/15-24). Toronto Ontario, Canada, Toronto District School Board.

Originally published in Education Week https://www.edweek.org/ew/articles/2012/05/09/30diakiw.h31.html

It's Time for a New Kind of High School

Our high schools are relics of the past. Based on an antiquated economic formula designed for the Industrial Revolution, high schools in the United States and Canada are ill-suited for the emotional and intellectual well-being of our young people and profoundly out of step with the needs of our contemporary economy. We have been tinkering with the high school formula for decades, but the recipe for innovation has yet to be written.

As academic and Phi Delta Kappan columnist Ben Levin pointed out in a paper in 2010: "Schools embody an industrial model of organization in a post-industrial world, and an authoritarian and hierarchical character in a world where networks and negotiations are increasingly prevalent."

And Sir Ken Robinson, the noted international education expert, said in 2006 at the TED conference that we have been "trying to meet the future by doing what we did in the past, and on the way we have been alienating millions of kids who don't see any purpose in going to school."

Minority children and those living in poverty are not playing the game. They are dropping out. In Indiana University's 2007 High School Survey of Student Engagement, 73 percent of the respondents said, "I didn't like the school"; 61 percent said, "I didn't like the teachers"; and 60 percent said, "I didn't see the value in the work I was being asked to do." About 30 percent of the students indicated they were bored because of a lack of interaction with teachers, and 75 percent reported that the "material being taught is not interesting."

Those students still in attendance are unchallenged, but they persist because it is the only game in town. Researchers have found that a high percentage of students dislike the place where they spend most of their learning time.

In the most recent Canadian national study, conducted by the Canadian Education Association in 2006, student attendance dropped from 91 percent in 5th grade to 58 percent in secondary school. More significantly, intellectual engagement reportedly declined from 62 percent in 5th grade to 30 percent in high school. What on earth are we doing to the 70 percent who have not dropped out? Realistically, school is not an ideal environment for providing all the necessary opportunities for becoming an adult. Instead, school is a particular kind of environment, honoring individualism and cognitive development. It imposes dependence on, and withholds responsibility from, students. We have lost sight of young people's potential for responsibility, and it can be argued that in doing so we have sacrificed many opportunities for growth and usefulness.

Teachers have difficulty providing meaningful, intrinsically interesting, and motivating experiences. Students see themselves as passive participants in an anonymous education system. This is learned powerlessness.

Years ago, John I. Goodlad wrote in *A Place Called School* that high school classrooms "possessed a flat neutral emotional ambiance where boredom is a disease of epidemic proportion." Ben Levin added, in the paper I referenced at the top of this essay, that the source of the disease is a "prevalence of teacher talk, which remains an enduring feature of classrooms around the world."

Despite what we now know about the power of learning through talking and doing, we persist in expecting students to learn by listening. The present disparity between teacher and student talk time is a profound hindrance to learning.

Walking through the halls of high schools in both the United States and Canada, one invariably hears the steady drone of teachers' voices in room after room. The sound of boredom is deafening.

We need to offer new kinds of schools and new kinds of classrooms. We need to revolutionize our basic high school structures: We need to tear apart the school day, the high school timetable, the school year, the four-year diploma. We need to rethink credit- and diploma-awarding authority, which need not be the sole purview of the high school. For instance, why can't we give this authority to nongovernment organizations and corporations willing to step up and offer academic credits in their workplaces relevant to the work of their institution?

We need to explode the boundary between the school and the workplace. Just for starters, we need to create 24-hour, year-round high schools; a grade 7-14, or six-year, diploma; a grade 7-8 half-day school/work internship; dual-diploma programs with high schools/community colleges; and a North American retooling of the German apprenticeship system.

In the United Kingdom, the remarkable innovation called Studio Schools has exploded. In them, disengaged 14 to 19-year-olds are assigned to project schools – e.g. television arts, food services – relevant to the designated theme of the studio, and in cooperation with local businesses. In these schools, work and learning are integrated.

Studio Schools are sure to be a major feature of our 21st-century school system, but they cannot be the only one. We need a multiplicity of alternatives, incorporating mentorships, internships, and apprenticeships to forge a new vision of education in our rapidly changing, team-oriented society.

We also need to look beyond high school to funding programs like Reading Recovery in 1st grade to reduce the eventual dropout rate in high school. We need to support and encourage emerging successful models, like the online Khan Academy, Flex schools in San Francisco that offer a hybrid online-and-in-school experience, and the Pathways to Education program in Canada that works to keep low-income students from dropping out. Likewise, we should back the schools working with the New Tech Network in the United States, which emphasize the use of more student-driven, project-based learning. New Tech schools focus on three principles: a project-based curriculum in which students work in teams; use of technology primarily, instead of focusing on textbooks and teachers; and a positive culture that promotes respect and responsibility.

With any of the emerging models, we need to provide radical new social-learning structures for youths. Educator Deborah Bial's brilliant concept of the "posse" of multicultural teams of student-leaders who are intensively prepared for college success can be applied across a wide variety of student ages and settings, not just for university-bound scholarship students. The need to form small, interdependent learning groups or teams is an important adjunct to online learning.

Whichever paths we take, classrooms have to change. If 70 percent of students are not intellectually engaged in classes, a revolution has to take place inside them.

The time has come to stop tinkering with an antiquated model. We are delayed in our thinking because those who were able to suffer through or even thrive in this dying high school model have grown up to be teachers and lawyers and businesspeople who now advocate for reforms through the prism of their experiences. But the vast majority do not have the same fond memories of those halcyon high school days. For these students, the "high school experience" has failed. It is not only an economic issue, but a moral one of providing the very best opportunities for our young at all socioeconomic levels to flourish in a rapidly changing world. Long live the new high school!

Originally published in Huffington Post. http://www.huffingtonpost.ca/jerry-diakiw/investing-in-disadvantage_b_9746274.html

Jerry Diakiw
Educator

Why We Should Be Investing In Disadvantaged Children

It is widely known that disadvantaged children perform dramatically lower on cognitive achievement tests than children from well-to-do families. In Toronto, for example, children from family homes earning less that $30,000 per year (disproportionately single moms), perform more than 30 points lower on test scores in reading, writing and mathematics, compared to children coming from homes with over $100,000 family income, on the EQAO provincial tests.

We know what the problem is. We even know what to do about it. But do we have the political will?

As Canada plans for investment of billions of dollars in infrastructure, it is worth noting that James Heckman (Heckman Equation), Nobel laureate in economics of human development, has shown that infrastructure has only a one to two per cent rate of return while investing in pre-school disadvantaged children has a proven record of yielding an eight to 10 per cent rate of return. As McKinsey & Company pointed out, achievement gaps, in evidence from birth, are "the equivalent of a permanent national recession."

Children who participated in the early childhood projects during the 1960 and 70s, called the Perry Preschool Project and the Abecedarian Project have been followed intensively now for up to 40 years and the results are powerful and instructive. They offer a bright beacon of light on narrowing the inequality gap and reducing child poverty.

Early childhood education delivered to disadvantaged children as young as one to four clearly promotes economic efficiencies and reduces lifetime inequalities.

In 1972, in North Carolina, the Abecedarian Project conducted a controlled experiment with 111 randomly selected disadvantaged high risk children, who were born between 1972-77, starting from infancy to age five. Ninety-eight per cent were Afro-American children. The 57 children were given a high quality education including important home visits focusing not only cognitive skills but socio-emotional soft skills such as: perseverance, motivation, risk-aversion, self-esteem, self-control. The important home visits by social workers and teachers impacted on the lives of parents that made positive permanent changes in the home environment that affected their children for years long after the program ended.

The lessons from this study of 57 children are remarkable. While the early IQ gains found in the Perry Preschool project evened out after four years (though the gains in achievement scores were maintained at age 14), the IQ gains from the earlier and more intensive Abecedarian project, carried on into adulthood.

While cognitive skills were important to both programs, socio-emotional development was central and key. Achievement tests do not adequately capture socio-emotional character skills. As James Heckman points out, socio-emotional skills have a 27 per cent life time earning impact, while cognitive test scores have only a seven per cent impact on life time earnings. Achievement test scores predict only a small fraction of the variance in later-life success. For example, adolescent achievement test scores only explain about 15 per cent of the variance in later-life earnings.

By the time children start kindergarten, those born into poverty are already at risk of dropping out of school, crime, and a lifetime of low-wage work.

The Abecedarian Project produced a phenomenal 10 per cent rate of return on investment compared to a standard 5.8 per cent average rate of return on investing in stocks.

Recently researchers at Duke University published a study that looked at what happened to five-year-old students, 13 to 19 years after they left kindergarten. The five-point teacher-rated social competence scale used was a powerful predictor of both positive and negative future outcomes in education attainment, employment achievement, criminal justice, substance use and mental health.

These studies, demonstrate that an early intervention for children in disadvantaged homes, focussing on these soft skills, have a direct positive effect on wages, schooling, teenage pregnancy, smoking, crime, performance on achievement tests, including a wide range of health factors and health choices. They are healthier, and make better life style choices. Both the Perry Preschool Project and Abecedarian Project reduced participation in a variety of social pathologies.

By the time children start kindergarten, those born into poverty are already at risk of dropping out of school, crime, and a lifetime of low-wage work. This is not only bad for all those born into poverty by the accident birth, and bad for society.

Common intervention programs offered by many government organizations such as adult literacy, job training, or prisoner rehab programs all have far lower rates of return. As well, no other remediation programs for older students come close to the returns from investment in preschool children.

A recent revised report of cost benefit from 40 years of data for the Perry Preschool showed that $15,895 spent for every child in the Perry Preschool Project saved $138,486 in social costs, for every dollar invested, a return of $8.74 at age 27, and over $14.00 at age 40. Within the targeted population, among many other outcomes, there was a pronounced reduction in crime, obesity, and heart disease.

Investing in disadvantaged pre-school children can dramatically raise tens of thousands of children out of poverty, narrowing the income gap, and giving thousands of marginalized children, born poor by the accident of birth, an equal opportunity to thrive and succeed in our society. It's part of a necessary anti-poverty pro-equality strategy that's good for kids and good for all of us.

VIEWPOINT

JERRY DIAKIW

Originally published in Education Canada, 2008. https://www.edcan.ca/wp-content/uploads/EdCan-2008-v48-n3-Diakiw.pdf

Thinking Outside the Box: The Post-modern High School

I am disenchanted by the contemporary high school, and I believe we can do better. For too many students, our large urban schools are vast, spiritless, unhappy places. Some are bored, some feel like outsiders, some feel intimidated, and most feel disconnected from the real world. Too many fall through the cracks and drop out.

I dream of a post-modern high school based on three components: innovative, alternative structures, close-knit, caring communities, and relevant new curricula – where social justice and equity permeate all aspects of the school.

Alternative school structures

All of the following alternative structures could be introduced without additional funding and would help make secondary school a successful experience for more students.

The 24 Hour High School. Why do we package schools into day schools, night schools, and summer schools? Why couldn't high schools operate like universities, offering courses all year, during the day or at night, on campus or online? These options would allow students to combine work and school and to pursue their education at their own pace, in their own time.

The Four-year, Grade 11-14 high school/ college diploma program, located on a community college campus. Many students would be far more successful in the community college setting than the current regimented high school system. Similar to the CEGEP option in Quebec, students could complete their last two years of secondary school during the first two years of community college and then go on to a diploma program.

The Six-year Grade 9-14, Co-op/apprentice-ship/internship program. A full day of school disconnects many students from the reality of the real world for too long. By taking longer to obtain a diploma, they could incorporate more real life experience into their formal education.

Grade 7 and 8 Co-op/apprenticeship/intern-ship program. Teachers have identified many students as 'at-risk' by Grades 7 and 8. For many of these students, an early introduction to co-op programs would help develop a positive self-image and improve their self confidence and chances for success.

Apprenticeships/internships/mentorships. Apprenticeships and innovative forms of hands-on learning would permeate all of the above, and they would be much more available and start earlier than they do now.

Last summer, I met a young framer for a local construction company. I asked if he had received his training through a community college apprenticeship program. He explained that he learned on the job after he left school at 15. Why can't we get young people like this man into formal apprenticeships earlier?

Years ago, I met two young women who were managing the high-tech sound and lighting system in a CBC studio. CBC had recruited them in Britain – after they had completed a BBC internship program – because there were no trained people in Canada. Why were we going to the UK to recruit young people who could just as easily have been trained here?

Internships are uncommon in our schools, but the opportunities are endless, from fine art galleries and sports venues, to law offices and research labs. We need to think outside the box.

Core Family Groups

I see one common element in each of the formats suggested above: a core family or home grouping who stay together over extended periods of time, with a core of group counsellors and therapists working with students as life counsellors, sharing and discussing everything from sex education and current events, to budgeting and family life, to course selection and career planning.

Many of us remember the sense of community we felt as our 9B or 9E class moved through Grade 9, then into 10B or 10E, and on into Grades 11 and 12. While we gained much in moving to the credit system, we lost that sense of belonging.

The groups I envision would fluctuate in size from perhaps eight to 60. In addition to creating community, they would attempt to build confidence, share concerns, bolster flagging spirits, and even permit peer brow beating. Occasionally, larger groups could promote democratic activities, or provide opportunities for celebrations, guest speakers, or special ceremonies suited to the goals of the program.

To validate their importance, these group sessions would be for credit.

Post-modern Curriculum

Our current high school subjects are not written in stone. We need new conceptions of knowledge, new ways of knowing. Jerome Bruner writes that argument and story are "two modes of cognitive functioning, two modes of thought, each providing distinctive ways of ordering experience, of constructing reality."[1] Our current curriculum is structured almost exclusively around the first of these modes, argument.

In the recent Massey Lectures Series, Alberto Manguel asks, "How do the stories we tell help us perceive ourselves and others? ...Is it possible for stories to change us and the world we live in?"[2] In my dream, the role of story emerges in innovative ways. For example, by using Bill Bryson's book *A Short History of Nearly Everything*[3], teachers can learn to use a narrative mode to teach science units, resulting in more engaged and excited students... and more of them.

Whatever alternative modes of knowing emerge, my post-modern curriculum would be interdisciplinary – theme and issue-based as opposed to subject-oriented, with critical thinking, problem solving and creativity at the core of every course. It would also reflect our multicultural heritage and incorporate taboo subjects, like racism.

Richard Rorty, the contemporary philosopher, said, "It is not so important to find the absolute truth of anything as it is to keep the conversation going." I share these thoughts in the hope that they will keep the conversation going about alternative ways to meet the needs of our students.

Notes

1 Jerome Bruner. Actual Minds, Possible Worlds (Cambridge Mass. University Press, 1986).

2 As quoted in Nathan Whitlock, "Massey Lectures," The Toronto Star, 28 October 2007, 105. 2007.

3 Bill Bryson. A Short History of Nearly Everything (Anchor Canada, 2004).

Put Bragging Rights on Hold, Canada

While Canada can feel smug about its recent success in international testing, the underlying effects of poverty on children's health, academic achievement, and society in general persist in disturbing ways.

Despite an all-party House of Commons resolution to end child poverty by the year 2000, the child poverty rate persists at 1989 levels, and, according to the Conference Board of Canada, the increase in income inequality has even been more rapid in Canada than in the U.S. since the mid-1990s[1] The relationship between social-economic status (SES) and school achievement has been clearly established, so it is instructive to examine the achievement of low-SES students living in Toronto, which has the Ontario's highest proportion of children living in poverty.[2]

According to Ben Levin, family income can account for up to 50 percent of differences in academic achievement. "Thirty years of careful social science has provided overwhelming evidence that socioeconomic status (SES) has been and continues to be the best single predictor of how much schooling students will obtain, how well they will do at their studies, and what their life prospects beyond school are."[3]

The most recent data published by the Toronto District School Board showed that only 16 percent of students who took most of their courses at the academic level in Grades 9 and 10 dropped out, compared to 56 percent of those taking most of their courses at the practical level. Students living in higher-income neighbourhoods dropped out at a rate of 16 percent, compared to 43 percent for students living in low-income neighbourhoods.[4]

Tracing achievement back to Education Quality and Accountability Office (EQAO) math and literacy results in Grade 3 reveals a 20-30 percent difference in achievement between students coming from families earning over $100,000 per year and families earning less than $30,000 – and the gap widens by Grade 6. These students come predominately from visible minority, immigrant families, where English is the second language. They are disproportionately single parent moms, boys, and/or from families with low levels of education.[5]

In Canada, we have narrowed the achievement gap between rich and poor by focusing on these injustices in society and developing programs to address them in schools. Whether it is the Aboriginal Schools, Songide'ewin, or Rising Sun in Winnipeg, or Pathways to Education in Toronto, we have proven that schools can make a difference – sometimes a big difference. Across Canada, the Reading Recovery program has proven conclusively that the reading level of children in poverty can be raised to match that of their advantaged peers,[6] and reading competency is the best predictor of academic – and economic – success.

Schools can do a lot, but they can't do it all. Child poverty persists as a cancer in our society, taking a toll on children's health, development, and school achievement – and on the public purse. The public cost of poverty in Canada in 2007 was low-balled at $24.4 billion.[7] Poverty contributes significantly to healthcare costs, policing costs, diminished educational outcomes, and depressed productivity. In 2004, the OECD concluded, "failure to tackle the poverty... of families and their children is not only socially reprehensible, but it will also weigh heavily on countries' capacity to sustain economic growth in years to come."[8]

As Ben Levin has pointed out, "Poverty is such an enormous negative influence, that it must be part of the educational reform agenda whether justified on grounds of economic interest or of social justice."[9]

Yes, by international standards we have made a lot of progress. But, as current statistics show, we still have a long way to go.

References
[1] Conference Board of Canada. Hot Topic: World Income Inequality. Is the World Becoming More Unequal? Accessed September 28, 2011 from http://www.conferenceboard.ca/hcp/hot-topics/worldInequality.aspx
[2] Children's Aid Society of Toronto. Greater Trouble in Greater Toronto: Child Poverty in the GTA Report. Fact Sheet, Toronto, 2008.
[3] Ben Levin. Educational Responses to Poverty. Canadian Journal of Education 20, no. 2 (1995).
[4] S. Brown. Making the Grade: The Grade 9 Cohort of Fall 2002: Overview. Toronto District School Board, 2009.
[5] J. O'Reilly an M. Yau. 2008. Parent Census, Kindergarten-Grade 6: System Overview and Detailed. Toronto District School Board, 2009.
[6] J. Douetil. At Last, Some Good News about Children in Poverty. Literacy Today, Summer, 2011.
[7] National Council of Welfare. The Dollars and Sense of Solving Poverty. Vol. 130, Autumn, 2011.
[8] Organisation for Economic Cooperation and Development. Messages from PISA 2000. (Paris: 2004).
[9] Levin, 21.

3 Racism and Multiculturalism

Articles about Race, Gender, Multi-faith Education, Multiculturalism

When I was a school superintendent I published a monthly newsletter called *The Diakiw Digest*, usually a capsule of my weekly education readings or topical education items. On occasion I would write one article for the whole digest. This is one example. I wonder how true these comments by Black students are some 20 years later.

the DIAKIW DIGEST

A Dialogue With Black Students

As part of the process of talking with students from wide variety of race and ethnoculturural backgrounds Paul DeLyon and I took the opportunity to discuss issues of racism with two groups of Black students in each of two of the secondary schools under my supervision.

The students who accepted my invitation were representative of all grades and were mostly high achieving students. Some of these Black students had roots for several generations in Canada, but most were born outside of Canada or their parents were. They were generally very positive and upbeat about their experiences in school and the community and in Canada. When we asked about their experiences of discrimination in Canada, they exploded with a stream of anecdotes about the kind of racism they experience in the community and in schools. They shared these stories.

- They told stories of shop keepers following them around closely when shopping for clothes; about being asked to leave convenience stores before they had a chance to buy things.

- Several told stories of being stopped by police when a group of them were in a car and going shopping or to a movie, or being treated rudely by police for no apparent reason when walking downtown with friends.

- Several cited systemic differences in treatment in schools. For example, they commented that when white visitors come to the school they are unquestioned, but when Black friends arrive staff come out of the woodwork to hustle them out of the building.

- Some students recounted being offended by guidance counsellors by telling them about how great the sports teams were in the school.

- Others told stories of being insulted by teachers who accused them of cheating when they got excellent marks. "Yes they think we're good for nothing but sports," said another.

- Teachers had low expectations of their ability. "I have to work 8 times harder," said one student.
- One student was hurt when a teacher called him an oreo cookie. "Black on the outside, white on the inside".
- Students described themselves as part of the "ghetto", compared to those who were "cottage country" or the "polo set". They felt their Canadian history, culture and literature was not part of the curriculum. "They don't teach me what I want to learn. I want to learn about my heritage."
- Another student complained that when a white student sang out, "Eenie meanie mynie mo. Catch a nigger by the toe", the teacher said nothing, even though the whole class heard it.
- Many affirmed racial jibes were ignored by teachers.
- Students complained vociferously about how difficult it was to get their music played over the PA or at dances, while white students music preferences were respected.
- Students told us many Black students transferred to other schools where there are larger numbers of Black students, because they didn't feel they were accepted at this school.
- Many felt that teachers were not sensitive to the fact that black students were treated differently than white students. Black teachers, too, confirm this.
- The tolerance for Black students' behaviour is much lower than for white students.
- Some experienced discomfort with comments about racial characteristics. "Like what?" I asked innocently. "Like your lips are so big you have to put on lipstick with a paint roller."
- Several resented they were never picked to be a group leader.
- More widely many expressed fear about travelling to the US. "It's such a hassle"
- Many complained about the way they were portrayed in the media including films by Black filmmakers such as, Boys in the Hood.

Say Goodbye Huck, Say Goodbye Shylock

Originally published in https://diakiwsdigest.wordpress.com/2016/01/15/say-goodbye-huck-say-goodbye-shylock/

This article was republished ten years after I retired, in Pathways to Equity, a newsletter of the Race Relations Coordinator for the York Region District School.

"The following is an excerpt of an article published in this newsletter in the winter of 1990. It was written by Jerry Diakiw, Superintendent of Schools, now retired from our Board. Has anything changed since? Are we having the same arguments to defend the 'classics'? Why? What drives this determination? Are we better at teaching these 'classic'? Are our students better at understanding these works? Do our current students of racial minority background feel less pain as they study these books? And the debate goes on... Here is the excerpt."

During the high school years, a student normally only studies formally between five and ten novels and five or six plays. Teachers and principals, with the approval of the Board, select this handful of "great works" from the thousands that are possible.

They, in a sense, "censor" hundreds of outstanding works through exclusion. They select titles appropriate to the age and needs of the students and the goals of the program. They select titles of high literary quality which speak to this generation, as well as to all generations. As our society changes, the choice of appropriate titles changes: *Pilgrim's Progress, Wuthering Heights, Silas Marner,* and *Great Expectations*, once mandatory reading for all students, are rarely seen on the curriculum today though they still hold a valued place on our library and classroom shelves. *Huckleberry Finn* and *The Merchant of Venice*, too, will always be treasured works. They may disappear from the curriculum for formal intensive study but they will always be recommended for small group and individual optional study.

Teachers will no longer teach these works, not because of public pressure to remove them, but because of their growing understanding on the role of the reader. Edmund Wilson said, "No two people read the same book." We have come to understand that the story the student is reading is not the same as the story the teacher has read.

One student wrote in his journal that "Twain made Negroes look so inferior, so stupid."

The teacher explained, "That's not what Mark Twain was saying."

"That's the way I read it," the student said.

Even the most sensitive and well trained teachers agree that it is difficult to overcome the way some kids feel when the sensitive content of the text is openly discussed in the class, whether the text is racist or not.

Many teachers are realizing the complexity of teaching these texts and asking themselves: "Is this text so important that it is worth hurting students?"

"I felt so isolated and separate from the class. Nobody saw it the way I did," said one Grade 12 student.

A disturbing effect of formally teaching texts like *Huckleberry Finn* and *The Merchant of Venice* in some communities is the increase incidence of racial taunts, jeers, and slurs beyond the classroom. When teachers understand how painful it is for many minority youngsters, they drop these works like a 'hot potato'. There are just too many other excellent works to use to achieve the same aim.

An issue of greater concern than the effect of individual titles on students in a classroom setting, is the cumulative impact of what has been unconsciously excluded from our student's literary experience. In examining the literature our young people encounter from kindergarten to O.A.C., the black experience, for example, is virtually absent.

Teachers have a difficult task selecting meaningful literature that strikes a responsive chord with the emotions of our young people. To do otherwise would render the program bland, boring, and without purpose. Few titles can be found that do not have their objectors.

There is a distinction, however, between objections by parents whose view is different from the accepted norms of the community and objections by students who find public discussions of the text in class humiliating and embarrassing. While this latter situation may occur with students on a wide range of sensitive issues, it is the visible minority student who cannot escape attention through silence. When racial issues arise in the class, they are front and central in the minds of all students. When other sensitive issues arise in a class, affected students can usually choose to remain anonymous.

Say goodbye Huck; Say goodbye Shylock. No one has really censored these text: Black students and Jewish students will still read them, but they will do so privately, when they choose, without the anxiety of having to discuss the text openly in class.

In fact, more and more classrooms are adopting the reading workshop model, whereby students select for reading, writing, and discussion from a wide selection of worthy titles, including *Huckleberry Finn*. Within this more flexible format, teachers can select titles that counteract the prevailing Euro-centric bias ensuring the portrayal of more positive images of minorities that offset the stereotype of simple black folk.

Whatever the method of organization of a program, however, teachers have a responsibility to provide a balanced ethnocultural viewpoint through the selection of quality literature from around the world. Minority voices need to be heard, not only to affirm the dignity and identity of minority Canadian students, but to enrich the literary experience of us all.

the DIAKIW DIGEST

In One Generation...

Thoughts on a night in Convocation Hall. As I waited to receive my doctorate in Convocation Hall at the University of Toronto on a chilly November day I was engulfed by waves of emotion. I had never felt such a personal sense of achievement and I had never felt so Canadian as I did that evening.

I first felt an emotional chill as we graduands crossed the commons from Knox College to Convocation Hall. In the late afternoon sun, we made our way into the hall in our flowing robes with our scarlet Doctoral hoods over our arms. We were joined by the platform party, with members wearing a striking array of robes, hoods and hats from universities all over the world. It was a splendid and colourful scene evocative of the medieval roots of the convocation tradition.

During the ceremony I scanned the faces of my fellow graduands, my own family and the sea of multiracial faces in the audience and I welled up with emotion.

It has taken a while to unravel those complex feelings with so many layers of meaning. I had returned to university to full time study after retiring from a thirty-five year career as a teacher, principal and superintendent. At the age of 57 I started back to school for the challenge of achieving a long held dream of completing a doctorate in education. My advisor told me that only 50% of U of T doctoral candidates ever complete their thesis and of those that do it takes an average of six years to complete the program! It took me six years. If I had thought that it would take me so long, I doubt I would have been so bold.

Having completed the arduous and demanding research and writing process and having successfully defended my thesis, the taste of success was sweet indeed. At the age of 63 I certainly felt the emotion of this achievement but it was superficial compared to the deeper emotions I was experiencing.

As I sat listening to President Pritchard before the illustrious gowned dignitaries on the dais and surveyed the faces in the audience, I was overcome with thoughts of my immigrant parents. They came from peasants families in Lapushna in the Ukraine in the 1920's and as they carved out a life in Canada, nothing was more important to them than providing for the best education they could for their three boys. As long as I could remember, my older brother was told he was to be a doctor and I was told I was to be a lawyer. As I sat in Convocation Hall my father's image stayed with me and under my breath I whispered through my stifled tears, "I am a doctor now, dad".

Similar stories were being played out by hundreds of families in the hall that night. The faces of the audience revealed a United Nations of eager parents and siblings; immigrant families from China, India, the Philippines and Latin America, boat people from Vietnam, black families from Jamaica, Trinidad and Nigeria, labourers with rough hands in suits, rarely worn. This was the Canada I love. The sons and daughters of these immigrant and refugee families were my fellow doctoral graduands in education, music architecture, laws, business, engineering and nursing.

In this grand hall the essence of Canada unfolded before me. We live in a country where, in one generation, immigrant children from humble backgrounds were able to achieve the highest levels of education. I was deeply moved by this realization. Our public education system had achieved one of the two highest levels of post secondary participation rates of any country in the world and these immigrant families were able to dream of an education for their children, and support and encourage them to achieve the highest level possible. Few of them in the audience that night would ever have believed their children would receive doctorates in their chosen field. We have developed a country where children of all races and ethnic groups have equal opportunities for the best education. It is not surprising that immigrants consistently reveal that the quality of education is one of the top two or three reasons why they like and respect Canada.

I realized that, as an educator, my own preoccupation with a quest for social justice and equity also lay at the heart of Canada's identity. Rightly or wrongly, I had long ago lost my hyphen and no longer called myself a Ukrainian-Canadian. While it was an important stage for me to go through, my identity, as a Canadian, is aligned with the continuing wave of immigrants. I feel I have as much in common with Asian, black and working class immigrants as I do with other Ukrainians. A pride in the wave of Ukrainian immigrants who so boldly opened up the Canadian West, who settled and built businesses in so many Canadian cities, merged with the pride I feel in the awesome achievement of black, Latino and Asian immigrants. Their entry into the mainstream of Canadian culture has been a heroic struggle. It is this third solitude with which I feel so closely identified. It is this group of immigrants that I feel so much a part of as we try to stake out a place for all Canadians.

On this graduation night, as a son of immigrants I felt a part of this group, intensely and emotionally. I was awash in the sense of pride in what we had all achieved and the hope that the rich variety of graduands from all races and ethnic groups in the graduating class would one day be reflected in the platform party.

In this very moving ceremony I received my doctorate on my knees before Chancellor Hal Jackman. I was humbled by the thoughts of how proud my mom and dad would be and how proud I was to be a Canadian. In one generation...

Our Culture's Native Roots

Originally published in The Toronto Star, July 21, 1992. Also reprinted in The Holocaust Era

The origins of Canadian culture and identity are tangled and knotted, but if you dig deeply, some surprising roots are revealed. Revisionist authors as widely divergent as McGill's Bruce Trigger, (*Children of Aataenisic*), feminist Paula Gunn Allen (*Who is Your Mother? The Red Roots of White Feminism*), and popular writers like Ronald Wright (*Stolen Continents*), are revealing the extent to which the genesis of our culture is grounded in native society.

We have always been led to believe that the richness of our culture is a product of the glory and achievement of Western civilization. It is humbling to realize that it is not a simple as that. Our social safety net, our ability and reputation as mediators, conciliators and peacekeepers and our democratic freedoms enshrined in our federal system of government, are three of the many conceptions of our cultural identity that intertwine and overlap to create a whole greater than the sum of the parts.

While these are considered sophisticated products of a European heritage, it is instructive to consider that they may also be deeply rooted in native societies.

The Hurons, for example, like other Iroquoian tribes, looked after their own from the cradle to the grave in a manner that smacks of our Canadian safety net.

When Etienne Brule wintered with the Hurons on the shores of Georgian Bay in 1610, Champlain guaranteed his safety by sending a Huron chief's son to Paris for the winter. When the young man returned and was asked what Paris was like, he explained to his disbelieving tribesman that people in Paris begged for food on the streets. That a society allowed this to happen was incomprehensible to the Hurons. He also described the appalling manner in which children were harnessed, spanked and beaten publicly, and the way citizens were punished or executed in public squares in the early 1600s. To the Hurons, the Europeans were savages.

Montaigne, the French philosopher whose writings strongly influenced the struggle for liberty, justice and equality in Europe and elsewhere, acknowledged the commentaries of other Iroquoian visitors during the colonial era, who were shocked at the gross inequities they observed between the rich and the poor in Europe. An ethnology of Iroquoian society written by Lewis Henry Morgan in 1851 was a popular treatise in Europe at the time. It outlined in some detail the workings of a matricentral society with an egalitarian distribution of goods and power, a peaceful ordering of society and the right of every member to participate in the work and benefits of the society.

Freidrich Engels reacted excitedly to this text; "This gentile constitution is wonderful! There can be no poor... All are free and equal – including women."

Certainly Karl Marx and other socialist thinkers at the time were similarly profoundly influenced by Morgan's ethnology. Marx's evolving ideas of female equality and women's liberation for example, though never achieved in practice, were fundamental to his socialist theories and can be clearly traced to the impact of his reading of Morgan's ethnology about the role of women in Iroquois society.

How these values informed Canadian identity is evident to this day. One of our most enduring qualities is our historic ability to mediate disparate points of view. Canada's evolution is a wonder of nation building. This immense land, with a divisive geography and a harsh climate, was united without military revolution, civil war or a war of independence.

The skills to achieve this remarkable feat have stood us in good stead internationally. Canada has long had a reputation as a peacekeeper for the world and we perceive ourselves that way. Canada's leadership and commitment to the United Nations, exemplified by Lester B. Pearson's Nobel Peace Prize, and our undiminished involvement as a peacekeeping force, are evidence of our conciliatory skills honed in nation building at home.

Confederation, itself, epitomizes our ability to unify a wide variety of disparate interests. We normally attribute this to the evolution of democracy and the parliamentary system, a crowning achievement of Western civilization. But the Iroquoian Confederacy, a political organization comprised of five distinct native societies, (later six), had a profound influence on both the American and Canadian systems of government. Paula Gunn Allen reminds us that we inherited slavery and vote by male property owners from the European democracies.

At the Treaty of Lancaster in 1744, Canasatego, an Iroquois chief, spoke for the Iroquois, "We are a powerful confederacy; and by your observing the same methods our forefathers have taken, you will acquire fresh strength and power."

In the audience was a young Benjamin Franklin, later a co-author of the American constitution. He acknowledged in his writings the influence of this confederacy: "It would be a very strange thing if Six Nations of ignorant savages should be capable of forming a scheme for such a union..."

But such a union they formed. The symbol of the Iroquois Confederacy was an eagle clutching five arrows in its claw – one for each of the Iroquois nations. The symbol of American independence was an eagle clutching 13 arrows – one for each of the 13 colonies. The American confederacy adopted the Iroquois system of distinct executive, legislative, and judicial branches of government and both Canada and the U.S. instituted the unique Iroquois system of three levels of government – local or municipal, state or provincial, and federal.

Through adopting this Iroquoian model, Canada was able to reconcile the many conflicting and divergent regional and cultural interests and bring about and maintain a confederation that more democratically represented the Canadian people. The fusion of the federal system and the parliamentary system is a unique Canadian approach to democracy.

The roots of our identity are indeed tangled and knotted but it is reassuring to realize the extent to which the First Nations have contributed to our uniquely Canadian culture. But it is less significant to untangle all the roots to ascertain their precise origins than it is to realize they are part of an integrated whole.

Originally published in https://ipolitics.ca/2016/04/15/want-infrastructure-spending-that-pays-off-spend-the-money-on-kids/

Want infrastructure spending that pays off? Spend the money on kids.

Jerry Diakiw is a former super-intendent of schools with the York Region District School Board. For the last 20 years he has been teaching courses on social justice and equity issues in schools and communities in the faculty of education at York University.

In Toronto, children from households earning less that $30,000 per year (disproportionately single moms) perform more than 30 points lower on Grade 3 and 6 provincial test scores in reading, writing and mathematics, compared to their peers from homes earning over $100,000.

We know what the problem is. We even know what to do about it. The outcome, as always, comes down to political will.

Our new federal government plans to spend billions of dollars on infrastructure projects. But according to James Heckman, Nobel laureate in the economics of human development, infrastructure spending only sees a rate of return of roughly 1 to 2 per cent – while investing in disadvantaged children before they start school has a proven record of yielding an 8 to 10 per cent rate of return.

Children who participated in two early childhood projects run during the 1960 and 1970s – the Perry Preschool Project and the Abecedarian Project – have been studied intensively now for 40 years and the results have been both powerful and instructive. The findings show how narrowing the inequality gap and reducing child poverty makes economic sense. Early childhood intervention delivered to disadvantaged kids aged one to four, and their parents, promotes economic efficiencies and reduces lifetime inequalities.

The Abecedarian Project produced a phenomenal 10 per cent rate of return on the initial government investment. Compare that to a standard 5.8 per cent average rate of return on investments in stocks.

In 1972, the Abecedarian Project conducted a controlled experiment in North Carolina with 111 randomly-selected, disadvantaged, high-risk children born between 1972 and 1977, running from infancy to age five. Ninety-eight per cent were Afro-American children. The 57 kids were given a high-quality education and home visits focusing on both cognitive skills and socio-emotional soft skills (perseverance, motivation, risk-aversion, self-esteem, self-control). The home visits by social workers and teachers changed the lives of the parents, making for positive, permanent shifts in the home environment that affected their children years after the formal program ended.

The lessons from this study are remarkable. While the early IQ gains found in the Perry Preschool project evened out after four years (though the gains in achievement scores were maintained at age 14), the IQ gains from the more intensive Abecedarian program carried on into adulthood.

While cognitive skills were important to both programs, socio-emotional skill development was key. Achievement tests don't adequately capture socio-emotional character skills. As Heckman points out, socio-emotional skills have a 27 per cent lifetime impact on earning, while cognitive test scores have only a 7 per cent impact on lifetime earnings. Achievement test scores predict only a small fraction of the variance in later-life success; adolescent achievement test scores only explain about 15 per cent of the variance in later-life earnings.

These studies, and more recent ones from other countries, demonstrate that early intervention for kids in disadvantaged homes, focusing on these soft skills, has a direct and positive effect on wages, schooling, teenage pregnancy, smoking, crime and performance on achievement tests. The children who benefit from early intervention are healthier and make better lifestyle choices.

Both the Perry Preschool and Abecedarian projects reduced participation in a variety of social pathologies. By the time children born into poverty start kindergarten, they're already at risk of dropping out of school, getting involved in crime and getting trapped in a lifetime of low-wage work.

Common intervention programs offered by many government organizations – such as adult literacy, job training and prisoner rehab programs – all have far lower rates of return. No remediation programs for older students come close to the returns from investment in preschool children.

A recent revised cost-benefit report based on 40 years of data from the Perry Preschool Project showed that every $15,895 spent ended up saving $138,486 in social costs – a return of $8.74 for every dollar invested – thanks to such outcomes as pronounced reductions in crime, obesity and heart disease.

Investing in disadvantaged pre-school kids can raise tens of thousands of children out of poverty, narrow the income gap and give thousands of marginalized children – starting with one strike against them by an accident of birth – an equal opportunity to thrive and succeed. When it comes to public investments, nothing else comes close.

4. Canadian Culture and Identity

Strengthening the Ties That Bind

Originally published in The Globe and Mail, 18 September 1990

Shared stories lie at the heart of any culture. Over time, arts and crafts, music, dance, film and poetry blend together to crystallize an image that says: "This is who we are."

The stories being shared give a culture its values and beliefs, goals and traditions. Their myths, legends, folk tales, histories and experiences bind any group of people together into a cohesive society and allow them to communicate with each other and to work together with a common purpose.

Canada today seems to be a nation without a clear sense of itself. A patchwork quilt of different regions and cultural and ethnic groups, it is groping for ties that can bind it together. Can its schools help? Should they?

British writer Ernest Gellner points out in his book, Nations and Nationalism, that history has shown that the school, not the home, has been the decisive factor in creating cultures for modern nations. He argues that the chief architects of the modern nation have been teachers; they helped create the modern nation-state, and they can perpetuate it, nourish it and make it thrive.

Of course, Canadians have realized this, to a point. Much time and effort has gone into discussing what Canadian content and literature students should study in high school. The problem is that this is too late. According to E. D. Hirsh Jr., writing in his book, *Cultural Literacy*, "The weight of human tradition across many cultures supports the view that basic acculturation should largely be completed by age 13. At that age Catholics are confirmed, Jews bar or bat mitzvahed, and tribal boys and girls undergo the rites of passage into the tribe."

This means the process of giving young people a sense of culture should begin in elementary school – and it wouldn't be particularly hard to do.

For example, is it unreasonable to ask all provinces to agree that, from kindergarten to Grade 8, every child should have 20 to 30 hours of instruction a year based on an identical set of stories, folk songs, poems, readings and tales about Canada. Over the course of 10 years, Canadian children would share between 200 and 300 hours of cultural content.

Granted, 20 or 30 hours a year isn't much of the 925 hours or so hours of instruction that students receive, but it would be Canadian and common to all. School children would know that, in every school from Whitehorse to St. John's, whether black, native, Chinese, anglophone or francophone, they are all learning the same things about their country. The stories, art, poems and films they would share could help to give Canadian culture a sound foundation.

Some outstanding resources are already available, but not enough. We must find new ways to tell tales about our heroes and heroines. Not textbook biographies but fireside tales about our native people, our explorers, our fur traders, our pioneer women, our Nobel laureates, our great athletes and scientists, the settlement of the West, the discovery of our minerals, our artists and musicians, the building of our railways and our international accomplishments.

We need to tell stories that capture Canada's multicultural heritage – the Jewish fur traders, the black people who outnumbered Scots in Nova Scotia two centuries ago, the Chinese workers who built the railways, and the English, Scots, Irish, Ukrainians, Finns, Germans, Sikhs and Japanese who have helped make this country what it is.

Given that storytelling has such power and important implications, wouldn't it be wonderful if we commissioned Canadian writers and storytellers to tell the story of Canada in short pieces appropriate to the age of elementary students? Taken together these quintessentially Canadian stories would create, like a patchwork quilt, a total image of Canada. IDENTIFYING the national culture may seem presumptuous, if not somewhat artificial, but the history of nationalism clearly indicates that it is not a radical notion. Indeed, Prof. Gellner argues that nation-building is by nature a selective process. "The cultural shreds and patches used by nationalism are often arbitrary inventions; any old shred or patch would have served as well."

Of course, some guidelines are necessary. Canadians currently confront three powerful needs: to recognize and support regional and ethnic identities, to create a national identity and to acknowledge our global interdependence as citizens of the world.

It may seem odd to suggest that Canada's national identity is rooted in a recognition of both regionalism and internationalism. But our federal system, bilingualism and multicultural policy certainly support and enhance regionalism. And our long history as global peacekeepers and mediators, our participation in international organizations, our long involvement with developing nations and our comparatively open immigration policies confirm our global commitment.

In a significant way, Canada is a microcosm of the world, where the forces of regionalism and ethnic identity (the Baltic States, India, Ireland and Quebec) are a counterpoint to the forces of globalism (the United Nations, free trade, a united Europe, and so on).

But these shouldn't be the only themes. There also must be stories about Canada as a nation of immigrants, including the risk-takers, adventurers and entrepreneurs among them; about the continuing struggles by natives, people of colour and French Canadians, and about Canada as a wilderness nation because, despite our largely urban existence, the wilderness preoccupies us.

These big themes are the "stuff" that myths are made of, the stuff that makes Canadians Canadian. By teaching them in our schools, we can reveal the Canadian identity and culture in a way that tells our children – all our children – that "this is who you are."

the *DIAKIW DIGEST*

Reconsidering Our Heritage

Luis Buñuel, the Spanish film maker, stated:

> "You have to begin to lose your memory, if only in bits and pieces to realize that memory is what makes our lives. Life without memory is no life at all... our memory is our Coherence, our reason, our feeling, even our action. Without it, we are nothing."

Our memory is our personal story, but we also have a cultural memory – the collective story of our people. It is our legacy. This remembered story lies at the heart of family heritage and cultural identity. Children need to know their family story. As well, they need to know the Canadian story; the shared story that inducts them into the Canadian "tribe"; the layer upon layer of Canadian myths, legends, folklore, historic tidbits, songs, symbols and images that together, create a collective Canadian consciousness.

For the sake of our multicultural Canadian society, this story needs to be "re-visioned" and broadened. An African proverb says "until lions have their own historians, tales of glory will be told about the hunter". Our recorded Canadian story has historically been shaped by the hunter. It has been largely a male Eurocentric perspective by those in power. The lions have yet to tell their tale. The voices of women, the poor, First Nations, people of colour and other minority groups are now being heard.

This re-visioning of our story is important for our children and their own sense of themselves as Canadians. When we consider that there were Jewish fur traders and settlers in Canada before the British, that there were more blacks in Nova Scotia two hundred years ago than there were Scots, that Sikhs opened up the timberlands in British Columbia at the break of the century, that Chinese laborers joined Canada "a mare usque ad mari" throughout the 1800s, our young people can begin to sense that these "other" Canadians are not a recent phenomenon. They are not outsiders. They are part of the Canadian story and have always been so. While we can appreciate and treasure the richness of our French and English heritage in the creation of our country, we can no longer exclude other Canadians who have always been a part of the Canadian Story.

Our curriculum has been institutionally Eurocentric since Canada's inception. We must change that. This does not mean we impugn western culture, nor do we eliminate from our curriculum the European history, culture, values and traditions that have been fundamental to the creation of our Canadian way of life, but we must also provide students with the opportunity of seeing the evolution of Canadian society through a non-Eurocentric perspective as well. The mainstream culture must become aware of our Eurocentric perspective, for example, when we use expressions like "we discovered America", "we conquered the west", while "the Indians massacred the settlers", or when we trivialize First Nation creation stories by asking children to write their own Indian myths. Would we ever ask children to write their own Adam and Eve stories? Or when we tell Native Canadians that they too were immigrants. Do we ever think of England as a nation of immigrants – the Celts, the Jutes, Saxons or Normans?

It is not reasonable for our students whether they are Caucasians or not, to go through their schooling either not coming across Black, Asian or First Nation characters in literature at all or seeing them only as servants, slaves, or seeing their lifestyles trivialized. We must see people of colour in every day situations engaged in normal family relations. We must see them in settings where we can benefit from a greater understanding of their culture. We must see them in realistic settings where they are confronted by racism and prejudice. We must see them in historical settings where we can begin to understand the integral part they have played in the evolution of Canada and North America from earliest times. We must see them in settings in the country of their cultural origins so that we can better understand their culture and can see that Canadian culture is deeply rooted in every nook and cranny on the globe. We must see Canadian history and contemporary events from their perspective, and not always from the Eurocentric viewpoint.

There is a Chinese expression that says "Every people view the world through their own keyhole". While this may have been true of Canada in the past, we can no longer look through one keyhole.

As educators we must provide leadership in creating a new multicultural paradigm that is anti-racist in intent; a paradigm that not only includes traditional mainstream culture and recognizes the role that Europeans have played in the evolution of Canada, but one that takes the Eurocentric "blinkers" off and allows Afro-Caribbean, Asian and First Nation citizens to feel that they, too, are Canadians and have always been Canadian. Their heritage in Canada must become part of our memory – "Our memory is our coherence, our reason, our feeling, even our action".

The School's Role in Debating and Discussing Our Canadian Culture and National Identity: Keeping the Conversation Going

A Multicultural Perspective: 2010

For the first time in long history of the influx of immigrants into Canada, the process of becoming Canadian is not working as it has in the past. For centuries while each new immigrant group held on to their own birthplace identity and values, as they slowly assimilated, their children, playing and learning together in mixed cultural and educational settings, assimilated at a much faster rate than their parents, often creating tension in the family over conflicting values. Second generation children of colour now feel less Canadian than their white immigrant counterparts... AND even their parents! Even white, third generation immigrant children feel less Canadian than their second generation counterparts! (Globe and Mail, Jan. 2007)

The study, (Statscan) based on an analysis of 2002 Statistics Canada data, found that the children of visible-minority immigrants exhibited a more profound sense of exclusion than their parents... It is also a warning that Canada, long considered a model of integration, won't be forever immune from the kind of social disruption that has plagued Europe. (Jimenez, Globe and Mail, 2007)

This is a perplexing and continuing dilemma as we welcome 200,000-300,000 immigrants each year, over 80% of whom are people of colour. It is an issue of both individual identity and national identity and as stated in our policy of multiculturalism, "National unity, if it is to mean anything in the deeply personal sense, must be founded on one's confidence in one's own individual identity." (1971)

I argue here that it is in our schools where this issue can best addressed and resolved over time and it must be through a process of debating and discussing our Canadian culture and identity in a systematic way in order "to keep the conversation going."

The argument that our Canadian identity is impossible to define remains a dominant theme with contemporary commentators and historians (Gwyn, 1995; Resnick, 2005; Bliss, 2006). Based on extensive research data Raney posits "that most Canadians have a strong national identity rooted in universal conceptions that everyone can share, such as citizenship. Data also show, however, that a growing number of Canadians define their national identity narrowly, such as through birthplace and religion." (2009)

Yet Resnick views Canada as a country without an identity, a nation in "perpetual self-doubt." (2005) Bliss describes Canada's nationalist project as a series of "failed identity experiments" (2005) and suggests that today's multicultural Canada is "no more sure of its role in the world than it is of its identity." (2006) Most of these condemnations center around Canada's remarkable approach to multiculturalism, coupled with the degree of national decentralization. It is widely believed that there is so much regional, cultural, ethnic, linguistic and religious diversity in this country that we do not, in fact, have a distinctive culture or identity.

However, even those who express this belief are quick to distance ourselves from our American neighbours and from our British and French roots. I argue that there are in fact powerful commonplaces in our culture and identity – shared values and characteristics that most Canadians can identify with regardless of racial, ethnic, and linguistic backgrounds, faiths, and regions. I also argue that the school is the most important place to explore, discuss and debate these commonplaces. They are not a written in stone but are offered here as a basis for generating debate and discussion about what makes us all Canadians and, as Richard Rorty argues it is not so important to find the objective truth of anything, as it is "to keep the conversation going." (Rorty, R., Philosophy and the Mirror of Man, 1979)

In fact, as I will point out, historically, in country after country, it has always been the school where a national culture has been promulgated. I will also explore how in most cultures it is in the pre-teenage, intermediate school years where the culture is infused and inculcated, not in post-adolescence. It is also my contention that it is not more Canadian history that we need but a broader inter-disciplinary cultural studies program that is needed, not more politics and history. Nor is it just a matter of including Canadian literature at the secondary school level, since historically it has been shown that it is in the early years that who we are, really comes into focus.

Schools in Canada and elsewhere have always conveyed cultural and political views, and they will continue to do so whether we like it or not. In the past, of course, these views were dominated largely by the white male European perspective of the most dominant powers in society; this is no longer true. The culture and identity we all share has become multi-faceted, multi-layered, constantly shifting and not dominated by any one group. Some have described it as the first postmodern state. It is complex and perpetually shifting. With each decade we morph into a more layered perspective and understanding of what is Canadian. The difficult task schools now face, therefore, is determining how to convey our culture and identity in a way that is inclusive of all Canadians, so that justice and equity are underlying principles of the curriculum.

How Cultures Have Traditionally Transmitted Their Values

In most culturally homogeneous countries or regions children grow up hearing and learning the stories that define their culture: myths, legends, folklore, historic tidbits, tales of heroes and villains, miraculous tales and tales of courage and achievement. These shared stories lie at the heart of a culture's identity. Literature, arts and crafts, music, dance, film TV, and poetry blend together over time to crystallize an image that says, "This is who we are." Countries with a common religion, language and history are defined as ethnic national identities." (Raney, 2009)

The shared stories provide a culture with its values and beliefs, its goals and traditions. The myths, legends, folk tales, histories, and experiences of any cultural group bind the individuals together to form a cohesive society which allows people to communicate with each other and to work together with a shared purpose. These common stories become the foundation of public discourse, and they are a source of pride in their community.

The education of children is central to this process. According to E.D. Hirsch Jr.:

> "The weight of human tradition across many cultures supports the view that basic acculturation should largely be completed by age thirteen. At that age Catholics are confirmed, Jews bar or bat mitzvahed, and tribal boys and girls undergo the rites of passage into the tribe." (1987)

Hirsch traces how Korean children traditionally memorize the five Kyung and the four Su. In Tibet, boys from eight to ten read aloud and learn the scriptures; in Chile the Araucanian Indians use songs to learn the customs and traditions of their tribe. The Bushmen children of South Africa listen to hours of discussion until they know the history of every aspect of their culture.

Hirsch also traces how the education system has been used to convey a national culture in modem nations. Traditionally on any particular day in France, for example, each child in each grade would be reading the same page in the same textbook. In the history of American education, the text book has been a constant source of debate over attempts to control the culture transmitted through the schools.

Hirsch cites an example of the influence of one particular document in defining a culture. This one document was also central to the development of Canadian education as it was widely adopted across Canada. In 1783, Hugh Blair, a Scot from the University of Edinburgh published Lectures on Rhetoric and Belle Lettres, intended as a compendium of what every Scot needed to know if he or she were to read and write well in English. This book had enormous impact on curriculum in school systems throughout the English-speaking world. Widely used in Great Britain, US and Canada between 1783 and 1911, the book went through 130 editions! Blair defined English literary culture for use initially by the Scots, later by colonials like Canadians and Americans; and eventually it became the standard for educating Englishmen and women.

In Nations & Nationalism (1983), Ernest Gellner argues that, viewed from a historical perspective, it has been the school and not the home that has been the decisive factor in creating national cultures in modern nations. Literate national cultures, he maintains, are school-transmitted cultures. He asserts that the chief creators of the modern nation have been school teachers; they helped create the modern nation state. They perpetuate it and make it thrive. The history of Europe has shown that the schools play a major role in the creation of a national culture. Even in the United States with its many disparate groups, the schools have done much to create a national culture through such common shared stories, both real and imagined, as George Washington, Daniel Boone, Tom Sawyer, and Casey at the Bat, as well as through the promotion of strong central shared values and symbols of patriotism.

The history of the evolution of nationalism in country after country indicates clearly that a national culture is an artificially created construct. Gellner says, nation builders use a patchwork of folk materials, stories of heroes, old songs, legends, and historical tidbits, which are selected and re-interpreted by intellectuals to create a national culture,

The cultural shreds and patches used by nationalism are often arbitrary inventions, any old shred or patch would have served as well... Nationalism is not what it seems and above all, not what it seems to itself. The culture it claims to defend is often its own invention (56).

While these authors have illuminated for me how culture has been transmitted throughout history, including more recent periods of colonialism and the creation of the nation states, they also have unsettling implications. Hirsch, for instance, laments what he sees as the disintegration of central core values and a shared common knowledge in recent years. He argues for the need to identify what every American needs to know, and works to promote a return to a narrowly Eurocentric curriculum based on the glories of Greek civilization, the British Empire, and the Bible. While the European civilizations, and in particular, British and French traditions, are an integral part of our own Canadian identity, they are but one significant facet among many.

Yes the school is, and always has been a major purveyor of a national viewpoint. But what kind of a viewpoint do we want to promote for the future? Any examination of the curricula of the past reveals a program of indoctrination into the culture and mores of those in power. The old African proverb is still true: "Until lions have their own historians, tales of bravery and courage will be told about the hunter." Or, as Napoleon put it more bluntly, "History is a set of lies agreed upon."(cited in Wright, 1992). History is written by winners (Wright, 1992). The winners write the school curriculum and decide what stories will be told and what literature will be read.

As the child of immigrant Ukrainian parents, during grade seven and eight in Toronto in the late 1940s, I vividly remember spending hours memorizing the Kings and Queens of England in chronological order. Later in high school I read the required stories and novels of Rudyard Kipling, Charles Dickens and Jane Austen, and the poetry of Tennyson and Wordsworth. I do not recall ever reading a single Canadian author. The children's books in the local library reflected this Anglo-centric curriculum. I grew up feeling that I was somehow an outsider in Canada despite the fact that I was born in the country. Nor was I alone: My research into the life histories of racial minority teachers in Canada reveals time and again that as students these young Canadians, while at last reading Canadian authors and learning about confederation rather than "1066 and all that". They still did not read about their own culture's remarkable Canadian history. They did not see themselves reflected in the curriculum of their schools. The experiences of these Asian, South Asian and Black educators, who were schooled in Toronto, illustrate how recently in our history, they clearly saw the transmission of traditional culture as a major function of schools. It was clear who the winners were, and they weren't at the victory party.

Revisioning the Traditional Culture

Since Prime Minister Trudeau proclaimed the policy of Multiculturalism in 1971, there has been a remarkable change in our official notions about our culture. Indeed, Trudeau said, "While we have two official languages we have no official culture, no one culture is more official than another." I have long celebrated Trudeau's statement; but the longer I ponder it the more I have difficulty with the words, "we have no official culture." It seems to imply what many have said for decades, that Canada has no cultural identity at all. The insistence on no official culture has resulted in a backlash against multiculturalism, while multiculturalists struggle to stem the tide of racism and disempowerment.

Education, then, is caught between conflicting demands. As Grossberg 1994) suggests,

> "On the one hand, there is the discourse of multiculturalism and liberation which calls for a democratic culture based on social difference and which is usually predicated on a theory of identity and representation. On the other side there is a discourse of conservatism based on canonical notions of general education and a desire to impose what it cannot justify – the existence of an illusory common culture." (10)

Simply, there is a lament over the loss of a culture rooted in Western civilization and values, while there is a cry for a multicultural perspective based on social justice and equity. Must there be a dualism? Is there an alternative to these two positions? Amidst the remarkable diversity of this country are there inclusive commonplaces? Can a patchwork quilt of our stories welcome all Canadians?

It is helpful to review some history surrounding some of these issues. We have been inundated the last few years with critical examinations of the meaning and purpose of multiculturalism and its affects on the curriculum in the school. Popular books like Hirsch's *Cultural Literacy* (1987), Bibby's *Mosaic Madness* (1990) and Bissoondath's *Selling Illusions* (1994) have promoted a return to a traditionalist view. In Henry Giroux's view (1992), they have "argued that multiculturalism posits a serious threat to the school's traditional task of defending and transmitting an authentic national history, a uniform standard of cultural literacy, and a singular national identity for all citizens to embrace." (1) The heated position of the traditionalists is best demonstrated by Roger Kimbal's (1991) provocative statement:

> "Implicit in the politicizing mandate of multiculturalism is an attack on the idea of common culture, the idea that despite our many differences, we hold in common an intellectual, artistic, and moral legacy, descending largely from the Greeks and the Bible, supplemented and modified over the centuries by innumerable contributions from diverse hands and peoples. It is this legacy that has given us our science, our political institutions, and the monuments of artistic and cultural achievement that define us as a civilization. Indeed it is this legacy, insofar as we live up to it, that *preserves us from chaos and barbarism*. And it is precisely this legacy that the multiculturalists wish to dispense with." (6; italics mine)

This position is widely held in Canada as well as we purportedly morph to an idealized, American style common culture. Many commentators already mentioned have argued versions of this notion that our cultural mosaic and regional and ethnic differences can promote "chaos and barbarism" often emanating form our perceived increasingly ghettoized enclaves. It is a form of extremism that is not useful in promoting a constructive dialogue.

The debate carries on, as the current immigration minister urges a move to a more American style "melting pot" and denying funding to heritage languages that have been traditionally allocated funds (Globe and Mail, March 26, 2009). A more positive alternative is to think of culture as, in Henry Louis Gates' words, "a conversation among different voices." (1991) Is it possible, by identifying a set of commonplaces, to balance the traditionalist objective, and yet incorporate a multicultural, inclusive and liberating perspective? Is it possible for diversity to be a source of cultural identity? Is the idea of multiple loyalties and identities possible within the framework of a national culture and identity?

I personally identify with my Ukrainian heritage, my Toronto and Ontario regional roots, with immigrant cultures, as well as feeling an overriding identity with Canada and even a pervading global outlook. Survey data indicate strong regional loyalties and identities in many parts of Canada, far stronger than any regional loyalties in the United States; yet the evidence shows that the stronger the regional loyalty, the stronger the identity with Canada. (S.M. Lipset, 1990)

As individuals we hold a complex set of loyalties and cultural identities, particularly in Canada. We have a strong bond to place – neighbourhood or community; often a strong affinity to our bio-region – the Maritimes or the Prairies, for example; often also a bond to our ethnic and/or our linguistic heritage, and to our religious group; and finally, to our country. For many Canadians there is even a strong feeling of loyalty to, and identity with, the planet. We move in and out of our various "tribes" with ease and comfort. The complexity of our "tribal" relations is in fact quite extraordinary. We are a mass of hierarchical overlapping, shifting, often contradictory and conflicting loyalties and identities. To cite one such conflict: When Canada plays Italy in a world class competition who does an Italian-Canadian root for?

Given this complexity, one might ask why national identity and culture are so controversial. Among many academics, nationalism is a concept in disrepute. At one extreme, David Trend (1993) declares, "Nationality is a fiction. It is a story people tell themselves about who they are, where they live and how they got there." (225) And in *Imagined Communities: Reflections on the Origin and Spread of Nationalism*, Benedict Anderson (1991) demonstrates how nationalism is only a recent phenomenon in human history. He finds its origins in the late eighteenth century, and points out three paradoxes about it. The first is "the objective modernity of nations to the historian's eye vs. their subjective antiquity in the eye of nationalists." The second is "the formal universality of nationality as a socio-cultural concept – the idea in the modem world that everyone can, should, will 'have' a nationality, as he or she has a gender..." The third paradox is "the 'political' power of nationalisms vs. their philosophical poverty and even incoherence." Anderson comments that, as Gertrude Stein referred to Oakland, one can quickly conclude with respect to nationalism that "there is no there there"(2).

But despite his unwavering scorn for the concept of nationalism, Anderson reflects on the continuing process:

And many 'old nations,' once thought fully consolidated, find themselves challenged by 'sub'-nationalism within their borders – nationalisms which, naturally, dream of shedding this sub-ness one happy day. The reality is quite plain: the 'end of the era of nationalism,' so long prophesied, is not remotely in sight. Indeed, nation-ness is the most universally legitimate value in the political life of our time. (3)

Why Culture and Identity Need to Be Addressed in the Schools

While many feel the concept of nation is an outdated notion harking back to a bygone era, but regardless of how we feel about this debate, as Anderson argues, nation-ness is with us. Nationalism is clearly not going to go away. It is unlikely we can do much about it. We can, however, make every effort to ensure that the manner in which our nation-ness is promoted in the school is based on democratic principles of justice and equity, concepts which also lie at the core of our Canadian commonplaces. As a pragmatist educator I am confronted with the problem of observing a gathering of fundamentalist, traditionalist and conservative forces which are erupting across this country and whose views are consistent with those of Roger Kimbal – that the legacy of western civilization and the Bible saves us from "chaos and barbarism", at the same time as we are presumably being swallowed up by American culture. They are fanning a backlash and are profoundly influencing the policy-makers and practitioners to bring back their "common culture," a move which they see as a return to essentially an exclusive Eurocentric Christian society, though cloaked in more expansive language. They view the schools as having a central role in transmitting their view of our common culture through a common curriculum

"Some argue that in an increasingly multicultural society there is a need for a common literacy; others propose that we are moving toward a culture of many literacies." (Trend 227) I propose bridging these two positions – that we work towards a common literacy as long as the common literacy is inclusive of all Canadians. But at least we should be arguing about it!

This sort of bridging of these positions requires a revisioning of our traditional notions of our culture. For example, we have to recognize the temporal character of culture. As Tomlinson points out, "There is no such thing as a single national culture that remains the same year after year. Nations are constantly assimilating, combining and revising their national characters." (as cited in Trend 229) In a speech given by Sheldon Hackney, Chairman of the National Endowment for the Arts in 1993, claims, "All ethnic groups have permeable boundaries, and the meaning of any particular identity will change over time... History has a way of changing who we think we are."

In short, there is a Canadian identity that is different from the identities of any one of the linguistic, ethnic or regional groups that comprise the Canadian population, that is inclusive of all of them and that is available to everyone who is a Canadian.

Commonplaces of Canadian Culture and Identity

In order to provide a starting point for these discussions I have contemplated what commonplaces there are about Canada that most Canadians would agree on... at least as starting points for debate. In struggling to identity these commonplaces I have asked myself: Do these commonplaces provide ample latitude to address critical issues in our society? Do they provide for a new multicultural curriculum that provides opportunities for students to become, in Henry Giroux's term, "border crossers." As he states:

"Teachers must be educated to become border crossers, to explore zones of cultural difference by moving in and out of the resources, histories and narratives that provide different students with a sense of identity, place and possibility."(1992. p 11)

And finally, do these commonplaces reveal that there is a Canadian identity that is different from any one of the ethnic or regional identities that comprise the Canadian population, and are also different from an American identity.

To illustrate, for example, two commonplaces, that reveal some of the common understandings about our culture that dominate discussions in Canada and that are deeply embedded in our identity, are on the one hand our powerful regional identities, Quebec, the Maritimes, the Prairies, and on the other hand, our perception of our international peace role and reputation – our global interdependence as citizens of the world. It may be simplistic to suggest that our national identity is rooted in a recognition of both strong regionalism and internationalism. Our federalist system with its strong distribution of powers to the provinces, bilingualism and our multicultural policy, certainly support and enhance regionalism. Our long history as peace keepers and mediators; despite our recent participation in the war in Afghanistan, our participation in international organizations, our long involvement with developing nations (currently declining), and our comparatively open immigration and refugee polices, confirm a global commitment as international or global citizens.

It may appear paradoxical to articulate a national identity or national culture based on the fragmentation of a country into distinct regions, two languages, distinct societies, First Nations, multi-cultures, and many faiths on the one hand, and striving towards global citizenship and responsibility on the other. Yet that is precisely what is happening today. Canada is in a significant way a microcosm of the world, where the forces for regionalism -former Yugoslavia, and the Soviet Union, India, Ireland and Scotland, and Quebec are a counterpoint to the forces for globalism -United Nations, G20, NAFTA, freer trade, GATT, a United Europe, OECD, and OAS etc. There is room for considerable debate and discussion here.

Other commonplaces that reveal some central truths about our country that would be included for discussion or debate are; Canada, home of our First Nations; Canada, a nation of immigrants – a nation of adventurers, inventors and entrepreneurs; Canada, a democratic nation with remarkable freedoms, but marked by equity struggles yet unfolding for First Nations, women, people of colour, and French Canadians; Canada, a nation with a strong sense of social welfare – a social safety net is part of our tradition, Canada, a wilderness nation, a land of awesome size and grandeur with savage beauty and obstacles – the 'true north strong and free'. Despite our largely urban existence our wilderness our north preoccupies our psyche, our literature, our arts, and our mythology. And finally, we define ourselves as NOT AMERICAN!

These big themes or commonplaces are the "stuff" that myths are made of. They are the stuff that makes Canadians Canadian.

I have played with these themes and have evolved a set of twelve commonplaces that emerge out of these simple notions. I believe they can provide the framework for a variety of approaches at the school level. They provide an alternative to the emotional discourse between the traditionalists and the multiculturalists. Not by resolving their differences entirely, but by providing a framework for constructive dialogue, for 'keeping the conversation going'.

The commonplaces included here are not intended to be definitive and may be considered only as a starting point. They are at best, tentative and exploratory. Perhaps they should never be fixed and complete, but are always to be viewed in draft form, in recognition of the fluid nature of culture formation. Each of the commonplaces is intended to capture a quintessential "given" about the nature of our Canadian culture and identity, at least for discussion purposes. While anyone conception may be characteristic of any number of countries, it is the unique layering of one conception over another, over another, that begins to merge into the warp and weft of the fabric of our Canadian identity.

Herewith is my initial set of 12 commonplaces:

- 1. Canada: A wilderness nation, a land of awesome size and grandeur, with savage beauty and incredible obstacles
- 2. A northern nation the "true north strong and free"
- 3. Canada: Home of our First Nations. Our Native roots are deeply entwined in our Canadian way.
- 4 Canada: A nation state founded on European traditions by the English and the French.
- 5. Canada: A nation of Immigrants. We have been a multicultural land mass even before the European colonization and has been ever since
- 6. Canada: A land of remarkable freedoms with a goal of equity for all, regardless of sex, race, age, colour, creed or disability enshrined in our Charter of Rights and Freedoms
- 7. Canada: A nation with a strong sense of social welfare, committed to providing a social safety net for all
- 8. Canada: A country of diverse and distinctive regions with powerful regional identities – Quebec, the Maritimes, the Prairies, for example
- 9. Canada: A land of adventurers, innovators and entrepreneurs
- 10. Canada: A land of rich cultural traditions
- 11. Canada: Peace-keepers for the world and a partner with all nations
- 12. Canada: Not American!

1. Canada: A wilderness nation, a land of awesome size and grandeur, with savage beauty and incredible obstacles

Despite our largely urban existence our wilderness preoccupies our psyche, our literature, our arts, our mythology. The majority of Canadians now live in urban centres strung out like a string of pearls along the southern border of Canada, but our vast, rugged wilderness and harsh climate dominate our history, mythology and our psyche. They form an indelible backdrop to our culture and identity.

Our legacy of art, from Group of Seven paintings to totem poles, and our literature, painting and native oral traditions reflect an intimate relationship, even a preoccupation with the land.

Canadians spend more money per capita on recreational equipment, such as canoes, skis, and tents, than any country in the world (Schafer, 1989). They visit provincial and national parks and conservation areas in higher numbers per capita than other countries. A Canadian wilderness summer camp is a traditional experience for children of the wealthy as well as many children of the poor. For many, owning a cottage or camp is part of the Canadian dream.

Our advertising and marketing campaigns capitalize on our penchant for the wilderness with images of shimmering lakes, majestic mountains and breath-taking seascapes, and the sounds of the call of the loon and pounding surf.

Our economy too, is deeply rooted in the land. Forestry, fishing, mining, furs and farming have established the pattern of our settlement, and each has contributed to our mythology.

In response to the immensity and the challenge of our landscape, Canadians have demonstrated remarkable ingenuity and innovation that has made Canada pre-eminent in many areas. Canada leads the world, for example, in cartographic expertise, and in innovation in telecommunications. The canoe, the kayak, the snowshoe, the snowmobile, CBC Radio, the Beaver Air plane and our contributions to satellite technology are all ingenious responses to coping with an immense and trying landscape.

Even our constitutional wrangling and our unique federal system is a political reaction to a vast and diverse land. Our size and unique regions have engendered a system that demands compromise.

The variety and majesty of our land is deeply embedded in our cultural identity and is a fundamental element of our mythology. William Lyon Mackenzie King (1936) captured an essence of Canada when he stated "If some countries have too much history, Canada has too much geography." The icons of our landscape, whether Atlantic or Pacific seascape, prairies or mountains, glacial north or lush St. Lawrence Lowland, are the 'ground' upon which we see ourselves, as well as the way we are viewed by others.

2. Canada the 'true north strong and free'

The North! Few people live in the true north, as 70% of our population living in our three largest cities along the Canada, USA border. In many ways we are more urban than northern. Yet we are a northern nation. John Diefenbaker, while our prime minister in 1958, had a great northern vision for Canada, "Sir John A. Macdonald gave his life to this party. He opened the West. He saw Canada from East to West. I see a new Canada – a Canada of the North... A new Canada... a new soul." (*A New Vision* speech by John G. Diefenbaker, Winnipeg, 12 February 1958.)

One could argue that this commonplace is naturally subsumed under our first commonplace: our wilderness nation, but our northern-ness is so unique that it deserves designation of a commonplace of its own. We are a northern country with as much in common with Sweden, Norway, Russia and Greenland/Denmark as we are with the United States. Geographically, the Canadian North can be divided into two natural zones: the Arctic and the Subarctic comprising the Yukon, Northwest territories the northern part of most provinces and now Nunavut.

Nunavut with less than 30,000 people is our most recent territory. It contains 20 per cent of our land mass, 20%! But as John Ralston Saul argues in, My Canada Includes the North: "These numbers only represent a problem if our few, densely populated areas – especially our big cities – see the country purely in population terms. If they do, well then, Canada no longer makes sense." (Globe and Mail, 2001)

Louis-Edmond Hamelin a Canadian geographer, developed the concept of nordicity, a measure of the degree of 'northern-ness' of a place, which takes into account both physical and human factors into account. His concept of nordicity has contributed to our understanding of how Canada is distinctive and unique, as well as reinforcing the natural ties we have with circumpolar nations of Russia Norway Sweden Greenland/Denmark and Alaska.

For most urban Canadians it is hard to grasp how much our north permeates not just our economy but our arts, letters, mythology and psyches. It has fascinated our most talented artists and intellectuals, from Glen Gould and Stan Rogers (his Northwest passage has been referred to as the unofficial Canadian national anthem), throat singer Tanya Tagaq's instrumental piece Nunavut, in music; to Farly Mowat, Margaret Atwood, James Houston, Roy Macgregor, in literature; the poetry of Al Purdy, Robert Service; The Spell of the Yukon, Gwendolyn MacEwen and the powerful enduring images of the north through the paintings of the Group of Seven, particularly Lawren Harris, and captured in raw, visceral, classic movie footage like *Nanook of the North* and recently *Atanarjuat*.

Polar explorations and the search for the Northwest Passage are enduring narratives that continue to capture our imaginations. The search for Northern passage, the Franklin Expedition in particular, and all the attempts to find evidence of its demise is part of our mythology and identity, explored in powerful ways by our best authors, for example Margaret Atwood referred to Franklin's expedition as a sort of Canadian national myth, that "In every culture many stories are told, (but) only some are told and retold, and these stories bear examining... in Canadian literature, one such story is the Franklin expedition." Other recent treatments by Canadian poets include a verse play, *Terror and Erebus* by Gwendolyn MacEwen, that was broadcast on Canadian Broadcasting Corporation (CBC) radio in the 1960s, David Solway's verse cycle, *Franklin's Passage* (2003).

Our arctic north is at the same time a mental concept as well as a physical one and an area of identification. It disproportionately permeates our mythology and our psyches. Our nordicity has contributed to our understanding of how Canada is distinctive and unique.

Glen Gould Canada's most noted pianist, captured this notion in a radio program he created called *The Idea of North*, "I've long been intrigued by that incredible tapestry of tundra and taiga which constitutes the arctic and sub-arctic of our country. I've read about it, written about it, and even pulled up my parka once and gone there. Yet, like all but a very few Canadians, I've had no real experience of the North. I've remained, of necessity, an outsider. And the North has remained for me a convenient place to dream about, spin tall tales about and, in the end, avoid."

As the prospect of a Northwest Passage operating as a major international waterway, a saving 7000 km from a trip now taken through the Panama Canal, sovereignty of the arctic has recently taken on both political and economic posturing by many northern countries various claims over the ownership and control of the Northwest Passage. Yet, "It's the Inuit who make our strongest case for Canadian control", Michael Beyers has argued, "It's their historic use and occupancy of the sea-ice that provides the basis for Canada's claim in the Northwest Passage. It's they who have given us all that they have, in pursuit of a quintessential Canadian dream... and that ice is the only dimension of our legal position that resonates with non-Canadians." (*Who Owns the Arctic*, Beyers, 2009).

Canada has a shameful record of the treatment of the nomadic Inuit; most notably the regrettable relocation, of 87 Inuit from Inukjuaq, Quebec, to Grise Fiord and Resolute, Nunavut, the northernmost settlements in Canada, as well as mistreatment of children in residential schools. Life in our Arctic outposts continues to be harsh and our institutional response has been inadequate for decades. Marie Wadden asks: "How can Canada claim to 'own' the Arctic when it can't provide adequate housing, health care and schooling for our Inuit, who number only in the tens of thousands." (Globe and Mail, 2007) Formal apologies from the Canadian government were made in June and continue to be investigated through the Truth and Reconciliation Commission of Canada begun in June 22, 2010. Mary Simon (President of the Inuit Tapiriit Kanatami), stated, "The Arctic... is a vital part of our country, and its peoples contribute to the cultural and social diversity that we value so dearly..."

With increasing economic activity brings additional problems in the Arctic, particularly over numerous concerns about the natural environment. The Arctic has been shown to be more vulnerable than elsewhere in the world, and control is also more difficult to achieve.

All of these themes and issues intertwine into the fabric of our identity. As Saul concludes, "Look at Canada as a whole. Its central, defining characteristic in global terms is to be the most important northern democracy. It is, or can be, the great northern nation." (2001)

3. Canada: Home of our First Nations. Our Native roots are deeply entwined in our Canadian way

Native Canadians have occupied the Americas for over 10,000 years and first migrated to North America as long ago as 30,000 years ago. Europeans first set foot in Canada only 1000 years ago (Vikings) and extensively only since Jacques Cartier, beginning in 1534. The imprint of native peoples on the evolution of Canada is profound. The early history of European intervention in North America was integrally linked with Native Canadian peoples, in many cases, as allies with the English or the French and often as adversaries in numerous conflicts.

The ingenious response of native Canadians to the demands of travel in such a vast and rigorous landscape led to their invention of the canoe, the snowshoe and the kayak. Only through mastering the skills of these inventions was it possible for Europeans to explore, exploit, and occupy Canada. Native Canadian foods from cultivated crops such as corn, beans and squash, and food preservation techniques such as dried meat (pemmican) and smoked fish, provided early travellers with the ability to survive the rigours of travel in Canada. They acted as guides, interpreters and negotiators for most of the early European explorations and trade and development.

Less widely known is the influence of the Iroquoian system of social organization on European thinkers like Montaigne, Hegel and Marx and on North American thinkers like Benjamin Franklin. The system of government in the United States and in Canada has its roots in the three level system of government practised by the Iroquois in the Iroquois Confederacy. Even the Eagle clutching five arrows in its claw (one for each of the five nations in the confederacy) was borrowed by the Americans as a symbol for the new nation. The American eagle now clutches thirteen arrows one for each of the original thirteen colonies. Canada's federal system of municipal, provincial, and federal governments was uniquely suited to uniting a large and disparate nation. The federal system in North America was unique among systems of government in the world at that time. Native words like caucus, a meeting of elders, have found their way into our political language.

Historic Native Canadian attitudes toward the treatment of members of the tribe less fortunate than others smacks of another conception of our Canadian identity – our social safety net. It is intriguing to trace this distinguishing characteristic back to our Native Canadian roots. Engels, for example, stated, "This gentile constitution (the Iroquioan social system) is wonderful. There can be no poor and needy... All are free and equal – including women." (as cited in Wright. 1992, p. 117). The Iroquoian social safety net provided and early system of protecting all members of the society "from the cradle to the grave". The role of women in Iroquoian society was at a level not attained in any country today.

In a variety of ways the influence of Native Canadian life has entered into our collective heritage. The traditional Native Canadian religion with its respectful holistic attitude towards nature and the environment are receiving increasing respect and study. Native art has long held an important place in our record of the visual icons of our culture. The totems of the West coast, Inuit stone carvings and contemporary prints and paintings have achieved world wide recognition and appreciation. Native elements of fashion and design, permeate in subtle ways contemporary urban, as well as, rural life – moccasins, fringed jackets, beaded belts and necklaces and native design elements in fabrics. Thousands of Native names permeate our Canadian landscape – Canada, Ottawa, Toronto, for starters. Strung together a list of names becomes a form of Canadian poetry. Just start at any point in the alphabet, for example: Abitibi, Aklavik, Algonkian, Alikomiak, and Assiniboia. Other words and phrases have entered the lexicon of everyday speech, for example, "passing the peace-pipe" or having a "powwow".

The Native Canadian way of life has entered the mythology of our Canadian ethos. It has become part of us all. The image of native Canadians plying the silent waters of a wilderness lake in a canoe is emblematic of a kind of Canadian Garden of Eden, when a blissful balance with nature was achieved. Linda Hutcheson (1988), for example, examines the importance of Natives for white Canadian writers in seeking their own roots.

The mistreatment of our Native peoples is an unfortunate but important commonplace of our history. The current legal battles over treaties, the social situation that exists on many reserves, and in inner cities and native Canadian struggles for self-government, attest to a response to an unfortunate record of misguided efforts (in the best of interpretations) or a record of ruthless, exploitative and racist actions. The reality of Native Canadians today trying to re-establish and rediscover their decimated way of life in the face of staggering rates of alcoholism, teen suicides, unemployment, and welfare is also part of our Canadian heritage. Native Canadians, as well as those south of the border, are at the bottom on most measures of mortality and social morbidity. (Richmond, 1988) It is only of comparative interest that it is clear that "native peoples have been better able to survive in Canada than in the United States." (Lipset, 1990. p.176)

But as Saul states, "We are a people of Aboriginal inspiration organized around a concept of peace, fairness and good government" (2008)

4. Canada: A "nation state" founded on European traditions by the English and the French

While evidence of Viking settlements exist at Anse aux Meadows dating back to 1000, the early voyages of John Cabot and Jacques Cartier set the stage for the full scale invasion and occupation of the continent, first by the French and then by the English. Through the long intertwining history of their colonization, through settlement, trade and resource extraction, these two founding nations irrevocably altered the face of the northern part of the continent. The patterns of settlement, whether the seigneury system of the French or the section system of the English imprinted the landscape with a network of roads, farm patterns and towns with a decidedly European familiarity.

While these early colonists were profoundly influenced by native American technologies such as the canoe, new foods and their method of cultivation and systems of government, they nonetheless firmly implanted their languages, religious values and institutions, the European form of democracy, in particular the parliamentary system, the tradition of both British common law and French civil law, as well as the system of schooling. A walk through any Canadian town or city reveals the unique juxtaposition of church, courthouse, town hall, banks and shops, school and residential streets characteristic of a European ordering of priorities.

Despite a long history of the migration of peoples from every corner of the globe and the unmistakable contributions and impact of this rich "melange" to the unique character of Canadian culture, yet the building blocks of our culture are firmly planted in the world view of Western European civilisation, particularly the English and the French. Many of the crowning achievements of our Canadian culture emerge from the interface of the British and French presence within this vast and awesome Canada. Our institutional infrastructure, the way our country works, and our power base, is still largely of British origin in particular, French in Quebec. Judeo-Christian ethics, mores and beliefs still underlie our institutions and community life. Our calendar year is organized around a Christian schedule. Our public holidays are largely Christian – Christmas and Easter. Our institutions often still attend to Christian rituals. The Bible is proffered to witnesses in the courts first before alternatives are made available, and Christian prayers are routinely recited at public meetings and meals.

Whether it be in the models born in the industrial revolution that were applied to every field of endeavour from offices, to schools, to research labs, or to the form of our free market economy, or our views on art, the family, time and gender roles, these European Christian notions became the warp and weft on the loom of Canada.

It is in Quebec that a unique "nation" has been created within the Canadian nation State. And while the Battle on the Plains of Abraham is still a sore point in Quebec and the provincial motto points a finger... "Je me souviens", "I remember", the rest of Canada is committed to keeping Quebec an integral part of the country. There has been a long, never-ending struggle for French Canadians to save their language and culture and several attempts to separate from the rest of Canada. It is important to think about how Quebec sovereigntists feel, and why they feel that way. We need to find ways for Quebeckers at every twist and turn in this tenuous balancing act of keeping Quebec inside Canada. To explore these commonplaces is to welcome Quebeckers unrelentingly into the Canadian family.

5 Canada: A nation of immigrants

Canada has been forged as a nation "a mari usque ad mari," since the first contact with Europeans, through a continuous process of conquest and cooperation with the existing First Nation and Inuit civilizations. The Vikings in the year 1000, John Cabot, Jacques Cartier and the early Spanish and Portuguese fishing crews began this long process. Viking, and French settlements including Jewish fur traders and farmers preceded the establishment of a British colony. The expansion and modernization of Canada was achieved through a remarkable process of immigration with wave upon wave of immigrant groups from England, Scotland, France and Ireland, United Empire Loyalists from the United States and Black slaves who arrived on the Underground Railroad. (There were more Blacks in Nova Scotia 200 years ago than there were Scots!) Successive waves of Chinese (as early as 1744), Ukrainians, Finns, Poles, Germans, Swedes, Italians, Portuguese and South Asians have all contributed to the very fabric of our country. Sikh and Indian settlers, for example, were among the very first to open up the B.C. timberlands in the late 19th century. More recently, immigrants from the Caribbean, South America, Africa, and other East Asian countries have increased the racial and ethno-cultural mix.

Even before colonization, our First Nations co-existed as a multi-cultural entity. The complexity of distinct tribal cultures, with fifty-three distinct languages such as the Inuit, Haida, Blackfoot, Iroquois, Huron and Beothuk, mirrored the mosaic that modern Canada has become. This multiracial, multicultural, multilingual multi-faith reality, from the very origins of human life on this continent, as well as from the inception of the nation is a central pattern in the fabric of our culture and identity.

The remarkable record is marred regrettably by many examples of racism, and while progress has continuously been made we are still not free of the destructive forces of racism. Dark moments in our history cast light on how we came to be who we are and are beacons to our future actions. It is important to study and explore how various groups have been marginalized and excluded from full participation in Canadian society while understanding the power and importance of our immigrant groups in the creation of a vibrant Canadian society

6. Canada: A land of remarkable freedoms with a goal of equity for all regardless of sex, race, age, colour, creed or disability

Canada has emerged as a democratic, multi-faith nation with equity is enshrined in our remarkable Charter of Rights and Freedoms. But, we are nevertheless, a nation marked by equity struggles yet unfolding, for First Nations, women, people of colour, gay and lesbians and even French Canadians. We often take for granted our democratic freedoms, but to the millions of Canadians who have immigrated to Canada over the last hundred years or so, it is one of our most cherished and distinguishing characteristics. The history of Canada is a history of the struggles to create a nation, a struggle for responsible government, for representative government, and for a confederacy that allowed for the regional, religious, linguistic and ethnic diversity that has come to represent Canada. The evolution of a parliamentary system in a confederacy modelled after the three level federal system of the Iroquoian Confederacy was a unique response to a vast land mass with diverse cultures, needs and interests in the population. It allowed for a greater democracy, a greater voice, by an ever increasing diverse population.

These gains have not been without their price. Canada does not have an untarnished record on human rights. We must not forget that in forging this modern nation it was at the expense of the First Nations. The demise of many native tribes such as the Beotuk, are symptomatic of a ruthless period of exploitation and imperialism at any cost. Canada was not without its period of slavery. Anti-Semitism and racism have plagued our history as it has many other nations. There was a time when it was acceptable for a public official was able to say "None is too many". (In reference to accepting Jews from Nazi Germany). The internment of the Japanese during World War II, Ukrainians in WWI, are examples of periods in our history when the bright lights of civil rights gains were extinguished. The rights of women, labourers and other minorities have similarly been thwarted at times in our evolution towards nationhood.

But few countries can claim a better record of emerging out of these dark days. Canada abolished slavery before Great Britain or the United States. It proudly became the terminus of the Underground Railway. Towns like Buxton became model black communities producing the first black lawyers, school teachers and preachers in North America. The first Black civil war commander came from Buxton. The first female editor of a newspaper in North America, Mary Shadd Cary was a Black woman who made her way to Canada during this period. Clara Brett Martin was the first female lawyer in the British Empire.

Emily Murphy was a Canadian women's rights activist jurist and author who became the first woman magistrate in Canada, and in the British Empire. She is best known for her contributions to Canadian feminism, specifically to the question of whether women were "persons" under Canadian law. Other female Empire firsts included the first female member of a legislature, the first cabinet minister and the first female speaker of a legislature (Nader, 1992). Female politicians have made significant contributions for many decades. Women lead our political parties and have led our country as both Prime Minister and as Governor-General. It is of at least symbolic significance that we have had a Canadian of Ukrainian heritage as a

Governor-General and both a Black and Chinese Canadians have held the positions of Governor-General as well as Lt-General in both Ontario and British Columbia.

Canada is a world leader in policy development in equity issues. The Canadian Bill of Rights and the Charter of Rights and Freedoms are landmark documents. Implementing them requires all our best efforts. The history of our constitutional wrangles, most recently Meech Lake and Charlottetown, while unsuccessful in achieving the goal sought by most Canadians, it is indicative of our relentless efforts of Canadians to try to achieve an accommodation of the varied regional, linguistic and cultural differences that comprise our complex nation.

Other equity issues, such as pay equity, mandatory race relations policies in all institutions and work places, equal rights for homosexual Canadians, and one the first nations to legalize marriage between gays and lesbians, demonstrate the persistent attitudes toward equity as a central characteristic of our identity. While Americans struggle over gays in their armed forces, Canadians, in typically Canadian manner, quietly implemented gay rights in the armed forces without fanfare or disruption.

While Canadians have proven to be more open to immigration by people of colour than almost any other nation, accepting now about 200,000 new immigrants annually, the attitudes of some Canadians reveal an underlying pervading discrimination, particularly to people of colour. It is instructive however, that in 1991, (not, I should note, during the subsequent recession), a Decima survey noted that 93% of Canadians thought that Canada was the best place in the world to live. The third most frequently cited reason for why this was so, was because of the way we received and welcomed new "immigrants". (Gregg and Posner, 1990)

While the equity culture in Canada is still evolving and gapping inequities still exist, it is important to trace the continuous improvement that has been made and recognize that this trait of seeking improved democratic rights for all is deeply ingrained in our collective psyches. It is upon this frame that the complex pattern of Canada's multi-cultural tapestry was woven.

7. Canada: A nation with a strong sense of social welfare committed to providing a social safety net for all

Canada is a nation that prides itself on its ability to look after all its citizens. Brian Mulroney as Prime Minister referred to this characteristic of our national culture and identity as "a sacred trust." One might argue that the roots of this tradition lie in the size of Canada with its small population resulting in the need for more government control. It was in Tory tradition of greater government control that arose out of the counter revolution that resulted from the American Revolution. It is interesting to note however that this tradition was long established in Canada by native peoples. When Etienne Brule, at Samuel Champlain's request, wintered over with the Hurons on the shores of Georgian Bay in 1610, a Huron chief's son was sent to Paris for the winter in exchange as an insurance for Brule's safety. When the Huron returned from Paris he shocked his fellow Iroquois with stories of the beggars on the streets of Paris, the brutal public treatment of children, and even the barbaric punishment of criminals in public squares. These practices were all so foreign to the Hurons whose traditions involved looking after all of its members – where no-one was destitute or everyone was. The notion of care "from the cradle-to-the-grave", has a long tradition in Canada, long before a European put his foot on our land.

Robertson Davies referred to Canada as "a socialist monarchy", while our neighbours to the south have always abided by Thomas Jefferson's adage that, "The government that governs best, governs least." Canada's social safety net certainly distinguishes itself from the United States. It is one characteristic of our identity that most Canadians would agree on. In a 1988 poll for example, 95% of Canadians preferred their own Medicare system to the American one, as did 61 % of Americans! (Lipset, 1990)

Canada early embraced comprehensive social welfare programs including compensation for widows and persons with disabilities, enriched unemployment insurance benefits, post-secondary education programs covering significant portion of student costs, universal old age pensions, man-power training allowances, subsidized housing, and family allowances, in addition to the universal Medicare system mentioned above.

Public support, as well as support by civil servants and legislators for social initiatives is very high in Canada. For example, Canadian conservative legislators scored much higher than even American Democratic legislators on a scale of support for economic liberalism or social welfare issues. Even in recessionary times when cutbacks to social services are often in evidence it is important to recognize the short and long term trends remain the same – Canadians continue to support this distinguishing characteristic of our identity and we continue to move inexorably forward. For example, just twenty years ago half the people living in poverty were over 65 years of age, by 1990 the proportion was less than 15%.

In a series of polls and surveys (Gregg and Posner 1990, Lipset, 1990, Adams, 2003), Canadians continue to view themselves as more tolerant, less violent, more concerned about the environment and the disadvantaged, both at home and abroad, and more peaceful than our neighbours to the south. When 93% of respondents indicated they believed Canada to be the best place in the world to live (Gregg and Possner, 1990). Ninety percent thought this to be true because of our health care system, 78% thought it was our education system and 74% thought it was because of the way we welcomed immigrants of different races, religions and cultures into our society. This type of prevailing attitude is indicative of the characteristic of a "quieter, gentler nation."

8. Canada: A country of diverse and distinctive regions with powerful regional identities – Quebec, the Maritimes, the Prairies, for example

Canada's distinctive regions, particularly British Columbia and the Rockies, the Prairies, the North, Southern Ontario, Quebec, and the Maritimes, have contributed to a unique character to Canada's cultural identity. Regional loyalties are powerful in Canada and regional cultures are distinctive. Confederation, with a carefully articulated division of powers between the provinces and the central government, recognized this diversity and enshrined this characteristic of our identity in a unique distribution of powers. The continuing struggles over these regional identities manifest themselves daily in everything from large scale examinations of power sharing at constitutional conferences, and inter provincial trade discussions, to squabbles between English-speaking Canada and French Canada, or between the West and Bay Street, the symbol of central Canadian power.

But aside from these perennial power struggles, Canadians generally cherish this regional diversity, as they have other forms of diversity. The icons of our regionalism conjure up the flavours of our nation. Majestic snow-capped mountains and deep fiords, totem poles, lush temperate rainforests, prosperous urban streets with a variety of Canadians including Sikhs, and Chinese evoke our Pacific region; the skyline of Quebec city, French Canadian villages centered in the seigneury system, around the local church, along the shores of the St. Lawrence, maple syrup runs, Carnival, Sovereigntists parading the streets on St. Jean Baptist Day, conjure up another. Our distinctive rugged sea-torn Maritime provinces rooted in Acadian, Micmac and Scottish cultures, our immense Prairies crowned with grain elevators, immense herds of cattle and oil wells, peopled by hard-working decedents of many central European countries – Ukrainians, Poles, Germans, Finns, as well as Chinese descendants of labourers from the building of the Trans-Canada Railway along with Blackfoot and Cree, reflect two other regions.

Some analysts argue that Canada has no distinct national style (Lipset, 1990) and that Canada is reflected more through its regionalism. As George Woodcock (1987) stated, "Canadian literature like Canadian painting has always remained regional in its impulses and origins." (p.32)

Saturday Night Magazine (January, 1987) in a special issue entitled *Our Home and Native Land* concluded that what makes Canada like no other is the variety of its regions and communities – in effect, that Canada's identity is defined by its regions. Certainly our regional richness has always been one recurring characteristic of our national identity and this reveals itself through our arts, our economy and our political process. Lipset(1990) argues that this emphasis on region in Canada results in a stronger sense of place than in the United States.

This strong regional loyalty has been apparent through many surveys, yet this strong sense of place regionally is positively correlated to high rankings of loyalty towards the country. David Elkin (1980) noted that except for Quebec Separatists, that Canadians' "deep and abiding sense of place covers both nation and province." (p. 209) Canada is more decentralized politically with stronger regional identities than the United States but still maintains a strong sense of Canadian loyalty. This is clearly one of our distinguishing characteristics.

9. Canada: A land of adventurers, innovators and entrepreneurs

Historically, this continent was explored, settled, and developed by unique individuals with a willingness to venture to a new land against unknown odds and under difficult circumstances. Canada shares with its neighbour to the south many of the same characteristics of adventurers willing to take on new challenges, to be inventive and innovative, a penchant for risk-taking and entrepreneurialism. The continuous wave of new immigrants, and refugees, has ensured an ethos of energy, renewal and risk-taking. While many argue that conditions in the United States have led to a greater spirit of adventure and risk-taking than in Canada, it is still only a matter of degree. By any standard world-wide, Canadians have demonstrated this adventurous spirit in many fields, i.e. Canada First. (Nader et al, 1992)

Certainly our mythology is replete with individuals that attest to this characteristic of our identity. Whether it be historic icons like Jacques Cartier, Henry Hudson, Samuel Champlain or Lief Erickson, the Coureur de Bois, the early Jesuits, the early pioneers of Upper and Lower Canada, the crew of the Blue Nose, the hardy men in sheep skin coats, the 'sod-busters' of the prairies, gold rush miners, the Chinese 'Coolies' working on the Canadian Pacific Railway, or Black American slaves escaping to Canada on the underground railway, they all share remarkable traits of courage and daring and a willingness to take risks.

Many Canadians have demonstrated this entrepreneurial courage and initiative through business enterprise and have become household names in other parts of the world. The Bronfmans, the Reichmans, Lord Beaverbrook, the Mirvishes, Rims, Jim Balsillie, Armand Bombardier and Lord Thompson of Fleet, and innumerable real estate barons are a few examples of Canadians who have ventured into the international arena with great fanfare and with remarkable success.

Canada has encouraged through its immigration policy, entrepreneurs from other countries. Chinese immigrants in particular have found Canada a conducive environment for entrepreneurial activity. Is it surprising that the Deans of the leading three business schools in the United States are all Canadian? Risk-taking is also a required trait for invention and innovation. Nader et al, in their book *Canada Firsts* (1992) and Brown in *Ideas in Exile: A History of Canadian Invention* (1967) have chronicled the remarkable number of inventions and innovations Canadians have made, including five Nobel prize winning scientists. From Fuller brushes, the zipper, the paint-roller, pablum, frozen and instant foods and Trivial Pursuit, to ground breaking medical discoveries by Banting and Best, Hans Selye and Wilder Penfield, to high tech communications firsts such as the first communications satellite, Telesat, the Blackberry, the Canadarm, the Imax film format and remarkable innovations in mapping technology.

The paradox exists that in comparison to many nations, Canadians are very conservative with their money. For example, they have higher insurance coverage per capita than other countries, invest in the stock market far less than Americans and have shown to be less inclined to participate in high-risk investments or to develop their inventions or innovations at home, often leaving development to their neighbours to the south. (Brown, 1967) But modesty is also a Canadian trait and we are less inclined to tout our achievements. Certainly the record stands of a highly inventive and innovative population with a long tradition of adventure, exploration and entrepreneurialism, even though it often takes an American like Ralph Nader to point this out to us.

10. Canada: A land of rich cultural traditions

Canada's unique history, its vastness and its complex multicultural mix has contributed to a rich cultural tradition. Cultural in this section pertains particularly to all of the arts, leisure and pastimes that occupy or entertain the citizenry: From the folk arts of fiddling, spoons and square dancing, decorated Easter eggs, totem poles, quilts and ceramics; to ballet, opera, symphony, theatre, movies and television, poetry and literature; as well as popular participative sports across Canada like curling, hockey, skiing, golf, bowling, softball and t-ball; to spectator sports like baseball, ice skating, football and hockey. One could also include a whole range of other popular activities or pastimes, from such diverse activities as camping, and canoe tripping, attending multicultural events such as the Highland Games in Nova Scotia, Caribbana, Gay Pride, Quebec Carnival, the Calgary Stampede and visiting art galleries, or attending rock, classical, jazz or choral and folk performances, picnicking, camping, watching television or jogging. The list could go on but the unique combination of these many activities by region and nationally paints a distinctive picture of who we are as a people. Though many of these activities are common to all North Americans, together in a particular place, in a particular combination they enter into a union with other cultural characteristics to provide a unique Canadian perspective and flavor. The culture of the hockey rink or curling rink presents a unique Canadian image.

Yet when the Toronto Blue Jays, playing the game the Americans call their own, played and won the World Series, in both 1992 and 1993 Canadians rallied round the Blue Jays from coast to coast, in a unique Canadian way, even though only one player was a Canadian. It was ironic that this American spectacle, the World Series, became such a unifying national event in Canada.

Our visual arts, in particular, evoke a powerful image of our nation particularly in its physical splendour. The work of the Group of Seven artists and painters like Emily Carr, Alex Colville, William Kurelek and Mary Pratt captured images of Canada that haunt us and delight us. More contemporary artists like Jean-Paul Riopelle, Michael Snow, and Jack Bush have contributed to new art forms and styles in a Canadian setting. Our many authors have described and contributed to our culture through story and have achieved world wide recognition in doing so. Margaret Atwood, Gabrielle Roy, Yann Martel, Robertson Davies, Rohinton Mistry, Margaret Lawrence, Austin Clarke and Michael Ondatje are a few recent names with such a claim. The legendary Northrop Frye and Marshall McLuhan, as well as Charles Taylor, have distinguished themselves in their respective literary fields.

The Canada Council has made a unique contribution to our rich cultural heritage. As a federal funding agency to support the arts, humanities, and social sciences, it has contributed millions of dollars to support individuals and organizations. Along with other provincial Arts councils and a variety of Canadian content requirements in CRTC, as well as other legislation, have reaped considerable rewards in the promotion and development of Canadian artistic talent. Many successful artists profess they would not have been able to carry on in their chosen artistic careers had it not been for the support of such legislation and government grant support.

Certainly the thriving regional theatre system, and the internationally regarded National Ballet, the Royal Winnipeg Ballet, Ballet Jazz De Montreal, the Vancouver, Toronto, Regina and Montreal symphonies, the Canadian Opera Company, and the Stratford and Shaw festivals would be hard pressed to survive without this kind of support. This public support for a wide variety of cultural activities from opera to rodeos is unique in North America. It is certainly in marked contrast to our neighbour to the south where the free market rules the arts or groups are dependent on private foundations.

A unique manifestation of this kind of support is the National Film Board created by an act of government in 1939. Famed worldwide for its documentaries and animation, it has won thousands of film awards. Fifty-seven films have been nominated for academy awards and nine have won. The work of the NFB in both the English and French divisions has been a remarkable achievement and has made a major contribution to our cultural heritage and identity.

CBC, the Canadian Broadcasting Corporation, has similarly had a profound influence on our Canadian identity. The creation of the CBC, initially as a radio network, was designed to link the country together by the airwaves. It has been a powerful antidote to the continuous barrage of American mass media that many Canadians feel puts Canadian culture at risk. For many English speaking Canadians, Don Messer's Jubilee, The Happy Gang, Fresh Air, As it Happens, and the Airfarce, This Hour has 22 Minutes, and Little Mosque on the Prairies are part of their cultural heritage. For French-Canada, the rich melange of programs on Radio Canada provides the same ties that bind. While television has not been as successful in creating a national image, nonetheless a legacy of outstanding programs linger on in our collective memory such Ann of Green Gables, the Famille Plouffe, and Sunshine Sketches, not to mention Hockey Night in Canada.

On both networks, radio and TV, the production of current affairs programming has always been exceptional; the National, Man Alive, Fifth Estate, Nature with David Suzuki, to name just a few. Northrop Frye (1982) noted that the NFB and CBC radio, had a significant influence on the maturing of Canada's culture and giving it a place internationally.

Native Canadian artists, authors and film-makers are increasingly creating a new artistic heritage to match their historic legacy such as rock paintings, totem poles, Inuit stone carvings and masks. Modern creations such as the work of Tomson Highway, the design of the Museum of Civilization, many fine Native Canadian films including the stunning documentary, Kahnestake and the rich variety of paintings and sculptures by contemporary Native artists such as Norval Morrisseau and Ashoona Pitseolak attest to a thriving renaissance of a Native Canadian voice.

While Canadian artists have often complained that it is difficult to achieve recognition in Canada, many have gone on to national prominence in the USA or elsewhere. Canadians do not often think of themselves as funny but the legacy of comics from Canada working in the USA is staggering, including; Michael J. Fox, John Candy, Dan Ackroyd, Eugene Levy, Leslie Nielsen, Martin Short, Mike Myers, Kids in the Hall, Andrea Martin, Tom Green, Rick Moranis, Howie Mandel, Sandra Shamus, Jim Carey, Seth Rogan and producers like Lorne Michaels. Less comic but equally visible on the major American national news networks are the large number of Canadian commentators and news broadcasters including Morley Safer, Peter Jennings, Mark Phillips, Hilary Brown, Ali Velshi and J. D. Roberts, and formerly Robert McNeil of the McNeil Lehrer Report.

As well there is a long history of Canadian actors and directors from silent screen stars like Mary Pickford, Walter Houston and Norma Shearer to contemporary Canadian actors. The list is endless but to name a few (young and old) include: Keifer Sutherland, Pamela Anderson, Carrie-Ann Moss, Neve Campbell, Victor Garber, Kim Catrell, Donald Sutherland, Genevieve Bujold, Colleen Dewhurst, Michael Cera, Kate Nelligan, Rachel McAdam, Kate Reid, Ryan Gosling, Margo Kidder, William Shatner and the legendary director Norman Jewison. As well, musicians like David Foster, Paul Anka, Dianne Krall, Nelly Furtado, Celine Dion, Avril Lavigne, Bryan Adams and Neil Young. The Guess Who, Burton Cummings, Shania Twain, and Rush have all contributed to our Canadian identity even when they have made their name and achieved their fame in the United States. Canada's talent pool of technical expertise in movie-making and recording and attractive tax/investment incentives has led to the development of a Hollywood North. Vancouver and Toronto vie for this title.

While many Canadians fear the loss of their identity in the face of the enormous media machine to the south, the reality is that we do share in many ways a common North American heritage and culture. Nonetheless, the complex web of relationships between the various conceptions of our identity in Canada continues to sustain a healthy and vibrant self-image that confirms for most Canadians the existence of a rich Canadian cultural identity including a French Canada with its distinct culture.

11. Canada: Peace-keepers for the world and a partner with all nations. Myth or reality?

Canadians have long prided themselves on their role as peace-keepers and their stature internationally as a nation that could be trusted and relied upon. It is fitting and appropriate that Lester B. Pearson received a Nobel Peace Prize in 1957 for his plan to provide the first UN peace-keeping force in the Suez Crisis in Egypt. All Canadians felt they shared in that award and Canadians have always looked on peace-keeping since that time with a 'proprietary air.' His achievement symbolised a role for Canada that Canadians have consistently lived up to. Canada has been involved in hundreds of successful peace-keeping missions on behalf of the United Nations, most particularly in Israel, Cyprus, former Yugoslavia and the Congo. Most recently Canada ha preformed a different role conducting a war in Afghanistan, a war ostensibly against terrorism but underlying that war is a powerful defence of civil liberties especially for the rights of women and girls. A major part of the budget for that war is for humanitarian endeavours. Beyond the front lines of border patrols Canada's reputation has led to Canada being called upon by other international organizations to serve in a mediator role, most notably in Laos and Cambodia as part of a three nation International Commission.

As well, Canada has a long tradition of peace movements from within its private citizenry. The Quakers and Mennonites in Canada, for example, have always spoken out against war and militarism. Dozens of organizations sprang up in the fifties and sixties such as The Pugwash Conference of Scientists, The Canadian Peace Research Institute, Voice of Women, Project Ploughshares, and Canadian Physicians for the Prevention of Nuclear War. These groups have had a significant influence on Canadian public opinion over the years and thus have made a contribution to the way this commonplace of Canada as a peace-keeping nation has entered into our cultural mythology. The fact that Superman was a Canadian creation perhaps symbolizes the fantasy of Canadians as defenders of good against evil – with not an aggressive bone in our bodies. Even Clark Kent, quiet and unassuming, seems to fit the image of the stereotypical Canadian.

But we are far more active internationally than just peace-keeping. Canada is committed to active involvement worldwide and we have made our mark internationally in a number of political ways. Our involvement in NATO, the OECD, OAS, GATT, G8, G20, represents a few of these involvements. Canada has also provided leadership to developing countries through CIDA, CUSO, and WUSC. All are well known acronyms world wide. Canada World Youth and Canadian Crossroads International have been successful youth initiatives with thousands of Canadians proudly listing those experiences on their resumes. Canadian involvement in assisting developing nations is quite remarkable and contributes significantly to our conception of Canada as a nation of global citizens. With citizens with relatives and heritages in every 'nook and cranny' in the globe, it is perhaps fitting that we show leadership in creating a single global perspective as opposed to our present preoccupations with nationalism. This view of ourselves as a peace-keeping, global nation is part of our identity.

Many are currently calling this attribute of our identity into question. They are revisioning our international role as peacekeepers and calling it a myth about the way we like to think of ourselves rather that the reality of our diminishing role on the world stage. Considerable basis for serious debate and discussion around this issue is possible.

12. Canada: Not America

"My name is Joe and I am Canadian." When Molson's Brewery first launched its great Canadian rants of ads in 2000, The Joe Canadian ad went viral see YouTube (http://www.youtube.com/watch?v=BRI-A3vakVg). It is a typical way of responding to what is Canadian. "I am not American!"

It seems very Canadian to define our identity by saying we are not American. Lipset (1989) however, points out it are in fact characteristic of many nations to define themselves by who they are not.

Several authors begin by reminding us of our most famous founding phrases. The American revolution in the declaration of independence proclaimed a defining goal and tribute of the American way as, "life liberty and the pursuit of happiness, while as an antithesis to that Canada followed by the words that form the heart of our confederation, "peace order and good government." What markedly different national cultures and identities evolve out such a few words.

Canada has been considered the historic country of counter revolution with a system put in place to preserve and ensure the well being of its citizenry while America is the country of revolution putting in place a framework to limit and control government. In America the notion of 'E Pluribus Unum' resulted in view of new immigrants as contributing to the 'melting pot' While Canada emerged as post-modern nation based on negotiation and a compromise of diverse and evolving interests of French and English protestant and catholic, native Canadian and merging to a nation promoting and proud of its bilingual, federal system and a policy of multiculturalism enshrined in the Canadian Charter of rights and Freedoms

No two countries have a stranger relationship. As Pierre Trudeau once said "Living next to you is in some ways like sleeping with an elephant. No matter how friendly and even-tempered is the beast, if I can call it that, one is affected by every twitch and grunt." Margaret Atwood described our border as the longest one way mirror.

One the one hand we are intricately entwined with our economy, sources of median information our defence and military. Some have argued we have given up and are increasingly becoming dominated by and absorbed by the USA while on the other hand, as Adams (2002) points out our social values are not only strikingly different but are diverging rapidly despite the unrelenting influx of American media to our country

Michael Bliss historian and one of the loudest critics of the Americanization of Canada summed up his lament when he said "What strikes me is that we are becoming more similar to the American in our culture and in our values". And polls tended to support him. When an EKOS(2002)poll showed that 58% of Canadian felt we were becoming more Canadian and only 9% felt we were becoming more distinct (National Post, 2002, Jan 18 p. b1). And Jeffrey Simpson in the Star Spangled Canadians writes: "Canadians whether they like or acknowledge it are becoming more like Americans... (Globe and Mail p. 6, 2000)

In 1960 I asked my six grade 10 history classes how many felt we would be better off if we joined America. Over 80% agreed, while the last time I asked any of my classes that question very few raised their hand.

Because the reality the pundits portray could not be further from the truth. Michael Adams has conducted an extensive series of research on the comparative values between Americans and Canadian over five successive, 4 year intervals (1992, 1996, 2000, 2004 and 2008). Not only are many of our values remarkably different but the divergence gets wider with each successive study. The British Journal *The Economist* in 2008, with a moose on its cover with sun glasses, titled *Cool Canada*, observed social and economic differences between the two countries, from our world leading deficit reduction to our legalization of gay marriage, decriminalization of marijuana, gays in the military and successful health care system.

In 2008 on survey showed that 83% of Canadians would have voted for President Obama if they had a vote, compared to 53% of American voters while only 17% of Canadians would have voted for John McCain. Of Canadian conservative voters 58% would have voted for Obama, prompting Jon Stewart of *The Daily Show* to say the closest example of Canadian politics in American politics would be the gays for Ralph Nader party!

Both countries believe in democracy free markets and the rule of law and have more in common than they do with many other countries in the world but as Adams (2008) reveals when you dig below the surface on each of these common values, striking differences emerge. To cite a few of hundreds of examples he reveals: they carry twice amount of credit card debt; their car is far more important to their style and image than for Canadians; they work longer hours and take fewer holidays; twice as many couples are co-habiting in Canada; they have three times as many murders per capita and 5 times as many gun murders... and the list goes on and on, despite the relentless barrage and consumption of American TV, movies and magazines. He explores the stark differences which continue to widen in our political attitudes: differences in church attendance, on consumption, differences in our attitudes to authority, spirituality, even the look and feel of our cities. When asked about our similarities, 54% feel we should try to be more distinct from our neighbours and only 19% feel we should be more like them.

Conclusion: Keeping the conversation going

I have stepped into controversial territory in daring to articulate ten commonplaces of our culture. I offer them up as suggestions for consideration. I believe it is possible to put forward a set of debatable commonplaces that reveal a Canadian identity that is different from any of the other ethnic and regional identities that exists in Canada, but that includes all of them. They are one initial attempt. If they promote further discussion and debate about Canadian culture and identity then I have achieved my goal. Bhikhu Parekh defines multiculturalism fittingly within the intent of my conception of the commonplaces of our identity:

Multiculturalism doesn't simply mean numerical plurality of different cultures, but rather a community which is creating, guaranteeing, encouraging spaces within which different communities are able to grow at their own pace. At the same time it means creating a public space in which these communities are able to interact and enrich the existing culture and create a new consensual culture in which they recognize reflections of their own identity. (As cited in Henry Giroux, 1992, p. 7).

We know that the school is a major purveyor of a political viewpoint. It always has been, and always will be. If we recognize this influence, we can promote a viewpoint that is reflective of all Canadians and that commits us to a continuing search for equity and a society for the new millennium that is free of racism and inequities. I believe these discussions can lead to a dialogue on the commonplaces of our culture that will further our democratic goals and provide a climate committed to social justice and equity. It behooves us to argue, debate, and discuss our commonplaces rather than to focus always on our differences.

The 'big' themes or commonplaces of Canadian culture and identity can assist us in suggesting an interdisciplinary core program for study or discussion that contributes to a truly just, equitable and inclusive society, for every grade from Kindergarten to grade twelve in every school in Canada. It is not our purpose to dictate what the Canadian identity is, but to create an open environment for debate and discussion, where we are not searching for a final definition.

Through this collective patchwork quilt of the shared stories, emerging from each of these commonplaces, we can create "a community of memory." (Bellah et al. 1995) We can reveal our Canadian culture and identity in a way that allows Canadians from all regions – French and English speaking, Native, of diverse racial and ethno-cultural backgrounds – to "recognize reflections of their own identity", in a way that says "This is who we are." Let us use this flexible framework of commonplaces for discussing our national culture and identity and "keep the conversation going". I have written elsewhere a variety of ways these commonplaces can be incorporated within the schools from K-12. (Diakiw 1996, 1997)

References

Adams, M. (2009) Fire and Ice: The United States, Canada and the myth of converging values. 2nd edition, Penguin Canada.
Anderson, B. (1991) Imagined Communities: Reflections on the Spread of Nationalism. (revised ed.) New York, Verso.
Atwood, M. (1972) Survival. Toronto, Anansi Press.
Bellah, R., R. Madsen, W. Sullivan, A. Swidler and S Tipton (1985) Habits of the Heart. Berkeley, University of California Press.
Benedict, A. (1991) Imagined Communities: Reflections on the spread of nationalism. (revised ed.) New York, Verso.
Bibby, R.W. (1990) Mosaic Madness. Toronto, Stoddart.
Bissoondath, N. (1994) Selling Illusions: The Cult of Multiculturalism in Canada. Toronto, Penguin.
Blair. H. (1963) Lectures on Rhetoric and Belles Lettres. Editor Harold F. Harding. Carbondale, Southern Illinois University Press.
Bliss Michael. (2003) National Identity Series. Dialogue with Brian Hutchison, National Post.
Bloom, A. (1987) Closing the American mind: How higher education has failed democracy and impoverished the souls of todays students.
Brown, J. J. (1967) Ideas in exile: A history of Canadian invention. Toronto, McLelland and Stewart.
Diakiw J. (1996) The school's role in revealing the commonplaces of our national culture and identity: A multicultural perspective. Multicultural Education: The State of the Art National Study, Report #4. Editor Keith A. McLeod. Winnipeg. Canadian Association of Second Language Teachers.
Diakiw J. (1997) Children's Literature and Canadian Identity, Canadian Children's Literature Quarterly, Fall, 1997.
Elkin, D. and Simeon, J. (1980) The sense of place in Small Worlds. Toronto, Methuen.
Frye, N. (1982) Divisions on a ground: Essays on Canadian culture. Toronto, Anansi Press.
Gregg, A. & Posner, M. (1990) The big picture: What Canadians think about almost everything. Toronto, McFarlane, Walter and Ross.
Gates, H. L. Jr. (1991) Multiculturalism: A conversation among different voices. Rethinking Schools, Oct/Nov.
Gellner, Ernest. (1983) Nations and Nationalism. Ithaca NY, Cornell UP.
Giroux, H. (1993) Living dangerously identity, politics and the new cultural racism.
Giroux, H. (1992) Curriculum, multiculturalism and the politics of identity. National Association of Secondary Principals' Bulletin 76 (5481-11).
Ghosh, R. (1996) Redefining Multicultural Education. Toronto, Harcourt Brace.
Globe and Mail (Jan 15, 2007) Editorial.
Grossberg, L. ed. (1994) Between Borders. New York, Vintage.
Gwyn R (1985) The 49th Paradox: Canada in North America. McLelland and Stewart, Toronto.
Hackney, S. (1993) Beyond the Culture Wars. Speech to the National Press Club. Unpublished.
Hirsch, E. D. Jr. (1987) Cultural literacy: What every American needs to know. New York: Vintage Books.
Jimenez, M. (2007) The Globe and Mail.
Hirsch, E. D. Jr. (1987) Cultural Literacy: What Every American Needs to Know New York, Vintage Books.
Hurtig, M. (2002) The Vanishing Country: Is it too late to save Canada? McLelland and Stewart, Toronto.
Hutcheson, L. (1988) Canadian post-modern: A study of contemporary English-Canadian fiction. Toronto, Oxford UP.
King, W. L. M. (June 19, 1936) Speech to the House of Commons. Ottawa.
Kimball, R. (1991) Tenured Radicals: a postscript. The New Criterion, Jan 4-13.
Lipset, S. M. (1990) Continental Divide. New York, Routledge.
Nader R., Conacher, Duff. Canada Firsts. Toronto, McLelland and Stewart.
Postman, N. (1984) Learning by Story. New Yorker. Dec, 119-124.
Raney, T. (2009) As Canadian as Possible... Under What Circumstances? Public Opinion on National Identity in Canada Outside Quebec. Journal of Canadian Studies. Vol. 43, Iss. 3; pg. 5, 26. Peterborough.
Resnick, P. (2005) European Roots of Canadian Identity.
Richmond, A. H. (1988) Immigration and ethnic conflict. New York: St.Martin's Press.
Schafer, D. P. (1990) The character of Canadian culture. World Culture Project, Markham, UNESCO.
Rorty, R. (1979) Philosophy and the Mirror of Nature. Princeton UP.
Saul, J. R. (2008) A Fair Country: Telling Truths About Canada. Viking Canada, Toronto.
Saul, J. R. (2001) My Canada Includes The North, The Globe and Mail.
Simpson J. (2000) Star-Spangled Canadians: Canadians Living the American Dream. Harper Collins.
Trend, D. (1993) Nationalities, Pedagogies and Media, in Lawrence Grossberg, Editor, Between Borders. New York, Vintage.
Woodcock, G. (1987) Northern Spring: The Flowering of Canadian literature. Vancouver, Douglas Mcintyre.
Wright, R. (1992) Stolen Continents. Toronto, Penguin.

Building Bridges Around the World
Canadian School Executive

June 1993. An Old Chinese expression says, "Every culture looks at the world through its own keyhole." With economic barriers, national boundaries and immigration restrictions disappearing, Canadians need fresh insights and many new keyholes. This article describes the York Region Board of Education World Issues Co-op Program in Thailand, whereby 17 and 18 year old students earn credits for their secondary school diplomas through a four and one half months placement in northern Thailand.

The York Region Board of Education recently hosted thirty-two educators from Thailand for nine days as part of a three-city Canadian tour. These educators were not just interested in visiting our schools, they wanted to stay in our homes. They wanted to experience our culture in our kitchens, from the other side of the bathroom door, and over the breakfast table. They feasted on our culture and our way of life. They didn't want to mimic Canadian culture; they wanted to understand it.

Seeing through many keyholes

My Thai guest had studied in Canada for a Master's degree in Education at the University of Alberta in 1967. His eldest daughter is completing the second year of her M.B.A. at the University of Indiana, and his 14 year old daughter is about to depart for Japan where she will spend the next 8 to 10 years in high school, university, and graduate school. It's not surprising that Thailand has the fastest growing economy in the world.

There's a Chinese expression that says, "Every culture looks at the world through it's own keyhole." Thai students, businessmen, and professionals are spreading out over the industrialized world, plugging in and establishing networks that will benefit all Thais. They know Thailand's future depends on making these connections. They are seeing the world through many keyholes.

At a time when economic barriers, national boundaries, and immigration restrictions are disappearing, Canadians need fresh insights and many new keyholes to understand better our own evolving multicultural society, to compete in the world economy, and to contribute to a more effective system of global interdependence. This time is ripe for Canadians of all ages to reach out and touch the world. In particular, we need to signal to our young people, through symbol and action, that they are not only a part of the world community, but that they too can play a role. Some powerful models for doing this already exist.

York students' "keyhole" on Thailand

Last year, fifteen 17 and 18 year old students (seven females and eight males) from nine high schools in the York Region Board of Education were earning their final four credits for their secondary school diplomas through a second semester placement of four and one half months in northern Thailand. They lived with host Thai families and worked in a variety of development projects such as agriculture, primary health, English language instruction, and rural development. All of these students had completed the World Issues OAC Course (Grade 13) in the first semester of the school year in order to qualify for this second semester program. In addition, they had studied the Thai language since October. This project was a joint venture of The York Region Board of Education, Interculture Canada, and AFS Thailand. It was funded with a grant from the Canadian International Development Agency.

I told students and their parents that this experience would change them forever, that they would never see the world in the same way again. Several students were place in the Royal Project, with the hill tribes in the Golden Triangle where the King of Thailand is personally financing a highly successful program to divert the hill tribes from the production of poppies for opium to the cultivation of cool temperate crops such as apples, peaches, lettuce, and cucumbers. In the areas where this project has underway, opium production has been reduced by 99% and the hill tribes are earning more money growing fruits and vegetables than they did producing opium. The students kept journal which they sent back to Canada. Trevor, a student who has been placed with the Royal Project wrote in this journal:

03/06/91 – After lunch I met up with a team of doctors who visit the hill tribes. They invited me along to help. It was quite the experience. They bring food, clothing, and medical attention to the needy hill tribe people. This team consisted of a doctor, pharmacist, nurse, dentist, hygienist and a barber. This service was funded by the Chiang Mai University. The Lahu hill tribe of Kap Dong really appreciated the help. I looked after the children. After dinner the medical group set up once more for Ang Khang staff. They received medical attention for free as well.

04/06/91- This morning I had breakfast early because I was going trekking up the mountains with doctors again. We went to Ba Loong village. This village is located within the Burmese border, I met more soldiers and I able to converse with them a little better. There was a soldier who was sick because he had eaten poisonous leaves. He died at 10:30 a.m. this morning as I took his picture. I was very sorry that there was nothing we could do for him. Since I sometimes cannot control my emotions, I could feel tears as they ran down my face. The soldiers were very kind to me because I was concerned. We paced up and we left Ba Loong to go back to Ang Khan. The doctors asked me if I wanted to go out with them this afternoon. I decided to decline the offer because I didn't want to see anymore death if there was no way of preventing it. This afternoon I went to a farm on the station. I saw a cow give birth to a healthy baby calf. I decide in my mind that this compensated for the death this morning.

Another student D'Arcy, who was placed in north-east Thailand, inquired about the future of the project:

"Do you have any idea about whether CIDA is interested in funding this program again? For what it's worth: This is without question the best eye-opening, thought-creating, It humanizing, and humbling experience that I think I will ever have."

Spin-off effects

These students were seeing the world through another key-hole. Not only did they benefit from this enriching experience but many of us are reaping the rewards:

- It was this project that led to the visit of thirty-two Thai educators to York Region. Twenty York Region teachers later returned the visit.
- More specialized visits are being planned; I have been party to a number of discussions of possible business ventures.
- New relationships are being forged between organizations within Canada (Interculture Canada, The York Region Board of Education, and CIDA) and in Thailand (The Thai Ministry of Education, AFS Thailand, and a host of Development agencies in Thailand).

More bridges need to be built

Our students where shining symbols of secondary schools they attended. They symbolized the value we place in participating in the global arena in a meaningful way. They signaled that high school students can reach out and touch the world. They demonstrated the value we place on co-operative learning in an international setting through the credits they earned toward their graduation diplomas.

We need to find ways to expand the opportunities for our young people to participate in this way. York Region's World Issues Co-op program in Thailand and exemplary programs such as Interculture Canada's "Year Away." Canada World Youth, and Canadian Crossroads International's programs, build little bridges around the world. Once those bridges are built it's amazing what ends up crossing them. If one truly believes our Canadian identity accrues in part from Canada's role in the larger world, and if we want to participate successfully in a global economy, we need to provide our young people with opportunities to build these bridges and to symbolize, for their peers, what can be done.

5. About This and That

Why We Travel: A Backpackers Ethos
Originally published on GoNomad. https://www.gonomad.com/5309-why-we-travel

I am a backpacker. I travel with a small pack to off-the-beaten-path countries. I travel with locals, eat with locals, and sleep with locals and other backpackers, mostly in hostel and dormitories. I travel overland using local shared vans, local buses, occasionally a train and often when transport is scarce or when I feel it is safe, I hitchhike. I am not unique. I am a member of a silent tribe of travelers from all walks of life, nationalities and ages. We unconsciously adhere to a shared set of common core values – what I call the "backpacker's ethos." While we do not have any written credo, word of mouth is our bible, yet we do have common shared texts – the Lonely Planet country guides may be our primary resource. We have our own internet forums such as "Thorntree", or "Boots'n'all". We recognize each other instantly on the street, in terminals or in airports. We have no high priests, no services, no organized dogma. When we meet, we instantly share tips, suggestions, and stories. The whole world is our temple.

We mostly travel alone initially, though not always, and will often match up with others for short periods of time, if mutually beneficial. We distinguish ourselves from "trekkers" who also carry a backpack, but theirs includes everything they need for survival, such as a tent, sleeping bag and often cooking gear, while we carry the bare minimum, buying what we need in local markets as we need them. They travel in the wilderness, we travel from country to country, city to city, town to town.

For example, in 2011, I backpacked overland from Capetown to Cairo. Last year, at 75, I traveled the Silk Road from Istanbul, overland through Iran to Tajikistan, over the Pamir Pass, to Kyrgyzstan and into the Takla Makan Desert in Western China; this year from the southern tip of India to the roof of the world in Katmandu.

I became a convert and became addicted to this way of travel when in 1963, before backpacking became popular, I backpacked overland, from Singapore to Beirut, over nearly ten months of travel, for a total cost for transportation and accommodation of $3.41 (in 1963 dollars!) I stayed in temples and monasteries almost the entire way.

A day never passes that I do not think of some experience I had on that trip. It changed my life forever. It transformed my career and my life in multiple ways. It even changed my personality. During that trip, crossing so many deserts of the Middle East inspired my desire to cross all the major deserts in the world alone.

Being Alone in the Wilderness

There is something spiritual about being alone in the wilderness. In the last ten years, I have made solo backpacking trips across the Gobi in Mongolia, the Atacama in Chile, the Sahara (3x), the Thar in India and the Kalahari, as well as crossings of Libya, Ethiopia, and Uzbekistan. The ethos of backpacking, however, is more related to reducing travel to the lowest, simplest, level – staying and eating in the cleanest, cheapest, accommodations and restaurants where the locals, as well as a wide variety of international travelers, stay.

Backpackers, today, include everyone from university professors, doctors, and teenagers to geriatrics like me. There is the challenge of doing it on the "cheap", to travel as long, and as far, for as little, as you can. For me I never make a reservation, I rarely know my route from day to day and though I sometimes have a destination such as Cairo on my trans-African trip, on other occasions I travel until I feel it is time to go home, such as my Silk Road trip.

Backpacking alone is particularly a way of meeting the local inhabitants. When you walk along the street alone you are frequently offered help, asked questions, invited for tea or coffee and sometimes to stay overnight in their homes. When you travel with another person you rarely are offered this kind of hospitality or opportunity to get to know them and their culture.

I have found that the backpacking "ethos" provides me the opportunity of seeing the world through a different prism: experiencing and living in each country closer to the way the local inhabitants experience life than any other way of traveling. I eat where they eat, I travel on the same buses and trains as they do, and I sleep where they sleep.

As Pico Iyer, a world traveler wrote, "I want to be moved and I want to be transported and I want to be sent back a different person." Backpacking accelerates this transformation.

While one normally thinks of backpackers as young men and women setting out to see the world before they settle down to marriage and a career, in reality, there is a whole backpacker culture out there, of all ages, from all over the world.

Local Cultures

Most have strong feelings of support and sympathy for local cultures and traditions, are usually environmentally sensitive, abhor cruelty to animals, dispose of refuse properly where often others do not. We travel to destinations that raise more questions than answers, destinations that "inspire questions that reverberate long after you leave" as Iyer says.

Traveling this way, especially, alone, results in a very reflective, often meditative, introspective look at one's life. I have remarkable adrenalin highs. My trip in 1962 across Asia started this life long journey and addiction to backpacking across deserts and continents. I felt on top of the world then and again now. I feel like I am a better man now for accepting this challenge and achieving my goal.

I feel I understand the world better, I stand taller. My knowledge and concerns for Africans and Central Asians are greater now. My thoughts for locals in emerging nations are visceral, and my dreams for their goals are greater, I understand them better, I understand the world better.

At another level entirely, I have often reflected on the grand sweep of historic and mythical travelers. In the reflective, dreamlike states, it is not me, but some mythical figures from some ancient script come to life to seek answers. The hero, who sets out on his journey to face many challenges and returns a transformed man, ready to take on the challenges necessary in his family and society. It is me, but, not me. Yet, I am transformed. In this dream-like reflection, it is the mythical me that ventures forth and then returns.

Holy man in India *Mongolia camel master* *Ubari sand sea in Libya* *Fatehpur Sikri India*

Pilgrims in Axum *Gobi desert nomads in Mongolia*

This superhuman, tireless, giant of a man who instantly blends in with the local population, lifts them up if only briefly; they feel good about themselves, see the progress they have made through the mirror I hold up to them. They feel and see the joy I see in their everyday living, the treasure and the joy of family. I feel their joy of a newborn child, of a good harvest, or a welcome rain.

Yes, a mythical giant roamed the hills and valleys of Africa and Asia. His name was Jerry and he liked what he saw. I like this man better than before. He is wiser and more empathetic.

Years ago this feeling of being a mythical man swept over me when I traveled around the world hitch-hiking for pennies. I seek to replicate that feeling every year alone on the road. The old story of, "Why would you climb Mt Everest?", "Because it is there", applies to my trips. "Why backpack from Istanbul to China or Capetown to Cairo?" Because it is there and there is a great feeling of exhilaration in accomplishing my goal as does any mountain climber attaining the summit of his chosen mountain.

I feel that following the backpacking ethos induces a more profound look at one's life, an introspective navel-gazing that can be both good and bad. The border between introspection and narcissism is blurred. But it is framed by the visceral experience of experiencing the life of locals, closer to their level of existence, when you eat, sleep and travel with them, especially when traveling in Asia or the developing world where there can be a dramatic, a mostly unconscious leap away from a Euro-Ameri-centric mentality.

Yes, one can experience this on an organized tour, but not at the profound level of a backpacker, in my opinion. It is a palpably different experience. Pico Iyer points out that "We travel, then, in search of both self and anonymity – and, of course, in finding the one we apprehend the other".

Abroad, we are wonderfully free of caste and job and standing. We are classless and without status and people cannot put a name or tag to us. And precisely because we are classified in this way, and freed of inessential labels, we have the opportunity to come into contact with more essential parts of ourselves (which may begin to explain why we may feel most alive when far from home).

Therein lies the essential dilemma. Feeling more alive when far from home. How can that be, when we love home so much? There is, for me, that essential living on the edge, life reduced to its basic survival essentials of finding a safe place to sleep, safe food to eat and how to get to the next destination.

I am free when traveling this way of all the pressures of home, whether it be seeking advancement in one's career, meeting the mortgage or even keeping up with the Jones'. Free of these nebulous goals, each day on the road is exhilarating because it is so full of successes of food, sleep and safe travel from A to B. Interactions with locals when communication is possible is often electric, charged with a strange instant bonding of two people meeting by accident on an empty planet. They are so pleased to know you, want more of you; a desire for reaching out from their world to touch someone in another.

I acquired all the rights and privileges that were bequeathed to me instantly on birth in Canada. How lucky I am and yet I see endless joy and happiness in what we would call deprived conditions. Suicide rates in Asia and Africa are way below Western rates, and I suspect mental illness rates and depression are well below ours as well. Their daily needs are so simple– put food and clean water on the table, clothe your family, and maintain and keep a safe place to sleep.

Compare that to our complicated lives, whether it getting further in debt with refurbishing the cottage or looking after aging parents, or even middle-aged children. As Paul Theroux wrote, "just experiencing the simplicity and primitivism of life can lead you to a destination you end up truly loving".

In backpacking hostels and on local busses I met hundreds of men and women from dozens of different countries of all ages who had stories to share, and I met hundreds of local citizens who have shared their culture, their hopes, and dreams for their families and their lives and their country.

Their life is a series of a multitude of simple joys and demanding hardships. I not only witnessed the relentless poverty, their struggles with the disease, and environmental destruction but at the level of a backpacker, I saw joy and hope.

Travel with locals also allows you to bring new eyes to the people you encounter and just as travel helps you appreciate your own home more, it helps you bring appreciative insights to share with people in the places you visit. You can reflect for them what they have to celebrate, as much as you celebrate what they have to teach you. We can provide them with a fresh and renewed sense of how special they are, the warmth and beauty of their country.

"Do You Like Our Country?"

The most frequent question I am asked wherever I am is, "Do you like our country?" It is important to me to have at the ready the things that have touched me, the beautiful places I have seen, the kindnesses of the people. They look at me with a sense of pleasure, at my pleasure and pride in the many good things they have. They see us on TV and in movies. For them, our differences are vast. But when I honor their cultures, their values, the beauty of their country, there is this look of triumph and joy, as if to say, "YES!"

For backpackers, learning about the people, their problems and dreams are as important, if not more important, than seeing the magnificent herds of African animals in Ngorongoro Crater, or the Pyramids at Giza or the great mosques of Samarkand.

So, yes, at 76, I am getting on, but as Paul Theroux said, "Years are not an affliction. Old age is strength." Age is about attitude, not chronology. I am a still a backpacker and a strong advocate for the backpacker's 'ethos'. I am still a practicing member of the silent backpacking tribe.

Dance In Toronto: East Meets West

On a Saturday in March, at a 2 pm performance of the National Ballet's, magical *Onegin*, in Toronto, my wife and I were enraptured by the visual treat of costumes, sets and spectacular dancing. From the fifth ring the dancers seemed to float, in constantly unfolding formations like a kaleidoscope. John Cranko's brilliant narrative style kept us mesmerized and engaged with the story for all three acts – a magnificent, exquisite, display of classical dance. Jennifer Homans, however, author of *Apollo's Angel's* writes, "I now feel sure that ballet is dying." But not at the Four Seasons Theatre, where there is no evidence of its imminent death, not by the enraptured looks of delight of the audience, most of whom happily paid well over $100 for the experience. More recently they have been enthralled by the sold out performances of the collaboration with the Royal Ballet in a new production of *Alice in Wonderland*.

We drove back to Markham by 6 pm. I had a quick dinner and, attracted by a 4 star review by Michael Crabb, I drove back into the city by myself to the Fleck Theatre without a ticket, hoping to see the final performance of the Indian Contemporary Dance festival, *Kalanidhi*. In the last row of the orchestra, I watched nine dramatically different dances. (four from Toronto, two from the UK, and a final set of three from India.) I was gasping for air from the astonishing performances, screaming 'bravos' along with a largely South Asian crowd (in a bewitching array of saris). These performances were all contemporary/modern dances based on traditional Indian dances. Nina Ranjani choreographed the dance called *Quick*, about 8 high finance cut throat investors, in business shirts and ties, trying to close a deal. It won the Bloomberg sponsored, Place Prize, which is the largest choreographic competition in Europe in 2006. She also did a second dance, *Bend-it*, a soccer game, including spectacular goals, fake injuries and crowd roars, all in the context of a dance routine based on an ancient traditional style of dancing. The final hour was the South Indian company *Kadam,* choreographed by a revered woman (guru), Kundulini Lakhia, sort of a Celia Franca/Betty Oliphant/Karen Kain combo who has evolved a modern version of thousands of year's tradition of dance in India called Kathak. Indian dance has its early roots back to 400 BC with itinerant storytellers and still thrives despite a period when it was frowned upon by Victorian administrators during the period of the British Empire.

This evening's program was a spectacular display of innovative modern dance based on ancient dance systems blending contemporary innovative Indian musicians, even incorporating western composers like John Cage, western themes and costumes and modern technology. Almost every dance displayed some cross-cultural, border-crossing element such as theme, content or form. It was an artistic embodiment of our city.

It was a day of five hours of spectacular classical dance... 2½ hours at the Four Seasons and 2½ hours at the Fleck Dance Theatre. It has forced me to do a lot of thinking about culture (sports, dance, opera, art) in a multicultural city like Toronto.

At the Four Seasons Theatre, it was the purity of classical ballet with its roots in renaissance France. At the Fleck Dance Theatre it was the explosiveness and inventiveness that surprised me. In the program notes, I read, "6 Tabla drums and laptop"... I was quite startled by that, and even more so when they started to play and the lead musician was drumming on his Apple laptop on a stool, amidst six tabla drums. The magical rhythms, riffs, and sounds emanating out of his Apple laptop over the powerful bass beat of the six tabla drums was indescribable. It's this surprising cross-cultural inventiveness that was apparent all night.

The history of civilizations has proven over and over, that in periods of great movements of people, ideas, and clashes of cultures, that wherever they meet there is an explosion in the arts, sciences and innovation in every aspect of society. And these dance groups are examples. Joanna De Sousa the classical Indian dancer, who danced with the Toronto Tabla Ensemble (who were commissioned to compose the intro music for CBC's Radio 1, *Metro Morning* show), has collaborated with a dozen varied cultural groups. She worked with First Nation singer, Sadie Buck, and Flamenco dancer, Esmerelda Enrique, as well as a Japanese ensemble, a West African dancer, a butch dancer, and has won and been nominated for several Dora Mavor Moore awards.

This is border-crossing at its best. It is an example of the merging of cultures. I love the experimental mixing of cultural traditions – multicultural schools, multi-ethnic neighbourhoods and food stores. And yet with all the mixing they are still able to maintain the purity of their own form of dance and music, or within the spirit of our multiculturalism, their own culture, There is an explosion in the arts in Toronto that is very exciting.

At another level, this spirit of experimentation exists at the National Ballet, through the genius of Karen Kain, who has become renowned for her innovative programming, mixing the traditional with the modern, fostering and developing new choreographers, and now creating an exciting new collaboration with the Royal Ballet. But I wondered how far can innovative ballet go? Other dance traditions with a longer history than ballet, many of them on view that Saturday night, have choreographers who are just as famous as John Cranko and yet we know little about them. And it is not as if they are way off in some foreign country, they are here. They are us! There is a firestorm of border-crossing creative activity in Toronto.

Half the people in the City of Toronto are now foreign-born, and half the GTA's population identify themselves as members of a visible minority. The United Nations for many years now has named Toronto the most ethnically diverse city in the world, more diverse than Miami, Los Angeles, New York City or London! There is an explosion of cross-cultural, inter-cultural, border-crossing going on in the arts and in every aspect of society. Interracial marriages in Canada are increasing at a heart-warming rate and are way higher in Canada than in the United States. We are fast approaching one million South Asians in Toronto, who have surpassed East Asians as the largest immigrant population in Canada. Indian film-makers and artists consider Toronto, Bollywood West. Toronto was been chosen to host the Bollywood film awards, India's academy awards in June.

Does it matter that the ballet appeals to a very narrow demographic? Or, that South Asians are absent at the National Ballet? Torontonians who attend the ballet, support all the arts in the city with their incredibly generous financial contributions, as well as for a host of multicultural events and venues like Harbourfront, Luminato, including the Fleck Dance Theatre, the host venue for so many international dance companies.

But in a provocative conclusion to her new book in *Apollo's Angels: A History of Ballet*, Jennifer Homan argues that ballet is not only dying but that companies have become "museums for the old".

Clement Crisp, the pre-eminent drama critic in the UK, too, has lamented "the dire state of ballet companies, worldwide; a shortage of classical choreographers combined with timid company management has led to repetitive repertoires", and again, "in an age when repertories are cloned and when the need for a troupe to preserve its own identity is often outweighed by the box-office allure of ballets people have heard of... It's a scandal. How can you put on Swan Lake 18 times?"

Karen Kain challenged this argument with her widely lauded Innovations program, breaking away from the classics, with three dances by young Canadian choreographers. As Clement Crisp effused "such rare adventurousness is the only way to ensure a future for a national company".

Alison Owen, the producer of the films *Jane Eyre* and *Elizabeth* with Cate Blanchett, hired Cary Fukanaga, a Latino, who had only done one film before, a Spanish speaking film about illegal immigrants, to direct *Jane Eyre*. She was questioned in a New York Times interview about why such a strange choice for a director. She said she learned a lesson when she did *Elizabeth*. She hired the Indian director Shekhar Kapur and it went so well. "It proved a great success to have a director from a different culture... you need to shake things up."

There is an explosion in Toronto of fusion in dance among non-Western dance and music, but not between classical ballet and Eastern dance forms. Why is this?

I believe if you dropped one of the dances at the Indian dance festival I saw in March, into a mixed National Ballet Innovations program, it would blow the ballet aficionados out of the water or if you commissioned a prize winning Indian choreographer to do a ballet for the National Ballet, it would take that one last innovative step, to not only take classical ballet into the contemporary world as they have done so successfully already, but to merge cultural traditions as well, just as film producer Alison Owen has done with *Elizabeth* and *Jane Eyre*. Is it time for classical ballet to forge some fusion with other cultural dance forms representative of our multicultural city?

What better place to do it than in the most multicultural city in the world – Toronto.

the DIAKIW DIGEST

SLIM CHANCE

As an educator committed to equity issues in our schools with many years experience both as a teacher and administrator, I am confident in my ability to implement an anti-racist policy and curriculum in a school or classroom. I know how to promote a positive multicultural school environment. I have learned slowly over the years how to deal with many issues of gender equity. I know how to accommodate students of varied abilities. Recently, I have come to realize there is one issue for which I am sadly lacking in an ability to cope, and for which I have little societal or institutional support.

I teach an introductory course to first year education students at York University. Students are required on paper to explore the most powerful forces of their identity, such as race, religion, ethnic origins, nationality, gender, and examine how these forces have shaped their attitudes and beliefs as they enter the classroom, and then consider how their life experiences can be used positively to create a just and equitable classroom. Despite the fact I never raised "weight" as an issue to explore in influencing their identity, it came as a surprise to me to read paper after paper from students who chose to write about their real or perceived weight problems. In a class of forty-six students, over a third of them, including several males, discussed the negative influence of being fat, or "chubby", or perceiving themselves as fat, during their school years. These were not passing comments or observations of their adolescent years, these were stories of pain, suffering and exclusion, devastated self-esteem, stories of ridicule, humiliation and discrimination, stories of anorexia and bulimia.

I was surprised by the number of those who suffered in their youth and with perceived or real weight problems. We struggle to combat racism, sexism, classism and homophobism in our society, but we are also a "fatist" society. There are two issues here. There is the problem of weight, and there is the problem of students who are truly overweight. We need to understand these issues better. Too many of our children are aspiring to the unrealistic ideal of the slim runway model or "waif" and "Hey Fatty" can be as hurtful and demeaning as intolerable as racist remarks.

I always consider offensive jokes and slurs in the context of where the power lies in our society and while racist remarks against any group are offensive and unacceptable, there is a categorical difference in severity depending on the power structures in society. "Hey n---r!" Is more offensive then "Hey Whitey! "Hey Yank!" Fat remarks fit into the same category as access to same opportunities as other citizens. They are highly visible and face daily humiliation through overt comments and innuendo, and have more limited opportunities for employment. Most of them understand that obesity is unhealthy, but they are physically and psychologically unable to do anything about it.

The process of socializing children to be thin begins very early. One teacher candidate wrote in our classroom internet conference:

> "I am placed in a kindergarten class. Just today, I received a sad, but serious taste of reality. A five year old girl – who by society's standards could be considered "overweight" – came crying to me that a classmate had called her a "a pig". When I confronted this female classmate she said to me "but that's what she is, look at her" (Needless to say I dealt with this girl accordingly, but my story doesn't end there.) This poor little girl, who was still sobbing, came to me and said "Why can't I be skinny? All the kids would like me if I was skinny. My mom puts me on diets and I'm still fat." This girl is a 5 years old for goodness sakes! She's been put on a diet, and obviously is already caught up on this "skinny is beautiful" campaign!"

Another student, a recovered anorexic, responded to this incident:

> "If you restrict a 5 year old's food intake, then all she will think about and want will be food. When she does get it, she will eat a lot and feel guilty, thus harming her already low self esteem. It is a vicious cycle... William Purkey has done studies on self concept and school performance showing that poor self image usually results in poor school performance. Girls constantly preoccupied with food tend to have low self esteem and will either do poorly in school or will excel to prove that they are good at something... the lack of nourishment in girls who are starving themselves will result in emotional mood swings and lack of concentration in class."

Discrimination, harassment and ridicule of obese students and the perception of being overweight by many students who aspire to emulate the skinny, unnatural body types promoted by the fashion industry and by the media are problems that are far more pervasive than I ever thought possible.

Unlike the unified public response to the problem of racism and sexism, there are no significant institutional, cultural, or community strategies to support teachers in the classroom. Strange as it may seem, it is almost as if discrimination against the obese is an invisible problem. The differently abled are supported by layers and layers of legal, institutional, media and community support. At the school board level there is a host of directives, policies, and curricula, such as anti-racist policies and procedures, gender equity initiatives and specialized programs for special education students, to address inequities based on race, creed, gender, and the physically and emotionally challenged. But, there is a silence, even an unconscious collusion of society's institutions with regard to the problem of discrimination against overweight students and citizens.

Perhaps even more significant is the problem of the number of students who perceive themselves as overweight and seek control of their bodies through starvation dieting. This often leads to a development of anorexia or bulimia. Again there is a societal collusion in perpetuating the ideal body type of the waif. The media and fashion industry relentlessly perpetuate the image of the pencil thin figure as an object of beauty. The tobacco companies promote the slimming effect of smoking, blatantly targeting the female teenager. (Virginia Slims). Magazines routinely feature photos of decadent desserts, articles about dieting, images of bulimic models with enhanced breasts, often all displayed on the same cover.

One education student, who continues to force herself to vomit regularly, wrote in her identity paper:

> I am a bit apprehensive to talk about such issues on paper. I am still afraid to share so much about myself. How do I begin? Well let's just say it all began in high school. I was always concerned by how I looked and how my appearance was viewed by others. I always considered myself "at" and would constantly talk about these things with friends. I can not pin point exactly when it happened I began to have a problem with my eating. I would not say I was anorexic but I remember not eating at all for days and then eating so much on others.

> As I got older, I was more in control of my life. I never ate breakfast and when I ate at all it would be in such abundance I would make myself sick. Then it happened. I began throwing up what I would eat on a regular basis. I do not know to this day what compelled me to do it but I found myself so empowered by it that I could not stop. I cannot describe the feelings for you, as you are crouched over a toilet holding your hair in one hand and sticking your finger or toothbrush down your throat provoking yourself to vomit. It takes several times before you actually accomplish it, but once you begin the ritual you can not break free from that position until it's accomplished... your body trembles and your eyes water as you hang your head further down the toilet and continue to stick your fingers in your mouth... I was scared my sister would hear me gagging or my mother would walk in on me. As I started doing it more regularly, it came much easier. I would eat and eat without even realizing it, and then end up in the bathroom throwing up all of it... I could not bear to find out that a child I teach now is going through the same things I went through, and am still going through."

Several of the male students wrote about the humiliation of being overweight, including the horrors of physical education classes where their problem was so blatantly exposed. As another student wrote "I don't think that people realize how damaging this teasing about weight and shape can be for a young person."

After I handed the papers back, I showed a powerful video about the problem called "Slim Hopes" and held an open discussion about what we can do as educators. One student who had not written about his problem in her paper, sent me and E-mail message:

> Well, I thought that I would write to share MY experience with this incredibly widespread disorder. Although women have obtained more control over their reproductive rights, and have made some progress towards equality in relationships, women are still being socialized to believe that in order to succeed, one MUST be beautiful. In today's society, weight preoccupation is now considered to be a part of a normal life. For myself, I suffered with anorexia and bulimia while in high school. My high school years were not "the best years in my life". The hours were filled with depression and self-scrutiny.

> Once I was on the road to recovery, I decided to do some research. The statistics paint a stark picture. I never knew that anorexia has a 20% death rate. For many, the eating disorder isn't truly about food. It's about self-esteem. Food is a metaphor, a type of replacement for everything that the anorexic or bulimic can't control. I personally never felt that I meet my parent's or society's expectations."

I feel quite helpless in knowing how schools can best address this pervasive problem. It is widely understood, but largely ignored. Yes, obesity is unhealthy. We are effective in schools in promoting healthy eating habits and we are bombarded with advertising about an array of diets and products to control weight. But we are ineffective in providing support for those who are obese, or think they are, and can't do anything about it. Our class talked about some of the issues the schools can address: the importance of fitness, the need to promote a positive and realistic body type, the difficulty of getting overweight students to take physical education when it becomes optional in high school, the need for curricular support for teaching about eating disorder and the need to analyze and deconstruct the media advertising. But somehow it seems overwhelming for the schools to do it alone. A colleague in the USA responded to my query about suggestions of what to do about situations like the 5 year old on a diet who was called a fat pig. It points out how complicated this can be.

> I was very touched by your student's experience with the 5 year old girl who wanted to be skinny. As a recovered anorexic and a scholar who does research in eating disorders, though, I cannot say that I was shocked. I have lots of resources for college students on eating disorders, but my suspicion is that there is little or nothing out there for this little girl.If I were your students, and, if I were comfortable with my position in this kindergarten, I would make an appointment with the girl's mother. This may accomplish nothing more than showing her how little she is going to be able to do for this little girl. If this little girl's mom is "putting" her on "diets" (goodness only knows what that means – I know a young woman who mom restricted her to 600 cals/day when she was 10 yrs. old), then the one with the body image disorder is the mom – who is passing it on to her daughter. This is very common. If I felt that I could speak to the mom, I would probably try to talk to her about her daughter's self-esteem.

> I would also try to convince her that "rounder" little girls, like her daughter, often grow into very pretty young women – of all body sizes. My strong suspicion, however, is that the little girl's mom will be a bit "heavy" herself and has real self-esteem issues that she believes she is "saving" her daughter from. Frankly, this little girl needs counseling and I imagine her mom does too."

This is a tough call. Are teachers really able to respond appropriately to the complex needs of students in this situation? Calling in a parent to talk about his child's problem is a bit beyond the skills of most teachers. It is often perceived as none of their business. With so many needy children in a class, unfortunately, the problem is more often ignored. The problem is far more pervasive and extends far beyond the school. While the school has a major role to play, the solutions lie in many areas of our society. There is just a slim chance we can harness all the institutions in our society to do that.

The unconscious collusion of the media and other institutions in our society persists in promoting an unrealistic body type for young girls The case of the kindergarten child illustrates how early the socialization begins. The prevailing image of the "Barbie Doll" early reinforces an unrealistic ideal. I was informed that if Barbie was 5' 5" tall she would need jeans that had a 16" waist and 40" legs, not to mention her 38" bust. Fat slurs and jokes are still tolerated in our society. We appear to close our eyes to the humiliation and discrimination that full bodied and obese citizens experience.

A young and vibrant full bodied high school teacher I know well, has outstanding credentials and recommendations. She has very specialized skills in computers and ESL. Her application for teaching yields "many" job interviews, but she continues to be rejected following the interviews. Down deep in my heart, I think I know why.

The Case for Extremes Taxes on Extreme Wealth

The rise of a billionaire class in North America is a staggering phenomena. North America is home to the super wealthy. It's hard to get one's head around what that means. Just eight men, (of the over 2200 billionaires) for example, own as much wealth as the poorest half of the world's population, that's nearly 4 billion people. Many of these billionaires earn over a million dollars a day (some as high as $3 million per day) or over $150,000 an hour. Four hedge fund managers made more than $1 billion in annual income last year.

There are over 11 million millionaire households in America – over 7% of Americans, more than the total population of Sweden. The number is growing... faster and faster. America has more millionaires than in any other country. There are also over 3 million millionaires in Canada. According to a report by Credit Suisse, the number of millionaires in Canada will jump by more than half in the next five years, a faster growth rate than other developed countries including the U.S.

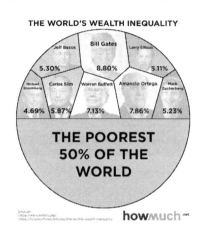

In many cases, with tax loopholes and incentives, interest forwarding devices, millionaires pay even less than their secretaries or cleaning ladies. Warren Buffett wrote an oped a few years back citing that he pays about 16% in income taxes, while many employees earning $100,000-$200,000 pay about 20% in taxes.

Yet, while 90% of 30 year olds in the 1970s earned more than their parents, now less than 50% of 30 year olds do. While the rich have been getting richer, wealth in the middle class has stagnated. While hourly wage rates lag behind the rise of cost living, workers struggle with stagnating incomes. The wealth of the super-rich has increased by an average of 11% a year since 2009. Yet this growth has failed to make a dent in the U.S. poverty rate. At 16.8%, it remains the third-highest among western countries (OECD nations) and is more than twice the rate in France. Canada's rate has dropped to 9.5% (2017).

Shouldn't you pay for the advantage of living in a country that fosters and supports entrepreneurs more than any other country?

If you are willing to pay the excessive costs of over $70,000 per year to attend Harvard university to obtain the accrued lifetime advantages from graduating there, is it not reasonable to pay excessive taxes on income over $10 million per year, as a hedge fund manager or Silicon Valley entrepreneur, for the advantages accrued from living and working within a unique economic system that provides myriad advantages to making a fortune that are not as available in any other country in the world. It is that unique combination of advantages, funded by public taxes, that has resulted in the greatest number of millionaires anywhere. Over half the world billionaires live in the North America, (including over 100 in Canada). North Americans are not uniquely genetically coded in their DNA to become richer than people living anywhere else. There are more rich people in the US because the American system of democracy, individual freedoms, capitalistic economy and the remarkable ease of doing business, is implicitly designed to generate great wealth. Shouldn't you pay proportionately to play in the system? Surely there should be a proportional price to the rich for living in a country that is so advantageous to entrepreneurial activity.

How the System Creates Billionaires

The ease of doing business in the US is described in the The World Economic Forum's 2018 global competitiveness report as "the closest economy to the frontier, the ideal state". The Forum's data indicates that the US is one of the highest ranking nations in measurements of business-friendly policies – "from ease of starting a business, obtaining credit, trading across borders, and resolving insolvent companies". According to Carl Riccadonna, Bloomberg's chief U.S. economist, the capitalist system in the America benefits from established bankruptcy law, relatively low taxes, and the protection of intellectual property. He claims the true edge for American capitalists comes from the country's public and private institutions of higher education. Top world talent is drawn to American universities providing a steady pool of some of the most creative, entrepreneurial talent anywhere. American universities were labelled as "Young Entrepreneur Factories", by Crimson Education. They argue that the US college system is more advantageous for entrepreneurs than almost any other in the world. Forty-one percent of Fortune 500 companies were founded by immigrants or the children of immigrants. More than half of Silicon Valley startups were founded by immigrants. Most were educated in America universities. The share of all Nobel prizes from U.S affiliated universities has climbed to 73% since 2000.

We pay through taxes for police protection, national security, our courts, our health system. Why should the wealthy not pay dearly for the advantages offered to them to make fortunes in business by the many unique advantages that facilitate and support making fortunes in North America?

While the republican/conservative mantra for cutting taxes has historically benefitted the super rich over the middle class, recently Liberals/Democrats in North America have argued for a variety of schemes of taxing the super-rich. For example, Olivia Alexandria Ocasio-Cortez has suggested taxing 70% of the annual income over $10 million. How much money do you need to be super-rich? Billionaires surely earn far more money in a year than is even necessary to act and spend like the super rich.

Bill Gates, the world's richest man, has seen his fortune rise by 50% or $25 billion since leaving Microsoft in 2006 without working another day and despite giving much of it away. It is proof of how surplus these excessive billions are. Warren Buffet, Bill and Melinda gates started the Giving Pledge, a commitment currently of 187 billionaires to give away more than half of their wealth to causes including lowering the poverty rate, refugee aid, disaster relief, global health, education, girls' empowerment, medical research, arts, criminal justice reform and environmental causes. Selma Hayek's billionaire husband,

Francois Henri Pinault donated $113 million to rebuild Notre Dame. His lifestyle and spending habits will not be affected one iota by this decline in total net worth.

There is the Atlas Shrugged metaphor, that over-taxing the creators, the producers, achievers, innovators, leads to the decline of the number of very people that produce this enormous wealth, that high taxes stifles entrepreneurialism, ingenuity and innovation. History suggests otherwise. Some of America's most productive, inventive periods occurred in period of very high taxes on the rich.

It's easy to forget how much the rich paid in the past. In 1950 to 1964 the highest marginal tax rates were over 90%! Earlier in 1918, the top rate of income tax was 77% on income over $1,000,000, to finance World War I. Laughably today, President Franklin D. Roosevelt even proposed a 100% tax on all incomes over $25,000. Imagine! While Ronald Reagan made massive reductions in tax rates, he did not reduce higher marginal incomes. The effective tax rate on the top 0.01% of taxpayers remained at 42.9% then. Sweden and Denmark have the highest average tax rates today hovering around 60%. It's not surprising that their citizens are among the healthiest, safest, best educated, living in the most sustainable environments and are the happiest people on the planet. They pay for it. And, Sweden is rated as one of the world's top 3 economies for innovation.

Today in the US, the highest income earners pay, 33% on income over $500,000, in a country with no national health plan. The Trump tax reform netted Warren Buffet's Berkshire Hathaway more than $29 billion in last year's tax return. The over 100 billionaires in Canada pay 53.53% on income over $220,000. While average wealth per Canadian adult in 2018 was at $288,260 it was almost 30% lower than in the U.S, but wealth in Canada is more equally distributed than in the US, for example, the median wealth per adult in Canada was $106,340, compared with $61,670 in the US. There is also a smaller percentage of Canadians with less than $10,000 and a larger percentage of those with above $100,000 than in the US.

The North American system leads to a billionaire class of unparalleled dimensions. They are throwing money around willy nilly in a scattered shotgun fashion, from funding the rebuilding of Notre Dame, to financing symphony orchestras, to paying the fees for all medical students at one university. All worthy endeavours but... they are so rich they are funding inconsistently, erratically, what most modern countries do systematically, like providing for national medical coverage, or reducing child poverty, or providing equal funding for every elementary student or providing for needed infrastructure repair.

It's time the super wealthy paid for all the unique advantages available to them to make their fortunes, just as many pay exorbitant fees at prestigious universities for the advantages that accrue from graduating there.

Thinking About Paris

For me, the shocking and hideous details of the Paris terrorist attack are symptomatic of seemingly world wide problem centred on unemployed, disaffected minority males between the age of 16-30. As I have mentioned before, my most enduring image, of my trip from tip to tip overland across Africa and on previous trips to Libya, Tunisia, Morocco, and most countries of the Middle East are the thousands of young men, many highly educated, lingering in mobs, loitering in markets, on streets, in cafés, at transport terminals, along all main roads, with nothing to do. Nothing. No work available. None! Millions of them and that is equally true in the poor suburbs of Paris, London, New York, Baltimore, Toronto and Los Angeles. (Particularly minority youth.)

Spinning off from this point it means not just lack of money to eat, to dress, but more important to me, they are terminally crippled in their ability to do what we are genetically coded to do, and that is to find a mate and create a family, raising children who will do better than we have done. What hope do these men with no money, self-respect, status have, of finding a permanent partner to create a family, our most enduring human need?

This catastrophic world wide dilemma is particularly rooted in racism and Islamophobia. The marginalization of Muslims in European cities, and the effect on unemployed male Muslims, with little hope, is a formula for extremism typical of the Paris attacks. (Just as it will, at some point, I feel, occur in urban America with up to 50% unemployment of young Black males.)

The solution, obviously, is not just targeting and eliminating ISIS and Al Qaeda, but long term social changes in finding useful employment, acceptance and inclusion for minority or Muslim youth in our world cities. Of course I am not offering anything new, but it does happen here in Canada to some hopeful degree.

Thankfully, Canada has the best record anywhere of integrating Muslim and other minority youth into the fabric of the country, while not obliterating their Muslim identity. In recent polls 91% of Canadian Muslims feel Canada is moving in the right direction, while only 71% of the rest of us do. 97% are proud to be Canadians after 15 years. (94%, fresh citizens.) Muslims in Canada feel far more welcomed and accepted here than they do in UK, France, Germany and the USA. Remarkably more so! But we still have a long way to go, 60% of Muslims still fear discrimination here. (Before Paris.) Here are a couple of my slide share slides from a lecture on Islamophobia.

Just my thoughts at this terrible time in human history.

JERRY DIAKIW AND NEIL BEATTY

A Superintendent and a Principal Write to Each Other

Using a dialogue journal helped these administrators learn firsthand what they were asking their teachers to do.

In September 1989, the York Region Board of Education, just north of Toronto. Ontario, implemented a new Supervision for Growth plan for all teachers. The new plan differentiates between an administrative track for probationary teachers and teachers seeking promotion and a growth track for successful teachers with a permanent contract. The administrative track involves a formal evaluation with a teacher rating. The growth track enables principals and teachers to explore a variety of innovative processes for carrying out a two- or three-year Supervision for Growth plan. Removing the annual evaluation with a rating results in a dramatically changed relationship.

The key to the success of the growth track is the teacher's ownership of the plan – what the teacher wants to do! It allows a principal to work as a catalyst, to help a teacher clarify an area that the teacher wants to improve. By giving both the principal and the teacher opportunities to develop an innovative program, explore a new area of expertise, or conduct research, the growth track shifts the teacher/principal relationship from a model of dependence and control to one of shared collegiality that leads to excitement, challenge, and growth.

But it is not easy to tell someone how to do this when you've never done it yourself. So we – a principal (Neil Beatty) and his superintendent (Jerry Diakiw) – decided to encourage reflective practice by starting a dialogue journal. We used a small 200-page spiral binder to write back and forth to each other reflectively.

> "A professional can go along nicely for years and suddenly catch fire and in some sort of 'Buddha moment' step up into a higher level of consciousness or awareness."

On average. we used it to make responses to each other about once every two weeks The following brief excerpts illustrate the process as we used it.

A Starting Point
Superintendent: I've been thinking about a starting point for identifying a direction for growth. Donald Schon suggested starting with questions such as *What do you like most about your job? What do you do, specifically, that excites you or rewards you most?*

Principal: I'd have to say that being able to effect change is, in a broad sense, what I most enjoy about the job. I've enjoyed helping to create a vision with the staff, then, via a deliberate, yet ever-changing plan, helping to move the staff step by step, toward that vision.

As part of this process I also enjoy the creativity which I've been able to express in the achievement of our goals and objectives – I never imagined how creative one could he as a principal but I now can see that the opportunities are endless.

Superintendent: "Enjoyment of our job as a process of change" surprised me because that's what I would say too. Inherent in the way both of us do that, however, is the way we try to bring

Writing to each other about hopes and dreams, fears and frustration is not always easy. Each person risks revealing hiw own imperfections and insecurities. But this principal and superintendent were able to confront serious issues, give feedback and support to each other and expand their understanding of both roles.

bring about change. We rend not to mandate, but rather create an environment for people to "buy in," to use a cliché. Introducing a new idea and watching people get excited about it. then implementing it, rewards me. A professional can go along nicely for years and suddenly catch fire and in some sort of "Buddha moment" step up into a higher level of consciousness or awareness Somehow I see this happening for me more often now than at any time in my career. Professional reading also gives me a lot of pleasure I was virtually a nonreader of professional literature 10 years ago. Now I read voraciously.

I've got to be close to the action. I've got to be part of identifying our own emerging needs. I've got to have my own pet projects to fight for. Starting, supporting. sustaining, and creating new initiatives gives me a great deal of pleasure. But perhaps more important than creating and supporting innovations is learning to create an environment where principals and teachers feel empowered to take risks to try something new that will hook them into an elevated state of professionalism – with or without an implementation plan!

Exploring Our Roles

Principal: One of the pleasant surprises I've discovered about the principalship is that I continue to be very much a teacher. The image of my staff as my class has become increasingly strong over the years. In my first year at the school I was fairly directive, establishing routines, structures, and expectations. Once established, I could loosen up, have some fun, and begin turning control for the direction of the school back over to the students and the staff. Now, with increasing confidence in myself and my "class," I am turning over control for decision making almost entirely to the class.

As I refine my teaching skills, I find myself wanting more and more to emulate these skills demonstrated by the excellent teachers I've had the privilege of working with. I guess ultimately I'd like to run the school in the way Jean runs her kindergarten.

You mentioned you would like to teach again someday But you've never stopped teaching' The principals are your students, and your influence spreads to thousands of students in our schools...

Superintendent: I agree, we never do stop teaching even as administrators. However, the ratio of teaching time to administrative time is significant. The amount of time I spend responding to complaints, incidents, unhappy parents, disgruntled teachers, and dealing with administrative detail preoccupies my workday...

Area superintendents can be so deluged with the onslaught of budgets, trustees, new schools, projections, boundaries, and staffing that they have little time for other things. The other side of the coin is that problem solving at a fast clip, creative thinking, effective delegating, and hard work can be intoxicating, invigorating, and satisfying. However, I'd quit if that's all I did. I try to force myself into an instructional role on the premise that "by your fruits they shall know thee." I want to be perceived as an educator, not an administrator, so I keep up to date on current learning theory. I meet with as many teacher groups as possible – lead teachers, librarians, and priority representatives to demonstrate current theories and instructional strategies and to urge risk-taking and innovation.

Bristling at Each Other

Superintendent: *[In response to an entry of the principal regarding the superintendent's administrative style]* Your last entry was provocative, and I think erroneous... You are an excellent principal, but you're still a little green and don't yet know what you don't know. Only a little more time will suffice. There's a touch of over-confidence, perhaps (I can remember the taste myself in my second year as a principal). It's largely to the good, but not all good. You remind me a wee bit of the sign I saw in an office over the holidays. "Hire a teenager now, while he still knows everything."

Principal: Yes, you're right, my statements about your style and mine were provocative and arrogant. Your response this week hit me like a slap in the face. I've had so little criticism in recent years that I fear I have lost perspective. It's very interesting, however, that you noticed this cockiness because I've seen it in myself... I recently set as another personal objective to practice my listening skills and bite my tongue more often. I'd hate to be perceived as a cocky know-it-all – but I may have recognized this in myself a little too late.

After having said all this, it bothers me greatly that I can't benefit from your immediate reaction, Have I gone too far? Have I been provocative again – without recognizing it? Have I any business asking these questions and saying my opinion of what you should do? Am I simply reinforcing your perception of me as a cocky "rookie" who has much to learn?

Oh well, such are the risks one takes in being candid and thinking out loud.

Superintendent: "A slap in the face" is rather a violent action. I hope my comments didn't smart that much! I detect a wee bit of the "I think I've gone too far" syndrome in your remarks. You are unnecessarily apologetic and deferential. Please don't ever defer to me. It's a form of anti-risk-taking.

Principal: [Added later in the margin of the journal.] These were significant statements for me – opening the door to further risk-taking.

Stretched Too Thin?
Superintendent: I throw this next point out for debate and discussion, Are you overextending yourself through your endeavors in the school and the board? You don't want to miss out on anything so you keep committing yourself and your staff to ever-increasing demands. Early Reading Intervention Project, Curriculum and the Learner Initiative, Transition Years, Primary Reading, Control Theory and Quality Schools. The Math/Science Priority, and Conflict Manager program, to name just a few. You have this way of rationalizing each new initiative that you take on by describing it as a subtheme of some other protect. In the process you end up being out of the school an inordinate amount of time.

Principal: Am I overextending my-self? This question has caused me to do a good deal of reflective thinking over the past week. My answer is *NO* Well, maybe, I'm not sure. Probably. No, I don't think so... ???

Yes, I can't seem to get enough action. Everything seems to interest me. I'm not sure why I keep taking on things. Partly it's pure interest, partly to learn something new which I can bring to my school, partly to be part of something exciting at the area or regional level, partly I suppose to build my profile (although I don't like to admit it).

I try always to watch myself and try to determine if I am losing effectiveness in other areas because of a project in which I'm involved So far I don't feel like this has happened to any great extent. I think I've been able to maintain my family time by being available almost every night and weekend to help take the kids to soccer, T-ball. and music.

I don't think superintendents should put a limit on what principals take on unless they determine that there is an actual problem. If you think my school is suffering, then tell me in what ways. If you think I'm suffering, then tell me. But to establish a general rule or quota doesn't make sense I've known principals who seldom left the school but were highly inept. I've also known principals who were out a great deal, but their presence was felt throughout the school whether they were there or not – and long after they moved on to another job.

Personal Disappointments
Superintendent: I'm shocked you didn't pass the Supervisory Officer orals examination. Surprisingly, if I had to say why they didn't pass you, I'd say it was probably a feeling that "he's so young, let him mature a year to two – he's got lots of time."

I don't agree with that position, but you couldn't fail it on your lack of knowledge and experience How do you feel about it – I mean, really feel about it?

Principal: When I was told I hadn't passed, I was totally shocked I felt so good about the interview I thought there was no way I wouldn't get it. I felt that I was totally prepared, and I presented myself with confidence, with a sense of humour and passion about issues I knew well. I'm sure I wasn't cocky, but I guess I was "green" and it showed.

It was very difficult for me to chair the curriculum meeting two hours after I heard the news. It was very difficult telling my wife and kids, my secretary and staff, my friends and colleagues, all of whom had been so supportive and so hopeful for me, But I did tell as many people as I could, as soon as I could in order to get that difficulty out of the way and out of my system.

The Planning Process
Principal: [As part of an ongoing debate about the dangers of over-planning vs thriving on chaos]... To be perfectly honest, I must admit that some of my best plans were created after the fact! Perhaps at this stage in my career. it's just politically astute to espouse the importance of a carefully, collaboratively developed implementation plan for change!

Superintendent: I was intrigued by your comment about writing a comprehensive implementation plan for the Supervisory Officers exam but that you don't have one in your school! Tch! Tch! It raises questions in my mind that have always troubled me—the technico-rational world of management by objective. strategic plans, and a logical, sequential "systems" approach vs. a clear vision coupled with "chaos" emerging to order and then vision fulfillment. I've always felt beaten to death by the former (and undervalued by the latter).

Bennis' book *On Becoming a Leader,*[1] which we have been discussing, explores this issue. There has to be a happy balance between action and planning. I like to make things happen and get things done. I have a bias for action— usually with a fair degree of innovation thrown in. I've loved that part of my career more than anything—the doing, the action. "Start small, think big" and "don't overplan or overmanage" were fundamental implementation principles for me long before they became catchy phrases.

Principal: It would appear that in the past five years in this school, this whole process has been deliberately planned by me. While I like to present it to others (principals, teachers, supervisory officers, anyone who will listen) as a carefully developed, long-term plan, it was really not so. It seemed to evolve based on an intuitive sense of what should happen next. But now that I look back, I think I could make use of such a plan when I move on to another school. The hard part will be determining where in the continuum the school is and being patient enough to take one step at a time to move in the desired direction.

Reflections on the Dialogue
Principal: While I've rambled on again I feel you've helped me get focused and develop a concrete action plan. Your comments and suggested readings are causing me to think hard about my concept of leadership and the change process. At the same time that I'm trying to figure out myself, I find myself trying to figure you out!

My half-hour drive to and from school each day is often devoted to reflecting upon what you said and what I want to say in response. Never having dialogued in this manner before, I am amazed at how much the process causes me to think and sort out my thoughts

The process of getting to know a person through a dialogue journal like this continually intrigues me. Since the last entry I've debated with myself how far I could/should go with my remarks to you. While I'd like to debate on equal terms, every once in a while I'm reminded of the fact that you are my boss – you can affect my career to become too chummy in our dialogue may become awkward for either of us. Based on your last entry I feel better about erring on the side of being honest, having fun, being provocative, and enjoying the "cut and parry" of debate.

I've been wondering what you get out of this process? Does it allow you to be reflective? Do you find it time-consuming? Do you do it primarily for me or for both of us?

Superintendent: Writing in this sustained manner over the last eight months has been a revelation.

I certainly have thought more deeply and more often on what I do, how I do it, and why I do it than ever before. Personal reflective writing of this type is an intense thinking, clarifying, and learning experience. When James Thurber was asked what he thought about something, he quickly replied "How do I know what I think until I write it down?" Exactly! Many times as I began my entry, I didn't really know what I thought. I do now. I'm certainly enjoying the experience a great deal

Credibility and Empathy
Neil Beatty is now using dialogue journals with several of his teachers on the Supervision for Growth track. Because both of us experienced feelings of alarm and uncertainty in our exchange, we can empathize with the teachers as they move from a supervision model of dependence and control to one of shared collegiality. But we also felt the excitement, challenge, and growth that can occur as this happens, and we can now recommend the use of journals to others.

W Bennis, (1989), *On Becoming a Leader*, (Reading, Mass Addison-Wesley)

Jerry Diakiw is an Area Superintendent of Schools, The York Region Board of Education, Area E Administrative Office, 36 Stornoway Cres., Thornhill, Ontario L3T 3X7, Canada. Neil Beatty is Principal of Buttonville Public School. He can he reached at the above address.

Is Oman the Canada of the Middle East?

December 17, 2018. On social media it has been debated whether Oman is the Canada of the Middle East. Culturally, politically and geographically, especially on human rights, there could not be starker differences. Yet at several levels, Oman is 'kinda' like the Canada of the Middle East.

Yes, differences are obvious. Oman is a absolute monarchy in a parched desert landscape, yet there are surprising similarities. Not only are they both oil-reliant, oil-producing countries but Oman has embraced modernity and rejected the fundamentalism of its neighbours, resulting in a tolerant, multicultural, peace-loving, cohesive society.

Almost half its current population comes from immigrants from India, Bandaladesh, Pakistan and Southeast Asia. Its constitution echos Canada's Charter of Rights and Freedoms, including among others, 'freedom from discrimination of any kind... freedom of religion and gender equality.' That's not the language of most of its neighbours. These rights emerge from a unique form of the Moslem faith called Ibadi Islam.

Diplomatically Oman has a Canadian-like reputation for mediation, peacekeeping and diplomacy. Oman, like Canada, is on friendly terms with everyone. Oman is even friendly with all its mutually antagonistic neighbours, Israel, Iran and Saudi Arabia. In October 2018, Prime Minister Benjamin Netanyahu met Sultan Qaboos bin Said al Said in Muscat. Shortly after, on October 27, 2018, Oman recognized Israel as a country. Oman also facilitated secret negotiations with Iran that lead to breakthrough agreement to denuclearize Iran.

On a recent backpacking trip the breadth of Oman, which once took three weeks by camel, I travelled on modern superhighways from the subtropical frankincense-sodden city of Salalah along the Yemen border, to the wild and desiccated Musandam Governate overlooking the strategic Straits of Hormuz across from Iran. I was surprised at the beauty, modern services and facilities of this idyllic land of frankincense, myrrh and gold, and Bedouin silversmiths. Oman was the home of Sinbad the Sailor, and the playground of the Queen of Sheba.

I marvelled at the paradox of this amazing country. A modern, successful, multicultural nation led by a benevolent despot, yet who rules with an iron hand. While travelling there last year, Oman celebrated its National Day of Independence, 47 years after a bloodless coup on November 15, 1970. The current Sultan Qaboos took over and banished his father to Delhi, India.

Before Sultan Qaboos assumed power, Oman was one of the poorest countries in the world. Slavery was still legal! There were only two primary schools and no secondary schools in all of Oman. Now Oman boasts a highly educated population, with world class universities and a modern medical system. Omanis experience a very high standard of living, longevity and very low crime rates. They pay no income tax! Women comprise 50% of university students, and 50% of practising engineers. While they have not yet obtained in practise the equity for women enshrined in their constitution, nor have we.

There are two reasons for Oman's success – the benevolent nature of Sultan Qaboos and the inclusive form of Ibadi Islam, which is practised by over 80% of Omanis. Sultan Qaboos bin Said al-Said, the Arab world's longest reigning monarch, is an unabashed Anglophile, a graduate of both Oxford University and the Sandhurst Military Academy. He is a highly cultured, composer who plays the organ and the lute, and manages his own symphony orchestra.

Still, Sultan Qaboos tolerates no dissent. Human rights abuses are still prevalent. There is no freedom of press. "Human rights... there is little respect for core civil and political rights such as freedom of expression, assembly and association." While homosexuality is illegal, Sultan Qaboos is widely reported as gay in the international press.

The second reason for Oman's modernity and success is the historic dominance of Ibadi Islam which honours the diversity of non-Muslims of all faiths. Ibadi Islam has a belief in equality between men and women. Oman has a long history of outreach. For four centuries Oman ruled over part of Africa, including Zanzibar and parts of Somalia.

As one blogger noted, "Yes, the Omani people are very much like the 'Canadians' of the Middle East. They are humble and kind and helpful.

On the dark side, it is *very* unlike Canada in the area of human rights. Their human rights violations are shocking and intolerable for a modern nation. Their treatment of immigrants, in particular domestic workers upon whom they so heavily rely, are surprisingly barbaric in some instances. On the bright side, like Canada, this progressive country has quietly and modestly built a modern, internationally-respected, officially tolerant, multicultural nation with a high standard of living, half of whom are immigrants. Sound familiar?

Getting Old: The Dark Side & The Bright Side
Aging Teachers: The Loss of Achievement Highs

Part 1. The Dark Side

My death is imminent. I have now passed the life expectancy for men in Canada of 80.2 years. (68.5 world wide for men, with the highest for Swiss men of 81.2 and lowest for men in Sierra Leona of 50.4) I am a statistic. I have a 1% chance of reaching 90. No matter how you shake it, the bottom line is my days are numbered… literally.

The simple story is, so what? I have lived past most. I can't imagine a more privileged life; a rich academic life, a rewarding and fulfilling teaching career, a happy marriage, (57 years of semi-bliss), two talented successful daughters who have married well, a granddaughter – a beacon of light. I have lived a life dominated by exciting world travel, enriched family life, bursts of creativity and innovation, and decades of lifelong learning and discovery. There is nothing left on my bucket list. If it is over today, I have no regrets. As the Inuit metaphor dictates, I could happily walk out on an ice flow with a smile on my face. There is no wailing for one more day, or one more year. Statistically it could all end in one day, or one year, or, 20 more years till 100!

Every day is living in each 'now' moment, one 'now' moment after another. As Maggie Smith (among others) said in the movie *The Most Excellent Marigold Hotel*, "I don't buy green bananas anymore". But having said all that I do not deny that being over 80 causes a lot of reflection on what happens to your mind and body as you age, and why.

Reactions to aging

Each person reacts differently, of course. Some fear death, some deny it and others can't stop talking about it. My nephew, Peter Diakiw, works as an eldercare worker in Seniors' Homes. He witnesses many different reactions to imminent death. He wrote: "I've met a few men who decide to isolate themselves as they wait to die. I've also met quite a few who have to live their last years alone. I also have experienced the absolute terror that getting near to the end causes some. I've also cared for the opposite. These people are surrounded by people who love and respect them. They still light up a room just by their presence."

Lillian Rubin, author, sociologist, and psychotherapist in her 80s, opens her book, *60 on Up: The Truth About Aging in America* with the declarative statement most of us can relate to, "Getting old sucks. It always has, it always will."

Writing about the heroism of old age, 87 year old Mary C. Morrison in her book *Life Beyond 85 Years*, through interviewing 150 seniors documents the dissipation of one's body and mind. "Old age is not for the fainthearted". One interviewee stated it simply, old age is "pure hell."

On the other hand as Maurice Chevalier quipped, "Old age ain't so bad when you consider the alternative."

Aging and physical decline

The most obvious sign of aging is growing physical disability. One way to look at the quality of life in old age is calculating how many healthy years are left, not just life expectancy. It is called, health-adjusted life expectancy (HALE). Currently, health-adjusted life expectancy at birth in Canada is 69 years for men and 71 for women. The average Canadian can therefore expect to live roughly 10.5 years with some level of disability. Failing health is a fact of aging.

For decades my mantra has been, "age is about attitude not chronology". But it is hard to maintain a youthful attitude if you can't get out of bed, or are losing your eyesight or are becoming incontinent. There comes a time when, as John Mortimer said, "There is no pleasure worth forgoing just for an extra three years in the geriatric ward". Or, as Woody Allen said, "You can live to be a hundred if you give up all the things that make you want to live to be a hundred". I'd rather follow Mark Twain's adage, "Age is an issue of mind over matter. If you don't mind, it doesn't matter".

Causes and effects of psychological issues: depression, loneliness and social isolation

But failing health can often be directly attributed to psychological and psycho-social issues, not just normal physical aging. While I accept my physical decline and the imminence of my demise, I have noted dramatic psychological changes getting to my ripe old age of 82. Psychological heath is critical to physical health in the elderly. "Depression, social isolation, loneliness are closely correlated to declining physical health. There is an increased risk of mortality with major depressive disorders". (Bruce, 1994) "Depressive disorders may also be associated with a reduction in cognitive functions according to other studies". (Speck et al, 1995)

Effects of Role Changes

After I retired as a school superintendent in 1993, I returned to school full time to complete a doctorate, the first item on my bucket list. Soon after, I began teaching courses on diversity at York University. I taught for another 20 years there till I was 78. While I changed roles from school administrator to student, then to university teacher, I felt no change in the challenge, rewards, or sense of satisfaction of my work. But when I stopped teaching and fully retired, the floor fell out beneath me. Suddenly I felt this overwhelming sense of the loss of 'presence', not just the invisibility that comes with old age, but of power, of status, of identity. Presence, as in: here, noticed, listened to, looked at, impacted by, changed by, interested in, appreciated, respected, better for… but NOT invisible! A chronic complaint of the elderly is their invisibility. We are routinely talked over, ignored, pushed aside, psychologically, even physically. After fully retiring at 78, I abruptly lost the identity of who I thought I was and how I thought I was perceived.

In one sense it is all tied up with change in roles. In social aging theory, role loss is one common component. Role theorists argue that having social power and prestige, and feeling in control of one's life is associated with good health and positive attitudes through the many roles we perform. As we retire, we start losing our natural and fulfilling roles as parents, employees, and spouses. Teaching is undoubtedly one of the most rewarding and fulfilling professions. It is not just the feeling of affecting young lives in positive ways, but teachers by nature are life long learners. As well, teaching is the gift that keeps on giving. Most of us are rewarded regularly through complimentary notes, emails, and accidental meetings in the neighbourhood.

But when coupled with the inevitable shrinking list of social interactions with friends and former colleagues, retirement results in feelings of loss of control over one's life. One's health is directly related. Research shows "that perceived social isolation [assuming that socially isolated people have few roles] is associated with a variety of altered physiological functions, such as blood pressure regulation... and immune reactions."

Certainly my identity as a father and spouse is one important role, but being a parent does not define one to the wider community. Nor are my parenting skills required any longer. My children are grown up, engaged in busy careers and do not need their parents any longer. A parental role is diminished, or sometimes, over. When I fully retired from teaching at 78, however, I felt an immediate loss of feelings of contribution and of being appreciated. I missed the satisfaction of solving problems, of interacting with students, generating innovative new ideas, constantly learning new things. I missed the collegial relationships of my career choice. I missed the feeling that I knew what I was doing was important. A career can be so deeply rewarding that nothing outweighs that loss. "You may walk all day and do sudokus all night once retired, but still miss the social and intellectual stimulation of the workplace," one retiree said.

My self-esteem plummeted.

Loss of 'Achievement Identity'

For many teachers, our work, our career role defines who we are. My identity is defined by my role as an educator. It is especially difficult to surrender our career's rewarding daily achievements. The loss of our 'achievement identity' is a health risk. It is accompanied by a loss of self-esteem. A UK Institute of Economic Affairs report concluded that 40% of retirees suffer clinical depression and 6 out 10 face declining health issues. Bruce Pitt in one study of aging reported about half of people 80 and over in the UK live alone, that dementia occurs in 20% of those over 80 and suicide rates peak in old age (for women in their late 60s, men around 80). So there are many psychological issues that are unique to the aged.

The loss of self-esteem, is one of the main causes of depression. It is a health risk.

Causes and Effects of the Loss of Self-esteem in Aging

The graph below shows how self-esteem evolves over a life span; from the loss of self-esteem in the teen years to a peak in 60s, and then a dramatic fall late in life. "Self-esteem is related to better health, less criminal behaviour, lower levels of depression and, overall, greater success in life," noted Ulrich Orth, PhD, the study's lead author. I see myself statistically at that 80 year old axis. I am aware that my 'achievement highs' are in the past, not in the future. My feelings of usefulness fade. My self-esteem suffered.

Figure 1. Mean level of self-esteem as a function of developmental period, separately for the total sample, males and females. Also plotted are year-by-year means, separately for males (open triangles) and females (open circles).

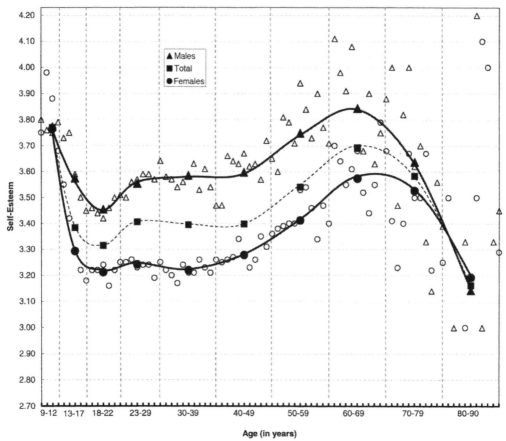

After completing the Rosenberg test of self-esteem used in many of these studies, I still do have above average self-esteem. I am not depressed (yet) but I must say, I feel the emotions that would pull one into a depressive abyss.

Common advice to the elderly is to stay connected, maintain happy relationships, engage with the community by volunteering. Certainly these are critical and convincing ways to ward of the dangers of psychological decline, loss of self esteem, or even depression, but the achievement high of a cardiac surgeon performing a heart transplant is not equal to his volunteer role stacking cans at a food bank in retirement. The achievement high of a kindergarten teacher, teaching one child for a school year does not equal volunteering at a local hospital for a year directing patients to their appointments. Kali H. Trzesniewski, PhD, of the University of Western Ontario, wrote however that "...being in a happy relationship does not protect a person against the decline in self-esteem that typically occurs in old age." Nor does being in a happy 'volunteer' situation, compensate for one's career achievement highs.

As can be noted in the graph, by the little circles and triangles, there are outliers at every age with individuals scoring way higher in self esteem (and lower). What has transpired in the lives of those high esteem individuals in old age? Why do I still have a high level of self esteem? Tune in to Part 2, The Bright Side. (It will explore Jungian theory about aging, Maslow's models of aging and other ideas emanating from Joseph Campbell's writing about the *Journey of the Hero*.)

Part 2. The Bright Side

Me! Lucky Me

How glorious it is to wake every day and look out of my bedroom window at a wide expanse of sky hanging over the lush greenness of the Rouge Valley and stillness of Walden Pond.

It is a gift to feel the rush of pleasure at the new morning light, the flight of a hawk, a thunderous cloud, another sunset.

How privileged to live and grow old in a country with such remarkable freedoms and enriching diversity, a nation comprised of all nations, with a social safety net of free medical care and a guaranteed income in old age.

The heart fills as I watch my children and grandchild blossom and surpass my finest moments and achieve an independence, both sad and exhilarating. It is a thrill to regularly feel the pull of the cosmic connections across time that I am fittingly a part of. To acknowledge anew that I was here in the beginning and will always be a part of this expanding universe. It is satisfying at times to feel this powerful sense of being one with the universe. These feelings do not go away with old age, they intensify and grow.

While I explored the Dark Side of Aging in Part 1, here I will examine the Bright Side. There are many of us who by the luck of birth are privileged to attain old age, whether by our country of birth, our level of schooling, our genes, and/or our personality type. There are many other factors that contribute to a happy, fulfilling, long life that we can do something about, including fitness and diet, but far more. It is encouraging to know there are factors that contribute to a long life, such as low self esteem or that a pessimistic demeanour can be unlearned.

It is inspiring to reflect on how some of the great minds who have envisioned a wise, meaningful and productive later life. The insight of Carl Jung, Erik Erikson, Joseph Campbell and Abraham Maslow challenge us to think about old age at a more spiritual level. Between 1900 and 2000, average life expectancy increased by nearly 30 years in Canada. What are we going to do with all those extra 30 years?

1. Geography and Nationality

Oh how lucky I am. How lucky we are! You were blessed if, by the accident of birth, you were born in the developed world, in the norther hemisphere, or in Canada. If you were so lucky, you have added years to your life expectancy. About half of the top twenty countries with the longest life expectancy are in Europe and another half in Asia (Japan, Singapore, S. Korea). Japan ranks number one with a combined life expectancy of 83.7, and in Canada, 82.2 (80.2 for men, 84.1 for women). The Health Adjusted Life Expectancy (years without disability) in Japan is 74.9 years and in Canada 72.3 years. Of course, women outlive men without exception worldwide.

While Canada's life expectancy ranks among the top 10 in the world, regional figures reveal important differences within the country. Regions of Canada with the lowest life expectancy have some of the highest rates of smoking, obesity, and heavy drinking, high long-term unemployment rates, lower levels of education, small immigrant populations, relatively large Aboriginal populations, and are situated in rural/remote locations. The urban areas of Canada have the longest life expectancies, notably, Toronto, Montreal and Vancouver.

2. Socio-economic factors

A. Income

How much you earn is a significant indicator of longevity. In the United States for example, there is a is 15 year longevity gap between the highest income earners and the lowest, which is about the same gap between the life expectancy in the United states and Sudan. For women, there is a 10-year difference between the rich and the poor, about the same difference in life expectancy between smokers and non smokers.

http://news.harvard.edu/gazette/story/2016/04/for-life-expectancy-money-matters/

The development of this trend is informative when looked at historically. Economists at the Brookings Institution found that between the top 10 percent of earners and the bottom 10 percent, there was a six-year difference in life expectancy for men born in 1920. That difference doubled to 14 years for those born in 1950. For women, the gap grew to 13 years for those born in 1950, from 4.7 years in 1920.

Sadly one can assume that for higher income earners born in 1970, 80, or 90 that same trend line will progress even more. Longevity for high income earners will continue to rise and at a faster rate than the lowest income earners. Researchers were surprised to find that those trends never plateaued.

https://www.nytimes.com/2016/02/13/health/disparity-in-life-spans-of-the-rich-and-the-poor-is-growing.html

B. Education

Education Researchers at the University of Colorado Denver, New York University, and the University of North Carolina at Chapel Hill estimates the number of deaths that can be linked to differences in education, and finds that variation in the risk of death across education levels has widened considerably.

http://steinhardt.nyu.edu/site/ataglance/2015/07/education-and-mortality-study-finds-less-education-reduces-life-expectancy.html

Lacking at least a high school education has been shown to be as deadly as being a current, rather than former, smoker. Studies show that a higher level of education is a strong predictor of longevity linked many factors, such higher income and healthier behaviours, and improved social and psychological well being. "Broadly, life expectancy is increasing, but those with more education are reaping most of the benefits," Virginia Chang said. By one study, college graduates can expect to live 13 years longer than a high school drop out. Post grads live even longer. The more education you have the longer is your life expectancy.

3. Psychosocial factors

A. Personality types

One of the ways researchers look at longevity is by personality type. There are dozens of studies of centenarians in several countries as well as the highly documented longevity study following a group of couples for over seven decades. Researchers believe that there are five core personality traits: extraversion, agreeableness, conscientiousness, neuroticism and openness. These five traits have emerged to describe the essential traits that serve as the building blocks of personality.

In *The Longevity Project*, one of the largest studies if its kind that spanned eight decades, Stanford researchers Howard S. Friedman and Leslie R. Martin found that conscientiousness beat out all other personality type when it comes to life expectancy. "The qualities of a prudent, persistent, well-organized person, like a scientist-professor – somewhat obsessive and not at all carefree" are the qualities that help lead to a long life." They found two traits to be predictive of longevity high conscientiousness and low neuroticism. The personality type 'conscientiousness' exceeded all other personality types. Conscientiousness includes, high levels of thoughtfulness, with good impulse control and goal-directed behaviours. Highly conscientious personalities tend to be organized and mindful of details. Conscientious people are efficient and organized as opposed to easy-going and disorderly. Conscientious people generally make healthier choices, the food they eat, careers they choose, their life partner choice, whether they smoke, follow doctors' orders, even whether to drive too fast.

As an example, a 2007 study, followed 1,253 men and women from California between 1930 and 2000, found that people who were conscientious as children and as adults lived longer than their peers who were not conscientious during either phase of their lives.

Another dominant personality type associated with longevity is low ratings on neuroticism. Neuroticism is a trait characterized by sadness, moodiness, and emotional instability. Individuals who are high in this trait tend to experience mood swings, anxiety, irritability and sadness. Those low in this trait tend to be more stable and emotionally resilient. They live longer.

Centenarians also tended to show high levels of extroversion. Extroversion is characterized by sociability, talkativeness, assertiveness and excitability.

A recent study of 243 people between the ages of 95 and 100 discovered that all of them were not only more conscientious than the average person, but were more optimistic and extroverted, were emotionally open, talkative sharing, and didn't 'bottle' things. They tended to laugh frequently.

B. Optimism

Lionel Tiger (1979) argued in his book *Optimism: The Biology of Hope* that optimism is 'one of our most defining and adaptive characteristics as humans'.

Researchers differ on how common optimism is as a prevailing attitude in the general population. Suzanne Segerstrom claims 80% of people are classified as optimistic, while Martin Seligman claims 60% of people are 'somewhat optimistic'. Optimism has been highlighted as being an important evolutionary part of survival. 'Optimism is correlated with many positive life outcomes including increased life expectancy, general health, better mental health, increased success in sports and work, greater recovery rates from heart operations and better coping strategies when faced with adversity.' Optimism is more what we do, than what we are, and thereby can be learned.

A couple of samples of dozens of studies illustrate the point. The first American study evaluated 839 people in the early 1960s. Thirty years later. when reexamined, optimism was linked to longevity. 'For every 10-point increase in pessimism on the optimism–pessimism test, the mortality rate rose 19%'. Another study from Holland evaluated 941 men and women between the ages of 65 and 85. People who demonstrated dispositional optimism at the start of the study, over a 9 year period, enjoyed a 45% lower risk of death.

Optimism can be learned. 'Learned optimism' was promoted by Martin Seligman and published in his book, *Learned Optimism*. He encouraged pessimists to think about their reactions to adversity in a new way, hence learn to be optimists.

'The resulting optimism – one that grew from pessimism – is a learned optimism'. He encourage optimists to examine failure: "What happened was an unlucky situation (not personal), and really just a setback (not permanent) for this one, of many, goals (not pervasive)".

Finally, Becca Levy at Yale, a pioneer and leading researcher in this area, found that older adults who held more optimistic age stereotypes lived 7.5 years longer than their peers who held negative age-related stereotypes.

C. Self Esteem

http://californiacounselinggroup.com/self-esteem-reflects-aging-process-and-longevity/

The MacArthur Foundation has recently divulged the results of a study that was conducted on the relationship between longevity, aging and self-esteem. It demonstrated the rapid fall in self-esteem after the age of 65. (see chart) Probably more than any other factor that causes depression and the slide into senility. This study was conducted on several thousands of people over the age of 50 years. It was discovered that self-esteem played the most important role in determining a person's lifespan and the quality of their life as well.

People who suffer from low self-esteem and think poorly of themselves tend to increase their chances of developing a number of illnesses. It has been discovered that their chances of death also increases threefold as well. It is for these very reasons that it is vitally important to look at the positive side of things in life.

How Can Self-Esteem Be Boosted? Seeing the vital role that self-esteem plays in boosting longevity and slowing down aging, you must do everything you can to boost it. Finding meaning, feeling a sense of worth, or doing something meaningful are essential to self esteem. I explore a number of programs that achieve this in my final section, Making Aging Positive.

D. Mindfulness

There are some findings to suggest that being mindful can actually have effects on lifespan. One such study looked at people attending a three-month stay at a meditation retreat and found that after the three months the meditators had on average about 30% more activity of the enzyme telomerase than the controls did, which is related to aging. The findings are very preliminary, but they suggest that the mind does have influence on the body.

E. Religion

https://www.psychologytoday.com/blog/the-human-beast/201302/do-religious-people-really-live-longer

The relationship between longevity and religion is a confusing one. There are dozens of highly religious countries in Africa and Asia that have life expectancy below 60, yet the two countries with the longest life expectancies, Sweden and Japan, are both highly secular countries, and have life expectancies that are the longest in the world. There is considerable research in the USA that active involvement with your church and faith can add years to your life. Some research, however, points out that when you separate out the faith component from the social component and compare church social life with life in a social club, the longevity benefits are equal, again affirming that social interactions are critical to longevity.

F. Social life

Being social is critical. This as well as diet and exercise are widely known as pillars of aging. Having a strong social group is associated with a longer life. Women tend to have stronger social networks, and that may be part of the reason women tend to live longer than men. Men in North America tend to scale back on their friendships as they age and become less social, while men in Mediterranean countries, for example, have a cultural tradition of elderly men gathering daily at clubs and coffee houses.

G. Relationship to Nature

Humans and nature, humans are nature, inseparable. Does it bear on longevity? One meta analysis shows that contact with nature can indeed be beneficial, leading to improvements in mood, cognition, and health... 'Those who are more connected to nature tended to experience more positive affect, vitality, and life satisfaction compared to those less connected to nature'.

Biophilia is a term that asserts that humans have an inherent inclination to affiliate with Nature. It implies an affection for plants and other living things.

Early hospitals in Europe were established in monastic communities where garden was considered an essential part of the healing process. Contact with nature has proven to have psychological benefits by reducing stress, and having a positive effect on mental restoration, as well as having direct physical health benefits, and not surprisingly, increased longevity.

Even viewing natural landscapes provides psychological and health benefits, including a reduction in stress. Having a hospital window with a view has been shown to improve healing, reflected in both the level of pain medication and the speed of recovery after surgery. One study showed that individuals who merely looked at a peaceful forest setting for 20 minutes experienced an average drop of 13.4% in salivary cortisol, a marker for stress. Subjects also benefitted from a lower pulse rate and blood pressure

All natural environments – forests, oceans, mountains – teem with negative ions that energize the body on a cellular level. Negative ions boost the flow of oxygen to the brain, increase alertness, and decrease lethargy. As well, walking in nature has been proven to increase white blood cells and lower your heart rate and blood pressure. The Japanese have capitalized on those benefits and even have a name for it, *shinrin roku,* or forest bathing. It is understood by all that shinrin roku has positive health benefits.

H. Physical fitness

No factor is more clearly understood to improve health and longevity than is physical fitness. Many studies have consistently shown that higher levels of physical activity result in decreased variety of coronary heart diseases, hypertension, colon cancer, non-insulin-dependent diabetes mellitus, and, even, breast cancer, as well as osteoporosis. We also would expect physical activity to delay mortality and enhance longevity. These studies prove that physical activity is effective in postponing mortality and enhancing longevity.

The surprising news however is how little physical activity is necessary to radically lengthen your expected life expectancy. The *New York Times* reported on the largest study ever carried out on fitness that proves even modest amounts of exercise can substantially reduce a person's chance of dying of heart disease, cancer or other causes. "The biggest health gain, surprisingly, came from just getting out of the most sedentary category, rather than seeking the fitness achieved by dedicated athletes".

The study found that people who engaged in leisure-time physical activity had life expectancy gains of as much as 4.5 years.

I. Diet

Eat your veggies. Enough said!

Part 3. Aging

Old Age. It's All About Transcendence... Gerotranscendence

"The adventure of ageing is nothing less than the opportunity to transcend the self which has lived its life up to now, and hence to transcend the decrepitude and death of that self. At its simplest that grand word 'transcendence' is about being totally at ease with ourselves, and hence at ease with others. Freed from self preoccupations and anxieties we can wholeheartedly serve others." Ken Jones Zen.

It's the afternoon. Old age. The afternoon of my life.

Carl Jung argued that, "The afternoon of life is just as full of meaning as the morning; only, its meaning and purpose are different... each of us has the opportunity to make the process of aging a positive and life-enhancing experience". (Yah! Good luck with that! Easier said than done.)

Afternoon is the culminating adventure of my life. All my earlier years have just been the preparation for this. As an adventure it suggests that it contains all the uncertainty, surprises, pain, delights and disappointments that adventures incur. It is ultimately exhilarating. (Maybe.)

In old age Jung felt that: "an ever-deepening self-awareness seems to me as probably essential for the continuation of a truly meaningful life in the aging, however uncomfortable this self-knowledge may be." It is a time for 'individuation', a term Jung used to reflect a process that takes place in the second half of life, 'by bringing the personal and collective unconscious into conscious', a process of integrating one's personality, a journey of self-exploration and inner discovery. It is felt to have a holistic healing effect, mentally and physically.

"Besides achieving physical and mental health, people who have advanced towards individuation, they tend to become harmonious, mature, responsible, they promote freedom and justice and have a good understanding about the workings of human nature and the universe". The key he argues, is to turn inward during the second half of life. This process of looking inward can open us to new ways of thinking about ourselves, our identities and the past.

Our old age is evolutionary, Jung argued. It is an essential part of the human condition. "A human being would certainly not grow to be 70 or 80 years old if this longevity had no meaning for the species to which he belongs. The afternoon of human life must also have a significance of its own and cannot be merely a pitiful appendage to life's morning."

There! It is said! We have the obligation as humans to make that part of our life significant and meaningful.

As he said, "An ever-deepening self-awareness seems to me as probably essential for the continuation of a truly meaningful life in any age, no matter how uncomfortable this self-knowledge may be".

For him, the aging process was not just as a passive observer to inevitable physical and mental decline and irrelevancy but rather a 'search for what is essential, an opportunity to redefine our self to achieve a new understanding regarding fundamental existential questions about life'.

Old age is a time, if truly desired, he urged, to find meaning and purpose through attaining universal wholeness and achieving wisdom.

Elusive as that is, I know I possess vestiges of wisdom, just from surviving 80 years, but not the kind he infers, I fret. "Hey Jer, you old fart! What are you up today?", a friend asks. "Shut up Jack, I'm working on my wisdom today."

Believe me, it is not an incremental steady upward process to this idyllic Jungian state of sublime peace along with deliberations of the 'fundamental existential questions about life'. It fluctuates wildly, in Eriksons' words, "from despair to integrity".

Both Abraham Maslow and the Erikson's (Erik and Joan) modified their models of psychosocial development when they actually lived into old age, and each added another stage to accommodate their lived experience. Their previous end stages were not deemed complete enough to describe the fullness of life experience. This later stage has come to be known as 'gerotranscendence', coined by Lars Tornstam but adopted by both Maslow and Joan Erikson. A stage at which an elder person is peacefully ready to move on to the next stage of existence.

Originally in Eriksons' model, Old Age, the last eighth – beginning at age 65 and ending with death is a stage where the struggle for integrity versus despair takes place.

It is a time of reflection on one's life in the midst of impending death. The positive resolution, integrity, is produced as a result of feelings of satisfaction and acceptance of one's life. But Joan Erikson, his Canadian wife and co-developer, captures it well in their ninth stage when she describes one's 80s and 90s as a time where the despair prevalent in stage eight is magnified by the experience of one's rapid deteriorating body and mind, which results in a lowering of self-esteem and confidence. "To face down despair with faith and appropriate humility," she wrote, "is perhaps the wisest. At this stage despair dominates not only by one's deteriorating decline, but along with the loss of friends and loved ones and especially the loss of autonomy and independence. As noted, self esteem plummets after 65 and hits rock bottom in your 80s. Depression is a concomitant condition of this loss. For many in their late 80s and up, decision making is removed by both family and care-workers. By one review, 49% of the elderly suffer depression and for those living in long term care setting, the figure reaches to 90%!

And yet, the Eriksons, and Lars Tornstam in their interviews with dozens of the elderly found those who overcame the despair and achieved a state of gerotrancendance.

At 80, I feel am still in Eriksons' 8th stage, not yet the 9th. Despite periods of dealing with bladder cancer, continuing deterioration of kidney functioning from polycystic kidney disease and recently heart interventions resulting in a cardiac ablation, they do not constitute a disability in any way. I do not view these constant physiological interruptions as anything more annoying than having a cold. They simply interfere with travel plans but do not end travel plans. They are minor annoyances that do not impact my sense of self or my belief in my ability to forge ahead.

But it is still, according to Erikson, "... a time when many engage in a life review to consider the worth of their experiences. Out of this life review the elder person arrives at either a sense of integrity that may lead to wisdom or to despair."

As I review my life, I reflect on what is it that sustains me in my old age, brings me satisfaction and a sense of integrity? Memories. I have been touched by thousands of students over my 56 teaching years, and touched by hundreds of acquaintances, here in Canada, and everyday citizens in the over 100 countries I have travelled in. I have been, and am, loved by perhaps a dozen family and friends. I have been touched by my students and friends humour, by their intelligence, by their kindnesses, by their trials and successes, by their gratitude, even genius. I have learned from them, been inspired by them, and moved by them. The accumulated agglomeration of these memories sustains me in my senility. I have in fact been shaped by all these interactions.

The beauty of all this, is the knowledge that I too have touched thousands through my teaching. Like all teachers, I know I have informed them, inspired some through my teaching or through example, or from my travels and life experiences. I know this because they tell me, whether through social media, email or social events and every day interactions.

What a gift it is to be touched and moved by so many and yet know I have touched and moved many in return. 'To touch a child is a gift of teaching'.

But of course nothing is more life-sustaining than the love of family and life long friends, that happy dozen who are there for you in your darkest moments and in all your many celebrations of life. And it is true that despite the many rewarding and rich friendships one has accumulated over a lifetime, the family rises to another level. It was Margaret Mead who said, "the only truly significant relationships one has in one's life time is with one's family". Significant may not always be positive, but for most of us that chain of familial relationships from grandmother and grandfather, to mother and father, to son and daughter, to grandchild is a powerful genetic link that binds us to the human family. There is no love that supersedes the power of that chain. One joy of old age is to holistically encompass that chain by looking back through time and forward to the future and see the universal links that tie one's grandparents to one's great grandchildren, to have known them all.

It is this reflection back in time to ancestry, family and friends that is a characteristic of old age as one makes meaning of one's life and begins to feel the cosmic connections that even go deeper.

It is upon reflecting on this sweep of my life's human contacts that I am reminded and relive 'peak experiences'. Like Erikson, Maslow also added another stage to his model of self actualization. He called it self-trancendance. As he stated, "At the level of self-actualization, the individual works to actualize the individual's own potential (whereas) at the level of transcendence, the individual's own needs are put aside, to a great extent, in favour of service to others".

I realize now, that after I retired as a school administrator I returned to teaching at university. My last twenty years of teaching till the age of 78 were dominated by the feeling that my teaching about social justice issues in schools and societies was important work and, whether received as such or not, was powerfully felt by me as a payback service to others. It was a way of focusing on some higher goal outside myself. Some examples Maslow gives for transcendence include 'altruism or spiritual awakening or liberation from egocentricity'.

As he wrote: "Transcendence refers to the very highest and most inclusive or holistic levels of human consciousness, behaving and relating, as ends rather than means, to oneself, to significant others, to human beings in general, to other species, to nature, and to the cosmos." (*The Farther Reaches of Human Nature*, New York, 1971, p. 269.)

Self-trancenders may have what he called peak experiences, in which they transcend personal concerns. "In such mystical, aesthetic, or emotional states one feels intense joy, peace, well-being, and an awareness of ultimate truth and the unity of all things." And yes, I do feel each and every one of these at some time.

Writing from a Jungian perspective, Tornstam describes a stage he calls 'gerotrancendence' a stage characterized by a natural evolution towards full maturation and wisdom. He believes that old age challenges us to take the opportunity to step through the door to a radically different way of seeing the world. Individuals he has found at this stage are less self-occupied and more selective in their social activities, they are less interested in material things and more inclined to mindful meditation. A period of life sensing "...an increased feeling of affinity with past generations." And like Jung's striving for wholeness, Tornstam posits that in this stage, "There is also often a feeling of cosmic communion with the spirit of the universe and a redefinition of time, space, life and death." If not thinking your way to this redefinition, at least feeling it, becoming one with it.

Contrary to much literature on aging, especially in America, where proponents almost command the elderly to: "Stay connected, maintain friendships, find new friends, join clubs, get involved, volunteer, square dance... or you die!"

Acceptance of Dr. Tornstam's work seems to vary by country. The American emphasis on activity – 'The vow that we're not going to retreat to a rocking chair on the porch' – can make it hard to listen to someone arguing that a rocking chair, and the contemplation and rest that accompany it, might provide a fine way to age. The University of Kansas gerontologist, David Ekerdt, coined the term "the busy ethic" to characterize the American view of aging.

Tornstam's research elders expressed a period of life, sensing as "... an increased feeling of affinity with past generations." I light up reading that and realize how often I demur and marvel across the generations, even the aeons. For the first time in my life I explored my family tree, had research conducted in the Ukraine on my behalf, and headed off at 80 to Ukraine for the first time to visit my parents' ancestral village and to track down as many cousins as I could find. We had lost all contact with Ukrainian relatives since 1945!

And like Jung's striving for wholeness, Tornstam also posits that in this stage, "There is also often a feeling of cosmic communion with the spirit of the universe and a redefinition of time, space, life and death." In the past my head would swim when I read language like that, even with many experiences living and studying in Zen Buddhist monasteries, at ashrams on the Ganges, or my resident visits to the Trappist monastery at Oka, even as an atheist. Now I feel this in my core. If not thinking my way to this redefinition, at least feeling it, becoming one with it. At least engaged in this process of self discovery. It is a search for wisdom and wholeness at a stage in life called gerotrancendance.

Tornstam argues if a person doesn't reach for wisdom, wholeness or gerotranscendence, and this new call for inner growth, there is a tendency to experience depression, despair, fear of death and regret.

Maybe that is what Jung understood when he urged us to use the later part of our lives to become more whole by discovering who we are and wisely sharing it with others.

Yes, it is the afternoon of my life. It is a fight to the death to confront the loss of friends, self esteem, depression, despair, but I am experiencing new levels of insights, moments of joy and ecstasy, deeper emotional connections, peace... and I am loving it.

Architecture as Symbols of Society's Changing Values and Power

Jerry Diakiw

I wrote a piece about architecture and cultural values on the bus from Bucharest to Sofia last month that got lost with my iPad upon arrival in Sofia at midnight. While I have recovered everything else, it got lost. I will try to recreate what I thought at the time.

While I am not a scholar of architecture and its cultural significance, I notice as I travel from continent to continent, the remarkable new emerging sources of power that result in new forms of architecture that deviate from the past and differ from continent to continent.

Gas stations! Mobile phone stores! Jewelry palaces! Evangelical churches! Why some places, and not others? What does it mean?

Of course, cathedrals, castles, temples, palaces, synagogues and monasteries for centuries have been the cornerstone of the works of master architects and still today these ancient edifices are the most dominant tourist attraction in major cities world wide.

In Ukraine, still a highly religious population, classic domed churches of every size scatter across the landscape like fall leaves. They are everywhere. In my ancestral village of Lopushna with about 100 people, the church built in 1909, where both my parents were baptized, dramatically stands on a rise above the row of simple centuries old peasant homes. There is nothing of note architecturally for miles in any direction.

Despite the remarkably high rate of church attendance, I never saw a single new church anywhere in Ukraine. I did see lots of flashy new architectural structures and striking, even daring, new store designs. It was surprising to me to see where new power lies. Really surprising!

It is obvious that there is a natural correlation between power, money and architectural monuments. Whether looking in awe at the pyramids, the Taj Mahal, palaces, castles, and cathedrals, the best architects were hired by the rich and powerful.

But these historic examples are in many ways symbols of the distant past. In more recent history, architects have found new sources of power. Since the days of castle building, two styles that come to mind are banks and court houses. Whether in the major capitals, like the Supreme Court in Washington, or in every small town in Ontario, courts are gems of architectural magnificence. For example here in Kingston.

The second area where talented architects have been hired in the 20th century are banks. Early banks a hundred years ago, too, replicated Greek and Roman buildings on the outside, and often on the inside they replicated church interiors.

And certainly that tradition carries on today as our city skylines are dominated by financial powerhouses. In Toronto, of course, with its trio of skyscrapers – the Scotiabank, the Toronto-Dominion Centre, and the Royal Bank Building.

But where do talented architects and designers find opportunities to create new masterpieces today? Travelling across India for example, I found two surprising and striking a new temples of power. In Kerala in southern India, while I saw no new Hindu temples under construction, I did see some modern avant-garde evangelical churches, clear signs of a renewed religious fervour, of a kind I least expected.

But even more prominent in every town and village in southern India were flashy, flamboyant, massive, new jewelry emporiums, ridiculously and visually out of place amidst traditional rundown surrounding shops and buildings. Here are two shots of mine taken amidst the hub-bub of bustling rickshaw congested town in Kerala, India.

The prevalence of these new architectural gems and the accompanying massive ad billboards everywhere, is indicative of an exploding middle class in India and a new source of power.

In Ukraine, Romania, and Bulgaria, I noted the proliferation of two surprising other architectural/design phenomena of emerging cultural power. While not radical by our standards, highway service stations stood out like sore thumbs on the post-Soviet, grey rural landscape, while just metres away local farmers were selling fresh garlic or squash in stalls by the roadside. These bold brassy new service stations lit up the landscape in prime colours, far more elaborate than anything in North America, with up to 5 different types and grades, and digitally flashing price changes by the minute. These small architectural/design gems are symbolically comparable I think to the stately railway stations of old and our ultramodern space age airport masterpieces everywhere.

The second startling sight walking along former Austrian-Hungarian designed historic streets, in ALL towns and cities, amidst drab but charming traditional shops, such as these, were the mobile phone palaces. The Samsung shop on the main historic Khreschatyk Street in Kiev left me speechless with its sci-fi design, in and out. And on Garibaldi Street in Sofia I snapped this example, while next door there was a small cramped convenience store not large enough to hold more than two people.

While it is true that in each of the major cities I travelled to, there were modern shopping centres with brand names comparable to ours, as well as sport stadiums monumental in size and design. It is also true that in capital city centres, striking new buildings were sprouting up with names like Microsoft, Apple, HP, Google. Hi-tech is the new king, the new high priest. Yet, it was in small towns and along rural roads that the car and mobile technology were obvious as new democratizing sources of power.

Architects and designers, of course, go where the money is and their creativity is evident through the ages, whether hired by kings, bishops or bankers and now by technology corporations. Whatever one may think of them, the products they've produced, such as the car and the phone, have unleashed remarkable freedoms and levels of communication, which have enabled an incredible democratizing potential. In contrast we have the symbolic significance of castles and palaces.

It has been interesting to me, as I travelled, that one way I found differences in the societal values and new sources of power in differing cultures was manifested by the new architecture I observed – jewelry stores and evangelical churches in Kerala India, and gas stations and mobile phone stores in Eastern Europe.